Pause Before The Pulpit

Personal Reflections For Pastors On The Lectionary Readings

Cycle B

William W. Helland

CSS Publishing Company, Inc., Lima, Ohio

PAUSE BEFORE THE PULPIT

Copyright © 2005 by
CSS Publishing Company, Inc.
Lima, Ohio

All rights reserved. No part of this publication may be reproduced in any manner whatsoever without the prior permission of the publisher, except in the case of brief quotations embodied in critical articles and reviews. Inquiries should be addressed to: Permissions, CSS Publishing Company, Inc., P.O. Box 4503, Lima, Ohio 45802-4503.

Scripture quotations are from the *New Revised Standard Version of the Bible*, copyright 1989 by the Division of Christian Education of the National Council of the Churches of Christ in the USA. Used by permission.

Library of Congress Cataloging-in-Publication Data has been applied for.
Library of Congress Cataloging-in-Publication Data can be found at
LCCN: 2005011731

For more information about CSS Publishing Company resources, visit our website at www.csspub.com or e-mail us at custserv@csspub.com or call (800) 241-4056.

Cover design by Barbara Spencer
ISBN: 978-0-7880-2373-6   PRINTED IN U.S.A.

I would like to dedicate this work to my wife and children who believe in me and have been so patient with me while writing this book. In addition to them, I dedicate it to the congregation of the Lutheran Brethren Church in Watertown, South Dakota, who inspired me to be a better pastor and writer, and has prayed faithfully for me throughout this project.

Acknowledgments

I would like to acknowledge and thank my wife, Sally, and a good friend of the family, Julie Radach, for their patient assistance in helping me put my thoughts on paper in a way that is readable and understandable. Without them, this project would have been nearly impossible and without God it would have been impossible. To him be all honor and glory if anyone is helped and blessed by this book.

Table Of Contents

Preface   11

Advent 1
Mark 13:24-37   13
1 Corinthians 1:3-9   15

Advent 2
Mark 1:1-8   17
2 Peter 3:8-15a   19

Advent 3
John 1:6-8, 19-28   21
1 Thessalonians 5:16-24   23

Advent 4
Luke 1:26-38   25
Romans 16:25-27   27

The Nativity Of Our Lord/Christmas Eve/ Christmas Day/Proper 1
Luke 2:1-14 (15-20)   30
Titus 2:11-14   32

Christmas 1
Luke 2:22-40   34
Galatians 4:4-7   36

Christmas 2
John 1:(1-9) 10-18   39
Ephesians 1:3-14   41

The Epiphany Of Our Lord
Matthew 2:1-12   43
Ephesians 3:1-12   45

The Baptism Of Our Lord/Epiphany 1
    Mark 1:4-11 — 47
    Acts 19:1-7 — 48

Epiphany 2
    John 1:43-51 — 51
    1 Corinthians 6:12-20 — 53

Epiphany 3
    Mark 1:14-20 — 55
    1 Corinthians 7:29-31 — 57

Epiphany 4
    Mark 1:21-28 — 59
    1 Corinthians 8:1-13 — 61

Epiphany 5
    Mark 1:29-39 — 63
    1 Corinthians 9:16-23 — 65

Epiphany 6
    Mark 1:40-45 — 67
    1 Corinthians 9:24-27 — 69

Epiphany 7
    Mark 2:1-12 — 71
    2 Corinthians 1:18-22 — 73

The Transfiguration Of Our Lord/ Last Sunday After The Epiphany
    Mark 9:2-9 — 75
    2 Corinthians 4:3-6 — 77

Lent 1
    Mark 1:9-15 — 80
    1 Peter 3:18-22 — 82

Lent 2
    Mark 8:31-38   84
    Romans 4:13-25   86

Lent 3
    John 2:13-22   88
    1 Corinthians 1:18-25   90

Lent 4
    John 3:14-21   92
    Ephesians 2:1-10   94

Lent 5
    John 12:20-33   96
    Hebrews 5:5-10   98

Sunday Of The Passion/Palm Sunday
    Mark 11:1-11   101
    Philippians 2:5-11   103

The Resurrection Of Our Lord/Easter Day
    John 20:1-18   105
    1 Corinthians 15:1-11   107

Easter 2
    John 20:19-31   109
    1 John 1:1—2:2   111

Easter 3
    Luke 24:36b-48   113
    1 John 3:1-7   115

Easter 4
    John 10:11-18   117
    1 John 3:16-24   119

Easter 5
    John 15:1-8   121
    1 John 4:7-21   123

Easter 6
John 15:9-17 — 125
1 John 5:1-6 — 127

Easter 7
John 17:6-19 — 129
1 John 5:9-13 — 131

The Day Of Pentecost
John 15:26-27; 16:4b-15 — 134
Acts 2:1-21 — 136

The Holy Trinity
John 3:1-17 — 139
Romans 8:12-17 — 141

Proper 6
Mark 4:26-34 — 143
2 Corinthians 5:6-10 (11-13) 14-17 — 145

Proper 7
Mark 4:35-41 — 147
2 Corinthians 6:1-13 — 149

Proper 8
Mark 5:21-43 — 151
2 Corinthians 8:7-15 — 153

Proper 9
Mark 6:1-13 — 155
2 Corinthians 12:2-10 — 157

Proper 10
Mark 6:14-29 — 159
Ephesians 1:3-14 — 161

Proper 11
Mark 6:30-34, 53-56 — 163
Ephesians 2:11-22 — 165

Proper 12
    John 6:1-21   167
    Ephesians 3:14-21   169

Proper 13
    John 6:24-35   171
    Ephesians 4:1-16   173

Proper 14
    John 6:35, 41-51   175
    Ephesians 4:25—5:2   177

Proper 15
    John 6:51-58   180
    Ephesians 5:15-20   182

Proper 16
    John 6:56-69   184
    Ephesians 6:10-20   186

Proper 17
    Mark 7:1-8, 14-15, 21-23   188
    James 1:17-27   189

Proper 18
    Mark 7:24-37   192
    James 2:1-10 (11-13) 14-17   194

Proper 19
    Mark 8:27-38   196
    James 3:1-12   198

Proper 20
    Mark 9:30-37   200
    James 3:13—4:3, 7-8a   202

Proper 21
    Mark 9:38-50   204
    James 5:13-20   206

Proper 22
- Mark 10:2-16 — 208
- Hebrews 1:1-4; 2:5-12 — 210

Proper 23
- Mark 10:17-31 — 212
- Hebrews 4:12-16 — 214

Proper 24
- Mark 10:35-45 — 216
- Hebrews 5:1-10 — 218

Proper 25
- Mark 10:46-52 — 220
- Hebrews 7:23-28 — 222

Proper 26 (All Saints)
- Mark 12:28-34 — 224
- Hebrews 9:11-14 — 226

Proper 27
- Mark 12:38-44 — 228
- Hebrews 9:24-28 — 230

Proper 28
- Mark 13:1-8 — 232
- Hebrews 10:11-14 (15-18) 19-25 — 234

Christ The King/Proper 29
- John 18:33-37 — 236
- Revelation 1:4b-8 — 238

Textual Index — 241

Topical Index — 243

Lectionary Preaching After Pentecost — 253

U.S. / Canadian Lectionary Comparison — 255

Preface

There is no other element in a pastor's ministry that is more important than his/her ongoing relationship with the God whom he/she serves. This intimate relationship which God desires to have with us is not maintained through sermon and Bible study preparation, a heavy schedule of pastoral care, or office administration. In fact, those important aspects of ministry most often drain the pastor, not only physically, mentally, and emotionally, but also spiritually. Regular time alone with God, where we are quiet before him with an open Bible to listen to what he wants to tell us, coupled with humble prayer where we talk to him about what we "heard," is essential for maintaining and growing our faith, knowledge, and maturity in Christ Jesus.

The purpose of this devotional is to help every pastor take the first step in sermon preparation, which is to let the text first speak to us. This book is not about how to preach the text, but rather about how the text relates to us personally. It is not an exhaustive exegesis by an expert theologian, but rather the thoughtful, prayerful, reflection of a colleague in ministry, sharing how the text stirred my heart and what I believe we have in common regarding its application to our personal lives and public ministry.

It has been my intent to bring you a balanced law/grace perspective of the truths contained in each text. Much more could be said on every one, I'm sure, but I pray that what I have written will convict you where conviction is needed, comfort where comfort is needed, and strengthen and encourage you spiritually where strength and encouragement are needed.

The Sundays after The Day Of Pentecost are listed as Propers in this book. A reference comparison chart is given on pages 253 and 254.

William W. Helland

Advent 1

Mark 13:24-37

As we begin not only the Advent Season, but also another church year, this Gospel Lesson implores us to be watchful and alert. I don't know how it is for every other pastor in the world, but I know how difficult it is for me (and some of my colleagues) to be as alert and watchful as we should be. I'm referring to not only the end times (which our text is in reference to) but also to our everyday life.

Ministry can be all consuming. Our heads are spinning with the needs of people, upcoming meetings, tensions that may exist in the church, a building program, sermons and Bible studies, and the list goes on and on; all of it consuming our thoughts by day and our dreams by night. On top of this, we are supposed to be alert to new needs and potential problems in the church. We are to be alert to the needs of our family, and we're expected to be alert in our driving and everyday activities. If we aren't, something or someone will probably catch us off guard.

The point I'm trying to make is this: When we are at our busiest in ministry (and we are beginning one of the busiest seasons of the church year), it is extremely difficult to be as alert and watchful as we should be toward everyone and everything around us. A failure to do so can prove to be painful and even fatal! This certainly is true in regard to the point our Lord was making in this text.

As he pointed out, an event is coming in the future which requires us to be alert and watching, for if we are not, it may well catch us off guard and possibly unprepared. This event is, of course, his Second Coming (or Second Advent). It will come on a day and time when we least expect it — sort of like a car suddenly coming out of a side street or some family crisis — catching us totally by surprise.

Could verse 34 also apply to pastors? After all, it was spoken to four of Christ's key disciples.

It is like a man going on a journey, when he leaves home and puts his slaves in charge, each with his work, and commands the doorkeeper to be on the watch.

Jesus is the *man* who went *on a journey*. The *slaves* who were put *in charge* make up the church. Now my question is this: Are we, as pastors, the *doorkeepers*?

Are pastors not the ones who have a better sense of who comes and goes from our churches? Are we not often the one constant figure who greets people at the door — if not when they arrive for worship, most often when they leave? Are we not the ones who watch over many of the affairs of the church, the most important being its spiritual affairs? In most of our church traditions, the answers would be affirmative.

Who then, above all people, is to be alert and watching?

We are. And in order to fulfill our Lord's urgent plea in this regard, we may want to make some changes in our own lives. Perhaps we will want to remove some distractions, simplify our lives, and delegate some duties.

If we are too busy and our minds too consumed with ministry problems, preparations, and details, so we cannot truly be alert and watching for our Lord's return, then we are doing our parishioners and our loved ones a great disservice. We cannot effectively preach alertness and watchfulness to others unless we are alert and watchful ourselves. Perhaps our Lord is asking us today, to free up some time in our busy schedules so that we can pay closer attention to this most important of all ministry tasks.

Has your life become too busy to even think about our Lord's return? If so, I urge you to take steps right now, today, with the help and guidance of the Holy Spirit, to become a *doorkeeper* who is alert and watching for our Lord's Second Advent.

A Pastor's Prayer:
Dear Lord,

You know how busy this time of the year can be and how much is on my mind. Please help me to know how to readjust my schedule and lifestyle so that I can pay closer attention to what is most important: that of being alert and watching for your return. I ask this, not only for my sake, but also for the sake of my parishioners, so I can help them learn this important discipline as well. Thank you. Amen.

1 Corinthians 1:3-9

What a wonderful, pastoral greeting our Epistle Lesson is! It would be a great way to greet our worshipers each Sunday. It is also an Advent text due, no doubt, to Paul's reference to the *revealing of our Lord Jesus Christ* and *the day of our Lord Jesus Christ*, both referring to his Second Advent. However, let us focus not so much on this theme as on the theme of "what God has given us" so that we can see the *day of our Lord Jesus Christ*.

To help us focus on this theme, I want to personalize this text in a way that hopefully will not take it out of context or change its meaning. I believe we can reread it in such a way that we will more clearly hear the wonderful promises to us personally, as we begin this busy and festive Advent season.

Grace to [me] *and peace from God* [my] *Father and the Lord Jesus Christ.*

I give thanks to my God always for [who I am] *because of the grace of God that has been given* [me] *in Christ Jesus, for in every way* [I] *have been enriched in him, in speech and knowledge of every kind — just as the testimony of Christ has been strengthened among* [my congregation] *— so that* [I am] *not lacking in any spiritual gift as* [I] *wait for the revealing of* [my] *Lord Jesus Christ. He will also strengthen* [me] *to the end, so that* [I] *may be blameless on the day of* [my] *Lord Jesus Christ. God is faithful; by him* [I was] *called into the fellowship of his Son, Jesus Christ* [my] *Lord.*

Please forgive me for taking such liberties with the text, but I hope you will agree with me, by reading it this way it becomes very personal. It no longer is merely a cordial greeting by the Apostle Paul to the Corinthian church, or a moving and heartfelt greeting that we might express to our congregation. Suddenly it becomes an intimate look at who we are, as servants of Christ Jesus in the ministry of the word.

Let me ask you: Are you going into the Advent season a bit "under the weather" spiritually? Sometimes this season sneaks up on us and we are not as prepared, inwardly or outwardly, as we would like to be and as others might expect us to be. Perhaps our own inadequacies or secret sins tend to get us down, and we feel less than excited about proclaiming the wonderful truths of the gospel during this season.

If I have just described you, allow me to cause you to pause and consider some wonderful truths from this text.

When was the last time you thanked God for who you are *because of the grace of God that has been given* you in Christ Jesus?

When was the last time you reflected upon all the ways you *have been enriched in him, in speech and knowledge of every kind*?

Have you taken conscious note of how *the testimony of Christ has been strengthened among* your "flock" due to your faithful proclamation of his word?

Are you more apt to complain to God about the spiritual gifts he doesn't seem to have given you, rather than praise and thank him for the fact that you really *are not lacking in any spiritual gift* according to the ministry he has called you to and equipped you for?

As you face the Advent season and the coming church year, are you going into it trusting in your strength, or trusting his promise to you that *he will also strengthen* you to the end?

What does it mean to you that you will, simply by faith in Christ Jesus, stand *blameless* before God on the day of Christ's return?

When was the last time you thanked God for calling you *into the fellowship of his Son, Jesus Christ*?

I hope you agree with me that now is a good time to pause and pray a prayer of praise and thanksgiving for who you are in Christ Jesus, and for what he has done, is doing, and will continue to do through your faithful service on his behalf.

A Pastor's Prayer:
Dear Lord,

(you fill in the rest as you feel led, based on the above questions)

Amen.

Advent 2

Mark 1:1-8

Just as last week's theme of "watchfulness" is a key Advent theme, so too, is this week's theme of "preparedness." Our calling, as proclaimers of the word, is to urge all who hear, to be watching and prepared for our Lord's Second Advent. In this way, our ministries are similar to that of John the Baptist.

Can you imagine being called to a ministry like that of John's? It would mean that every day, instead of going to a comfortable office, you would go out to the countryside, along a major river, and wait for people to come to you. You wouldn't be dressed in comfortable clothes that matched the styles of the day, but instead, you would wear itchy, coarse garments more common to a homeless person. You would not enjoy meals of rich delicacies, but rather, natural foods that would come right from the fields of your surroundings. Seem odd? Certain things about John and his ministry did seem odd!

However, John was not trying to be eccentric, for this was who God had called him to be; where God had called him to serve; and what God had called him to do. His ministry (as short as it would be) was for the specific purpose of preparing the way for the Lord.

Each pastor has a calling that is somewhat unique and different from anyone else, as well. The way in which God called us to ministry might be quite different from others. The gifts he has given us and the way in which he wants us to employ them might be different from that of others. The setting that he wants us to minister most often is different from anyone else's, and our means and style of ministry is often unique to each of us. No two pastors, nor their ministries, are identical.

However, the overall purpose for which we were called into ministry is identical. Like John, we were called to prepare people for Jesus. His ministry of preparation was linked to Christ's first coming to earth and earthly ministry. Our ministry of preparation is linked to Christ's Second Coming and heavenly reign.

We can see additional similarities between John's ministry and that of pastors today. First, John proclaimed a baptism of repentance for the forgiveness of sins. We too, through faithful proclamation of Law and Grace, emphasize the importance of repentance for the forgiveness of sins. We too, practice baptism (in one form and tradition or another) in relation to repentance and the forgiveness of sins. John did this faithfully, in his setting and style, so that his listeners would be prepared for the day that Jesus would walk into their lives. We are to do this faithfully, in the setting and style that God has given us, so that our listeners will be prepared for the day that Jesus returns for all who believe in him.

Secondly, John dealt with the confession of sins. One can only imagine what he heard by way of confession from those who were coming out to listen to him and be baptized. John didn't judge these people, but rather proclaimed, to those who were truly repentant, the forgiveness of sins! That is an important part of our ministries today — the ministry of confession and absolution. The way we do this, and where we do this, may be different in various church traditions and differ based on the various needs of people, but the bottom line is that we are called by God to be his ears and lips — to listen to people as they confess their sins and, for those who are truly repentant, to proclaim the forgiveness of those sins on the basis of the blood of Christ.

Last of all, I'm moved by John's humility, which ought to be characteristic of each of us. John recognized that Jesus was more powerful than he. He recognized the greatness of Christ to the degree that he felt unworthy to even stoop and untie the sandals on Jesus' feet. He also recognized that his ministry was only a visible reflection of the real, invisible work of the Holy Spirit.

May our ministries be characterized by such humility. May people not be drawn to us, our personalities, and our gifts, but rather through us, be pointed to Christ who is infinitely greater than us!

A Pastor's Prayer:
Dear Lord,
    Thank you for calling me to proclaim your word. May your Holy Spirit work through me to prepare many people for your Second Coming. May my ministry be characterized by true humility whereby you alone are glorified. Amen.

2 Peter 3:8-15a

I don't know about you, but patience is not one of my strong points! In fact, my lack of patience is often detrimental to my effectiveness as a pastor, husband, and father. In the church, I want people to grow and mature now! In evangelism, I want people to come to faith in Christ now! In the home, I want my family to understand me and comply with my wishes now! In the wake of all this impatience, people get hurt and my ability to relate to them is hindered.

Notice what our Epistle Lesson has to say on this. Peter pointed out that it is a *fact* that God is patient. Why? Because he does not want anyone *to perish, but all to come to repentance*. Peter wanted the church to know that time is not the important issue when it comes to evangelism and spiritual growth. All too often we get this confused. We think we need to save the world today and that everyone should grow up immediately, because Jesus could return at any moment. The imminent return of Christ is a reality that we live with, but it is no reason for panic and impatience when it comes to our ministries. This has been a hard reality for me to deal with, and possibly for you as well.

What is important to God, over and above the element of time, is that people would not *perish*, but rather *come to repentance*. Since that is God's primary focus, it ought to be ours as well; and it takes divine patience since people (ourselves included) can be so slow to come to a point of genuine repentance.

The urgency in this matter, lies not so much in the "when" of Christ's return, but in the absolute *fact* of his return. There is a Second Advent coming just as there was a First Advent. Both will usher in a new age. His First Advent ushered in the age of the church. His Second Advent will usher in the eternal age of a new heaven and a new earth. Those who are not ready for his Second Advent will be destroyed, which is exactly what God does not want to see happen. Therefore, he has employed us in this ministry of preparing people so they can, simply by faith in Christ Jesus, escape the coming and certain destruction of everything as we know it.

Peter then proposed to his readers that there is an appropriate way for us to live our lives in the interim. They are to be lives marked by *holiness and godliness*. They are to be lives lived in *waiting*, not so "heavenly minded we are of no earthly good," but lived with loose attachment to the things of this life, which will all be destroyed anyway. Peter emphasized these things by urging his readers to *strive to be found by him* (God) *at peace, without spot or blemish.*

Again, this text, like all of scripture, forces us to reflect on who we are and our relationship with this patient God, before we speak of these truths to others.

Are our lives marked by *holiness and godliness*? The good news of the gospel is that, by faith in Christ, God chooses to see us as holy! That, in turn, ought to be what motivates us to follow Paul's directive, *to lead a life worthy of the calling to which you have been called* (Ephesians 4:1). This is what it means to live a godly life.

Are we living life loosely attached to the material things around us that will one day perish at the Lord's return? It isn't just the unbelieving world around us, nor carnal Christians, who get attached to material things. We in the ministry can, too. Often we are tempted to find comfort and significance in the people and things around us.

Is our devotional life, our professional life, and our private life seen by God, and others, as a *striving to be found by* [God] *at peace, and without spot or blemish?*

The answers to these questions are best found in humble prayer before God, as we honestly ask him to search us and know our hearts, to test us and to know our thoughts (Psalm 139:22).

A Pastor's Prayer:
Dear Lord,

Please forgive me for my impatience with you and with others. Help me to know how to live with this tension of urgency, by not focusing on time, but on the importance of repentance and preparedness for your Second Coming. Help me to live a life of peace and lose attachment to material things, without spot or blemish, which brings glory to you. Thank you. Amen.

Advent 3

John 1:6-8, 19-28

Who are you?
"What?" you ask. "What do you mean, 'Who are you?'"
That was the question asked of John the Baptist in this text. It's a good question to ask ourselves, for it might shed some light on how we view our calling as a pastor.

John was asked if he was *the Messiah*, or *Elijah*, or *the prophet*. Now think with me how it would have affected his ministry, if John had thought himself to be *the Messiah* or *Elijah*. I'm sure he would have presented himself much differently. No doubt his message would also have been different. Perhaps his way of relating to people would have been different, and no doubt they would have responded to him differently. Worst of all, John would have failed miserably at carrying out God's purpose for his life and ministry.

So I ask you again, "Who are you?" How you answer that question is a direct reflection of how you view yourself, your position in life, and God's purpose in calling you. For example, if you see yourself largely as an administrative pastor, you will fill your day with administrative details and become annoyed with most everything else. Sermon preparations and preaching will be something you do because you have to, not because you feel called to.

Let's suppose you see yourself as primarily a visitation pastor. You love to visit people, whether in their homes, at a restaurant, in the hospital, or in nursing homes. You would spend all of your time visiting people if you could. Now, on the one hand, that is commendable, for much good ministry takes place in visitation and how well you do in this area can make or break your ministry. However, as in the previous example, if this is primarily how you view yourself, sermon preparation and preaching will be something merely to be tolerated since you have to do it.

Brothers and sisters in Christ, who have been called by God to be ministers of the glorious gospel of Jesus Christ, our primary calling is still very similar to that of John! We are called to be *the voice of one crying out in the wilderness*. The Apostle Paul put it well when he wrote to the church in Rome: *Everyone who calls on the name of the Lord shall be saved. But how are they to call on one in whom they have not believed? And how are they to believe in one of whom they have never heard? And how are they to hear without someone to proclaim him?* (Romans 10:13-14).

I urge you to put your name in the appropriate places in verses 6-8 of our text so that it might read something like this:

There was a [person] *sent from God, whose name was* (name) . [He/She] *came as a witness to testify to the light, so that all might believe through* [his/her preaching]. (Name) *was not the light, but came to testify to the light. The true light, which enlightens everyone, was coming into the world.*

When I read the text in this way, it clarifies for me who I am and what my primary purpose as a pastor is. The difference between the day in which we minister, and John's day, is that in John's day, *the true light was just coming into the world.* In our day, *the true light* has come. There is no mistaking who he is and the immense value of us *testifying about* him.

Don't get me wrong; administration, visitation, and everything else that is expected of pastors have their place, but anything that diminishes the importance of our calling to proclaim the gospel and testify for Christ is distorting our identity and hindering our ability to quickly reply, as John did, to the question, "Who are you?"

Many in the church today see little or no value in the pastor's role and identity as a proclaimer of the word; therefore we must defend it with conviction and the authority of God's Word.

A Pastor's Prayer:

Dear Lord,

Thank you for making me who I am. Thank you for the privilege of proclaiming your word to a world that is searching for *the true light* that has already come into the world. Please forgive me for times I have taken the importance of this calling too lightly. Help me to give it first priority in my ministry and to know how to communicate to my parishioners, not only your precious truths, but how important this part of my ministry is. Amen.

1 Thessalonians 5:16-24

These "final exhortations," in the Apostle Paul's first letter to the Thessalonians, are delightful gems of truth for all Christians, but especially significant and meaningful for those of us in ministry. Let's carefully examine them to see how this is true.

Our text begins with this quick, almost shocking exhortation: *Rejoice always!* Really? Even when I'm having a bad day? Even when the whole world seems to be against me? Even when I feel like I'm ineffective and accomplishing nothing? Yes, even then — and especially then! You see, the Apostle Paul had learned how to do this, as he pointed out further in his letter to the Philippian church. In that letter (ch. 4) he wrote about rejoicing and being content no matter what circumstances he was facing. Where does such joy come from? It doesn't come from people, successful programs, good sermons, more money, or anything temporal. It only comes from a deep and personal relationship with Jesus Christ.

His next exhortation is just as brief and startling: *Pray without ceasing!* What? How do we find time for that? I'm sure we've all taught this verse to parishioners who reacted similarly to Paul's challenge, and so we know he doesn't mean that we should pray 24/7. However, we don't want to just brush this off as hyperbole either, for he does mean something by this. The meaning of this, and its fulfillment in our daily lives, is seen and experienced by being in such an intimate relationship with God that at any moment we burst into conversation with him. So, for example, when stuck on a difficult Bible passage, or facing a tense situation in a meeting, or confronted with a hard counseling issue, we can, at that moment, talk to God (at least in our thoughts) and ask for wisdom, comfort, peace, or whatever we need. That is praying without ceasing. It becomes our way of life and ministry.

Paul's third exhortation is a bit longer, but as shocking as the first two: *Give thanks in all circumstances; for this is the will of God in Christ Jesus for you.* Oh how hard this has been for me, and still is yet today. Does he really mean *every* circumstance? Am I to give thanks for difficult people? Am I to give thanks for personal crisis? Am I to give thanks when giving or attendance, or both, are down? Well, again, remember who wrote this and how he probably faced more discouraging circumstances in his lifetime than a whole district of pastors combined! Paul had learned from experience that difficult circumstances are good for us, as it is in the heat of trials that faith and godly character are developed. That is something to be really thankful for!

The fourth exhortation doesn't so much shock us, as it causes us to pause in thoughtful reflection about its meaning and significance for our life and ministry: *Do not quench the Spirit.* You mean to say, I might do that? I can somehow hinder his working in me and my parish? Absolutely! And that ought to be a sobering thought for all of us. Perhaps the remaining exhortations in the text shed some light on this, for if we *despise the words* of God's prophets, if we don't *test everything* for truth or falsehood, if we don't *hold fast to what is good*, if we don't *abstain from every form of evil*, and if we don't allow God to sanctify us entirely — keeping our *spirit, soul, and body sound and blameless* until the coming of Christ — we will most definitely quench the Spirit of God who is at work in and through us.

If there is anything I have learned over fifteen years of ministry, it is how desperately I need God's Holy Spirit in every area of my life and ministry. But how easily and quickly I can quench his work in and through me due to sin. We, in ministry, cannot afford to preach, teach, and beseech our parishioners without the help of the Holy Spirit. If we attempt to do so, we will eventually fail.

Our human nature often rebels when confronted by such blunt truths as these Pauline exhortations, but they are for our good and hold the key to successful ministry.

A Pastor's Prayer:
Dear Lord,

Please help me to take each of these exhortations to heart and to allow your Holy Spirit the freedom to work in and through me. I want to *rejoice always, pray without ceasing, give thanks in all circumstances* and think, say, or do nothing that will *quench* your Spirit's work in me, nor the ministry you have called me to. Thank you. Amen.

Advent 4

Luke 1:26-38

Since childhood, I have always enjoyed the gospel texts that unfold the Christmas story. This one is no exception. I've always marveled at how (and why) God called this young woman, Mary, to such a huge and responsible position as that of being the mother to the Son of God. When we think about it, what a daunting task! In more recent years, as I've read and reread this text to preach and teach it, I've become increasingly impressed with certain elements of it that I believe parallel our calling, as proclaimers of Christ. This calling, which we have all responded to (provided you are in the ministry for the Lord and not self), is also a daunting task! So let's look closer at this account and see how it might apply to us, personally.

The first thing that impresses me is that God sent the angel to a most unlikely candidate for such a high calling (at least "unlikely" in the eyes of the world). Why did he select a young, single woman from the despised community of Nazareth? Why not select an older, more mature woman from Jerusalem or Bethlehem, or better yet, from a royal family? But that is not how God usually works. When calling men and women into his service, God often calls those whom the world would consider the most unlikely candidates. The Apostle Paul wrote about this in his first letter to the Corinthian church: *Consider your own call, brothers and sisters: not many of you were wise by human standards, not many were powerful, not many were of noble birth. But God chose what is foolish in the world to shame the wise; God chose what is weak in the world to shame the strong; God chose what is low and despised in the world, things that are not, to reduce to nothing things that are, so that no one might boast in the presence of God* (1 Corinthians 1:26-29).

I have found great comfort in this passage as I am a farm boy turned preacher. One of my seminary professors tells the story about how, after first meeting me, he didn't think I would ever make it through seminary, much less become a pastor! You see, God often calls the most unlikely candidates, and maybe you are feeling that you are one of them. I urge you to find comfort and hope in the fact that he called Mary to be the mother of his Son!

Secondly, I am impressed with the angel's words to Mary: *Do not be afraid, Mary, for you have found favor with God.* Imagine how frightening it must have been for Mary to have an angel suddenly appear before her! Imagine how frightening to hear of God's call upon her life and how nothing would be as she and Joseph had originally planned their future to be. And what did it mean that she had *found favor with God*? Dear friends, God's call to serve him is not something to be taken lightly. To serve the one, true God is an awesome privilege and responsibility!

You see, God calls those who *have found favor* with him. Not because we were so good or deserving of such a high calling! No! To find favor with God is purely an act of his grace and will! It is a mystery! Why did he call Mary to be the mother of the Son of God? Why did he call you and me into the ministry of the gospel? It's a mystery! But we shouldn't be afraid of it.

Last of all, Mary asked: *How can this be, since I am a virgin?* And the angel replied: *Nothing will be impossible with God.* May we find great comfort and confidence in that reply. How can it be, that I, a farm boy, should preach the gospel? It's because nothing is impossible with God! To the seminary professor, it looked nearly impossible, but with God all things are possible. How is it that God can use you to accomplish great things for his kingdom? Because nothing is impossible with God.

May we respond to these truths with the same spirit and faith as that of Mary. Her humble surrender to God's call upon her life resulted in the birth and life of the Savior of the world. Our humble surrender to God's call upon our lives, will (and is) resulting in the salvation of many souls. To God be the glory!

A Pastor's Prayer:
Dear Lord,

Here am I, the servant of the Lord; let it be with me according to your word. God, you have called me to serve you for a specific purpose, at a specific time in history, to a specific group of people.

In spite of my shortcomings and inadequacies, I thank you that you have chosen me and will accomplish your purposes through me. To you be all the glory! Amen.

Romans 16:25-27

This text is the "final doxology" to Paul's letter to the Roman church. It is brief, but contains wonderful truths for the church and for those of us who "shepherd" the church.

Just as Paul was closing out a powerful, doctrinal letter, so too, we are closing out a powerful season of the church year — the season of Advent, which marks the beginning of the church year. As we do so, our attention is directed to end times — the Second Advent of Christ. The season of Advent also gives way to the season of Christmas, whereby we hope and pray that the first has prepared us to properly observe the latter.

Paul, in this final doxology, desired that all glory go to God. We could sum up this short paragraph this way: *Now to God be the glory forever! Amen.* But Paul wasn't this brief, as he wanted his readers to understand why all glory should be given to God and no one else. It is equally important that we do the same, and Paul tells us why.

First of all, God deserves all the glory because of Jesus Christ. The gospel is centered around Christ and not us. The message we proclaim is Christ crucified for sinners. The church needs Christ and not the other way around. Far too often, individuals (some pastors included) and even whole congregations, think that all glory should go to them. They believe they are God's gift to humanity, but they are deceived. Jesus is God's gift to humanity. We, as individuals and congregations, are the recipients of this great gift and all glory should go to God.

Secondly, God deserves all glory, for only he can strengthen us and the corporate church. People and congregations who try to carry out ministry on their own strength can probably go for awhile, but eventually they will burn out and their ministry will be proven for what it was — an effort to bring glory upon themselves rather than to God. An effective pastor, lay person, and/or congregation, is that which constantly looks to and relies upon God for strength. This strength comes through the gospel and the proclamation of Christ Jesus.

Thirdly, God deserves all glory for the revelation of the mystery of the gospel that had long been hidden. How thankful we can be that we live and serve the Lord on this side of the cross! Can you imagine being a priest, serving God under the Levitical code? For hundreds of years God's prophets and priests served him under this cloud of mystery, knowing there was some fuller meaning and purpose to all of it — longing to see it, but never allowed to. But the disciples, and the whole Christian church since their time, have been blessed and privileged to see the clearer picture of God's grace and mercy to mankind! Not that there isn't still some mystery, for there is; but thank God — and to him be all the glory — that we can know, understand to some degree, and proclaim the gospel of Jesus Christ!

Fourthly, God deserves all the glory for bringing salvation to the Gentiles! No doubt most of us who minister in North America are Gentiles. What if Christ had been only for the Jews, as Peter and others believed so deeply for a time? Thank God — and to him be the glory — that he revealed the universal nature of the gospel as being for all people, Jew and Gentile alike, and that it came about by his eternal command! In other words, it always was his purpose that the gospel should go to all the world and not just the chosen nation of Israel.

Last of all, God deserves all the glory, as he is the only wise God. There is none besides him. All other gods are a figment of humanity's imagination. The truths we've shared during Advent are God's truths stemming from his wisdom. The truths we will share during Christmas, in all their marvel and majesty, are God's truths, stemming from his wisdom. The truths we will share throughout the church year, mysterious as some of them are and at times difficult to preach and teach, are all God's truths, stemming from his wisdom. Due to his wisdom, he deserves sole position as the one to be worshiped, now and forever.

A Pastor's Prayer:
Dear Lord,
 I praise you for who you are! I thank you for Jesus and desire that he be at the center of my life and ministry. Please strengthen me and your church to carry out your purposes. And I praise you, and thank you, for bringing salvation to me and all who believe. To you be the glory forever and ever! Amen.

The Nativity Of Our Lord/Christmas Eve/ Christmas Day (Proper 1)

Luke 2:1-14 (15-20)

What a marvelous story our Gospel Lesson is! Every time I read it, all sorts of images and memories flood my mind: images and memories of nativity scenes, Christmas plays and services, Christmas goodies, music, and fellowship. The joy of Christmas!

Yet there is a down side to all this for pastors and that is staying fresh and original, especially in our preaching, when year after year we proclaim the same Christmas story. How many different ways can we tell it and present it? And is there not the pressure at times to somehow present it in bigger and better ways than last year? As a result, we are tempted to stretch the story, delve into speculation, and take people into places of the imagination that run the risk of distracting them from the central truths of the story.

In addition to this, after telling something over and over again, it can lose its newness and excitement for us. We get tired at this time of year and feel the pressure, at home and in the church, to be happy and make everyone else happy. All the while, a subtle cynicism begins to sneak up on us and we find ourselves thinking (if not saying aloud): "I can't wait until this season is over!"

If I have in any way come close to describing you, I urge you to revisit this text with me. Let's look closely at two scenes which can help us keep our perspective during this season.

First is the statement made by the angels: *Do not be afraid — for see — I am bringing you good news of great joy for all the people: to you is born this day in the city of David a Savior, who is the Messiah, the Lord.*

May we never forget that the Christmas story is always good news! In a world where the media constantly bombard us with bad news, we have the privilege and opportunity to bring to our people good news. And it is good news of great joy! We minister to people who, for the most part, are unhappy. They are continually told by the world around them that happiness is found in relationships with the right people, or in having the right things, or in looking good and staying young. But we have good news that does more than make people happy; it brings people joy — deep-down, genuine, heartfelt joy! And this good news is for all people — for all who will receive it by faith. May we never tire of sharing the good news of Jesus Christ, even if we share it the same way year after year.

Secondly, I want us to notice the behavior of the shepherds after they had been to the stable to see the newborn Christ Child.

When they saw this, they made known what had been told them about this child; and all who heard it were amazed at what the shepherds told them.

The shepherds returned, glorifying and praising God for all they had heard and seen, as it had been told them.

If we want to effectively lead our parishioners in glorifying and praising God this Christmas, we need to first of all have a very real and personal encounter with him ourselves. The shepherds did not go out, talking about what the angels had told them, without first having had an encounter with the child and his parents. Only after they experienced for themselves that everything was just as the angels had told them, did they testify about it to others.

How important it is for us, each and every year, to be alone with the Lord and this text before we preach it. No matter how many times we have read it and shared it with others, God desires that we marvel again and again at what it says, at what it means, at what took place, and at its significance for us and others. As a result, I believe you will find that many people who listen to you this Christmas season will be amazed at what you tell them, no matter how many times they have heard this story; for you have been impacted by it, and amazed at it, before you told it to them.

A Pastor's Prayer:

Dear Lord,

Thank you for the "Old, Old Story"! May I not simply go through the motions of preaching this text, but rather speak about it with joy and passion as your Spirit touches me once again with its glorious truths and significance. May I go into our Christmas worship glorifying and praising you for all that I have "seen" through the eyes of faith and "heard" from your precious word. Amen.

Titus 2:11-14

In our devotional on the Gospel Lesson, I urged us to recapture that same wonder and marvel in the birth of Christ that the shepherds had. This is so important, not only for us spiritually, but also for the benefit of our listeners during this wonderful season of the year!

Here in our Epistle Lesson, the Apostle Paul reminds us of the grace of God that appeared to the world in the person of Jesus Christ. The goal of God's grace is that he might have a family of believers who are zealous for serving him.

I think it would be safe to say that the shepherds in the nativity exhibited a fair amount of zeal! Would it not make sense that God's children also have a fair amount of zeal? How about you? How zealous are you for serving God? If you've lost your zeal (or never had any in the first place), there's probably a reason, and I think our text can identify it for you.

Paul wrote, *For the grace of God has appeared, bringing salvation to all, training us to renounce impiety and worldly passions, and in the present age to live lives that are self-controlled, upright, and godly.* He here points out three things about the grace of God that has appeared in the person of Jesus Christ.

First, this grace brought *salvation to all*. Obviously, when understood in the whole context of scripture, that does not mean that everyone is automatically saved, but rather that salvation has been made available and possible for all who will receive it by faith. In order to be zealous about Christ and passionate in preaching the significance of his birth, life, death, and resurrection, it is essential that we believe, and receive, his salvation for us personally. It is hard to imagine that anyone would go into Christian ministry who has not received Christ's salvation, but it happens. If they have any zeal for what they do, it is probably either an effort to work their way to heaven, exercise control over people, or provide an "easy" way to make a living!

Secondly, Paul wrote that the grace of God appeared for the purpose of *training us to renounce* certain things. He specifically identified *impiety* (which is to be irreverent or profane) and *worldly passions* (which are passions for things of the flesh rather than for things of the Spirit). If we in the ministry are not willing to renounce sin in our own lives, or to tactfully and prayerfully renounce it in the lives of others, we will, either due to hardness of heart or cynicism toward others, lose our zeal.

This training to renounce our sin is a gracious work of the Holy Spirit. If God's Spirit didn't convict us of our own sin, or give us, through the word, insight, and boldness to renounce it in the lives of others, how would sin ever be addressed? We would go on living painful lives like the unbelieving world around us, never knowing why the things we are thinking, saying, and doing are causing us, and others, pain.

Thirdly, Paul pointed out that another reason for the grace of God appearing in the person of Jesus Christ is to enable us to live godly lives. His grace saves us, then it trains us to renounce sin, and last of all it enables us to live a lifestyle that we could not possibly live on our own. He characterized it as a life that is *self-controlled, upright, and godly*. If we ignore this enabling work of the Holy Spirit to live a godly life, we may, again, lose our zeal.

One of the things I have agonized over, as a pastor, is that I am as human and sinful, and in need of God's grace, as my parishioners. However, the beauty of God's grace is that, through Jesus, he *redeemed us from all iniquity and purified for himself a people of his own who are zealous for good works.*

May that be the spiritual condition of each and every one of us, as we proclaim the wonderful good news of Jesus this Christmas and in the year to come.

A Pastor's Prayer:
Dear Lord,

I confess to you that I desperately need your grace as much as the "worst" sinner that I might minister to. Lord, please give me that zeal which comes from being in a right, saved, and obedient relationship with you. Thank you! Amen.

Christmas 1

Luke 2:22-40

The two main characters of this text, Simeon and Anna, are fascinating people. Every now and then, a pastor is blessed to have one or two (and extremely blessed is the pastor and congregation who have more than that!) of these deeply spiritual and insightful members in their church.

I've often marveled at the prophetic words these two people shared with Mary and Joseph that day. They were words that *amazed* this young couple. But I've marveled even more at Simeon's and Anna's character and what it was that shaped them to be so deeply spiritual and insightful.

I want to encourage us to pray for, be quick to spot, and involve in our ministry, seniors of great faith, spiritual depth, and godly insight. They will provide you with much needed prayer support and have a stabilizing effect on your ministry and the congregation you serve.

Notice, first of all, the kind of man Simeon was. We are told by Luke that he was a *righteous and devout* man. His righteousness, no doubt, could be characterized by that which Abraham was known for — a righteousness that came simply by believing God. Notice, I did not say "believing IN God," for a lot of people (then and now) believe IN God, but don't necessarily *believe* God. There is a difference and scripture makes that clear. One who believes IN God has head knowledge about God's existence, but someone who *believes* God, goes beyond believing in his existence to believing his very words. Simeon believed the words of God, and lived his life accordingly.

Oh how we need men and women in our churches who not only believe IN God, but also believe God's Word. The failure of church leaders (including some pastors) to believe and hold to God's Word has had a detrimental effect on the church. But we also need people who, like Simeon, are *devout*. In other words, they are sincere in their relationship with God through faith in Christ Jesus. They read their Bible and spend time in prayer. They regularly attend worship and Bible studies. They use the gifts God has given them to serve him in his church. Simeon was like this in his relationship with God and in his service in the temple.

But there is another important thing about Simeon that I want us to notice: his close relationship with the Holy Spirit. We read that *the Holy Spirit rested on him*, that something had *been revealed to him by the Holy Spirit*, and that he was *guided by the Spirit*. One of the marks of a truly righteous and devout man or woman is their relationship with the Spirit of God. You can tell when the Holy Spirit rests upon someone. His fruits will be clearly seen in their words and lifestyle. They will share God's truths with others, for they allow the Holy Spirit to reveal his truths to them. And they are a people who are clearly guided by the Holy Spirit, for they tend to sin less than others and they generally make wise, Spirit-led decisions.

I'm also greatly impressed with Simeon's confidence. There is no indication in the text that he questioned whether this was the long awaited Christ Child. He just knew it and spoke confidently about it. "How could he do this?" we ask. He could do so, because of his intimate relationship with God. Simeon was so close with God; there was no doubt in his mind that this small child that Mary and Joseph held would be the Savior of the world. Much of the same could be said of Anna as well.

Could these things be said of us: that we are righteous and devout? Could it be said of us that the Holy Spirit clearly rests upon us and that he is guiding us? Could it be said of us that the truths we share and the pastoral care we give are truly a work of the Holy Spirit revealing these truths to us for our benefit and the benefit of others? I pray (and may you as well) that these truths will make themselves evident in our daily lives.

A Pastor's Prayer:
Dear Lord,
   Please make me more like Simeon and Anna; a person who is so intimately connected with you that I am absolutely confident in speaking your word and with your authority. Lord, if it be your

will, please give me more people in my congregation like them — people who are righteous and devout, living by your Spirit. Thank you. Amen.

Galatians 4:4-7

Perhaps we've all been asked, by inquisitive minds: "Why was Jesus born when he was?" Well, this text has the answer: He was born in *the fullness of time*! Quite an answer, isn't it? If anything, it raises more questions! If it tells us anything, it is this: Jesus came to earth when the time was full (or just right) in God's eyes. It doesn't matter if it fit into the time frame of the Jewish people or of historians around the world. What matters, is that he came exactly when God planned it in fulfillment of his prophetic word.

With little more to be said on that, I want us to look at a wonderful truth contained in this text for each of us. I'm referring to the significance of being God's children versus being Satan's slaves.

Paul explained to the Galatian church that Jesus came to redeem us, so that we might receive adoption as children. In the Fall, in the Garden of Eden, Satan corrupted the innocent, pure, parent/child relationship God had with his newly created humanity. I liken it to the end result of a messy divorce with an ugly, child custody battle, which I've had the unfortunate experience of witnessing on more than one occasion. Perhaps many of you have as well. It grieves our hearts to watch what happens to the children when parents fight over them — at times for no other apparent reason than to inflict pain on the other parent.

The devil never wanted us, because he thought he could love us more or take better care of us than God could. He wanted us under his control so he could inflict pain on God, and that is exactly what happened. God was grieved over what happened in the Garden of Eden and he has grieved over the sins of humanity ever since. Yet that is not the full extent of his pain. As a loving parent, he was faced with the painful situation of having to sacrifice one child in order to save the rest of them. In other words, God gave up his own Son, so that the rest of us could be redeemed (or bought back) into his loving family. What an incredibly moving story!

Christmas, therefore, is not only about Christ's birth, but also about our adoption! All who believe in Christ's death and resurrection, for the purpose of their redemption back into God's family, are no longer slaves, but children of God! Just as children in an orphanage are absolutely helpless when it comes to finding a family to love them, and are completely dependent on someone coming in the "fullness of time" to adopt them and make them a child in a family again, so too, we, who were orphaned by Satan's lies and deceptions, are absolutely helpless and unable to make ourselves a part of God's family on our own. We needed God to take the initiative; to do the "paperwork" which frees us from slavery and gives us identity once again as a child of God. And that is what happened. What a miracle! What a wonderful story for Christmas!

Not only have we been adopted, but we have been gifted, big time! We have been given all the rights and privileges of a natural-born child of God. Jesus is God's Son and one with the Father and the Spirit. We are God's children through faith in Jesus who then sends his Spirit into our hearts, opening the way for our relationship with the Father to be as intimate as it is between him and his Son. What a privilege that is! We are invited and enabled to call out to God, *Abba, Father.* We can call him "Daddy." Few things give adoptive parents more joy than when the child they adopted calls them "Daddy" and "Mommy." It gives God great joy to hear us do the same.

Better yet, Paul pointed out that we are not only children in an intimate relationship with our Heavenly Daddy, but also heirs of all that God has. Imagine the riches of God! Paul wrote to the Corinthians: *No eye has seen, no ear has heard, no mind has conceived what God has prepared for those who love him* (1 Corinthians 2:9). We can't even begin to imagine what we have already inherited by being a child of God! This truth is better than any gift we could ever receive at Christmas.

A Pastor's Prayer:
Dear Lord,

Thank you for sending your Son in just the right time for me and all of humanity. Thank you for redeeming me and adopting me as your child and making it possible for me to have an intimate, Father/child relationship with you. Thank you for the incredible inheritance that awaits me in heaven! For all of this I am deeply grateful! Amen.

Christmas 2

John 1:(1-9) 10-18

The child in me still loves opening gifts at Christmas. One of my favorite experiences while opening gifts is what I call "The Shocker!" You know it is a "shocker" when the one opening the gift stops and gasps in surprise as they see what is in the package! Then when they pull it out of its wrapping, everyone gasps along with them, exclaiming, "That is beautiful! That is awesome!" Turning their attention to the one who gave it, they ask, "Where did you get it? That must have cost a fortune!" or "How did you make it?" (depending on the gift).

I see this Gospel Lesson as similar to a "shocker" gift, for when we first peek into the Gospel of John through this text, we might find ourselves making similar exclamations and asking similar questions. "This is beautiful! This is incredible! How did he do it? Is it really true? This is mine to keep? It must have cost God a fortune!"

John is introducing us to (and will unfold throughout the rest of his gospel) the wonder and marvel of who Jesus is, and the incredible significance of that for all who believe. The whole idea of the Word becoming flesh in the form of Jesus is a brainteaser. None of us have ever seen our words take on human form. How can this be? It is a mystery that is outside of our ability to fully comprehend it. However, that does not make it any less true, nor does it mean we can't in some way experience this truth, for we can.

There is great significance in this for us who proclaim God's Word week after week. First of all, it is so important to remember that God's Word is alive. Yes, it took on living flesh in the person of Jesus Christ, but yet today it is a living word. It is not merely a book about God, or about the history of the Judeo-Christian faith. It is the living and active Word of God which touches the hearts and minds of men, women, and children who read or hear it. It affects change in the lives of those who will submit to its authority and do what it says. It is timeless truth that never changes, nor becomes outdated or obsolete. If we see God's Word through any other lens, we diminish it's effectiveness in our ministries.

Secondly, it is absolutely essential that we recognize and emphasize, in our preaching and teaching, that God's Word is full of grace and truth. Many people feel (and it is always people who are feeling guilty) that the Bible is too harsh and demanding. They see it merely as a book of do's and don'ts. Unfortunately, they are not listening to the grace that comes through from cover to cover. Just as Jesus was full of grace (for he was God's grace in the flesh), so too, God's Word is full of grace. It is, in fact, God's main, primary, number one way of delivering his grace to us. When we ignore the Word of God, minimize it in any way, or diminish its significance and importance for all people everywhere, we are doing a grave injustice to this inexhaustible source of grace.

Equally as tragic, is the fact that fewer and fewer people (pastors included) are upholding the Word of God as absolute truth. Through what has become known as "relativism," more and more people are making the arrogant assumption that truth is in the eye of the beholder; that what is true for you may not be true for me. Anything can be true then, no matter how big of a lie and deception it really is. This way of thinking also destroys the effectiveness of God's Word to bring salvation to a lost world and hope to the hopeless, for it has lost its God-given distinction as being the timeless, unchanging, source of truth that it is.

If Jesus was full of truth — and few would dare make the claim that he was anything but truthful — then God's Word is also full of truth.

We in the Christian church have been given an incredible gift that ought to cause us to gasp as we open and read it. When we reveal it to others, there ought to be a sense of awe and amazement as well, for we are, through God's Word, being given grace upon grace, which is absolutely amazing and absolutely true!

A Pastor's Prayer:
Dear Lord,
Thank you that you and your word are full of grace and truth and absolutely true. Please make your word alive in me today and enable me to preach in it all its truth and authority. Amen.

Ephesians 1:3-14

Perhaps this Christmas you had loved ones or parishioners (or better yet, both!) lavish you with gifts of love and appreciation. I have personally been deeply moved, again and again, by the way my wife and children, and many appreciative parishioners, have lavished me with gifts — whether at Christmas or at other occasions. It seems the more lavish the gift, the more deeply moved I am. Yet, whenever I read this Epistle Lesson, I find myself asking, "Do I respond with the same sense of gratitude and humility toward the grace of God that has been lavished upon me, as I do toward earthly gifts that are given me?"

I know I have often failed to appreciate God's grace as I ought. Oh, there have been those "mountaintop" experiences when I have been moved to tears by God's grace and mercy and the forgiveness of sins, but for the most part, I know I take it for granted. Perhaps the reason for this can be better understood when we consider the gifts that family or parishioners might lavish upon us. If they are once-in-a-lifetime gifts, or annual expressions of love and appreciation, then we are more likely to be moved and appreciative. However, if those lavish gifts were to become daily provision, would we not begin to grow accustomed to them and take them for granted? I know I would! Thus a passage like this is good for us, and those whom we minister to, as it reminds us of how lavish and extravagant God's gifts to us are. Let's look closely at them by way of reminder.

First of all, let us remember that we have been *blessed with every spiritual blessing!* We haven't been given a part of the package, but the whole thing! And it is all ours simply through faith in Christ! Notice that God always intended, *before the foundations* of the earth were even laid, that we would be chosen (in Christ) *to be holy and blameless!* What an incredible gift! Try as we may, we can never on our own stand holy and blameless before God to the degree which God requires, so he planned to choose us as his very own holy and blameless children through a personal relationship with Christ. Only those who receive this gift, of course, actually know the joy of having received it.

The same point is repeated in the next verse, only with different words, as Paul announced our *adoption as children* of God, again through Christ, but emphasized that this wonderful gift was according to the *good pleasure* of God's *will*, which he *freely bestowed* on us. Can't you just see the excitement in God's eyes as he holds out this glorious gift of grace to one person after another? It's similar to (yet greater than) that sparkle in the eyes of those who are about to lavish a very meaningful, and possibly expensive, gift upon us.

However, an expensive, lavish gift, as generous as it may be, doesn't mean much to us if we don't know what it is or its purpose. So Paul reminds us what God's grace is all about and what it is for. It is for the purpose of redeeming us back to God from Satan and for the *forgiveness of our trespasses*. If we tend to take this gift of grace lightly, then we would do well to consider what life and eternity would be like without it! Do we want to face the full weight and consequences of our sins on our own? I sure don't! Yet I am so guilty of taking this precious gift for granted.

Once in a while we are given a gift in which the giver did not fully think through what they were doing and merely acted out of emotional impulse. As it turned out, they really couldn't afford it. But Paul reminds us that God did his giving with *all wisdom and insight*. He knew what he was doing then and he still knows what he is doing today as he gives us his grace over again and again.

Lastly, Paul goes on to remind us of a wonderful *inheritance* that is ours and the free gift of God's *Holy Spirit* as well. Space does not permit me to sufficiently describe the full extent of all God has lavished on us, but I'm sure you get the point by now and see that there is no other proper response, but to praise him daily for all he has given us!

A Pastor's Prayer:
Dear Lord,
    I praise you and thank you for all you have lavished upon me ... *(pray through the text)*. Forgive me for how I have taken all of this for granted. Teach me to appreciate it as I should. Amen.

The Epiphany Of Our Lord

Matthew 2:1-12

These men, who came looking for Christ, have always impressed me. They had to have been working with rather sketchy information, and yet they pursued their mission with great determination. And what amazes me is that no one in the land of Judea seemed to have a clue! It reminds me of how we can be looking for our car keys, but just can't find them. Then somebody comes into the room and finds them right away, only to point out that they were "right under our nose" all the time! So, too, the child for whom the Wise Men were looking was "right under the nose" of the Jewish people and yet they never noticed him.

We see in our text that the *chief priests and scribes* knew something about the potential birth of Christ, for they quoted out of their own prophet's writings and were able to steer these travelers, from the East, to Bethlehem. This scene (in vv. 1-8) amazes me, for if the chief priests and scribes knew where the Christ was to be born, why weren't they out looking for him? Why didn't this peculiar situation cause them to go and make a diligent search for the child?

I wonder if we, in ministry, can become as careless and filled with apathy as the religious leaders of that day? In other words, is it possible that people might come to us, filled with curiosity about the claims of Christ and the truths of scripture, and we simply brush them off or tell them to look for answers on their own? Is it possible for us to be too familiar with truths of God's Word that we lose our interest and curiosity, and no longer pursue these truths with those who are searching? I fear it is. And that ought to grieve us deeply!

The chief priests and scribes, if they had been on the ball and doing their job, should have not only told the Wise Men what their prophets had written and where they believed the Christ Child to be born, but they should have gone with them and looked for him also. They should have had the same faith and passion that these Gentile travelers had. But they didn't, and as a result, they missed out on an awesome discovery.

Notice the emotion that the Wise Men felt when they realized that they were being divinely led to this wonderful discovery: *they set out; and there, ahead of them, went the star that they had seen at its rising, until it stopped over the place where the child was. When they saw that the star had stopped, they were overwhelmed with joy.*

When was the last time you were overwhelmed with joy over a rich discovery in God's Word? When was the last time you were overwhelmed with joy, realizing that God's Spirit had just opened your eyes to something you had never seen in his word before, or enabled you to understand a passage that you had never understood before?

I have noticed, over the years, that often someone who has not grown up in the church is more excited about coming to faith in Christ, or discovering some new truth from the Bible, than most people who grew up in the church and have been reading their Bible all their life. Should we not be just as overwhelmed with joy at the message of a Savior for all who believe? Is it not still good news for us, too, and not just the unbelieving sinner? Is not the story of Christ's birth just as good news today as it was then? The answer to all those questions is, "Yes!"

Perhaps one way to renew and recapture that joy once again, is to do as the Wise Men did: to worship Christ once they found him. Jesus is, as we sometimes say, "only a prayer away." Therefore he is not hard to find. When we find him, may we be quick to worship him, whether privately or publicly. As we do so, and others see the joy that is ours as a result of having found him and worshiped him, it will be contagious. Others will want to look for Jesus, too, and hopefully we will not only steer them in the right direction, but actually "go there" with them and make the discovery with them all over again, no matter how many times we've done this.

A Pastor's Prayer:
Dear Lord,

Please fill me with an overwhelming joy over your birth and arrival here on earth. May I never take lightly the significance of your birth for me, but be quick to worship and praise you for who you are and for what you have done for me. Thank you! Amen.

Ephesians 3:1-12

The season of Epiphany is all about revelation, and specifically the revelation of Christ Jesus to the world as the Son of God. In this Epistle Lesson, the Apostle Paul pointed out that God had commissioned him to be a servant in this revelation process. Paul had an Epiphany experience on the road to Damascus and since then God's Holy Spirit had been revealing more and more of Christ to Paul. Paul clearly understood his calling to be one through whom the Holy Spirit would reveal Christ to the world.

We too have been called to help with this process. As we proclaim the Word of God, the Holy Spirit is speaking through us to those who either have never heard, or who have, but never understood what they heard.

What we proclaim has its share of mystery to it, but not to the extent that it held for those who lived before Christ. There had been an understanding that the Messiah would one day come, but exactly when, no one knew. In addition to that, a major element of this mystery, which had been concealed up to this time, was the revelation of Christ to the Gentiles so they too might *become fellow heirs, members of the same body, and sharers in the promise in Christ Jesus through the gospel.*

Although this text was Paul's commentary on what God had been doing in and through him to advance the gospel, it can be (and should be) ours as well. Read with me, verses 7-10, and I think you will agree:

Of this gospel I have become a servant according to the gift of God's grace that was given me by the working of his power. Although I am the very least of all the saints, this grace was given to me to bring to the Gentiles (or we might add the name of our community here) *the news of the boundless riches of Christ, and to make everyone see what is the plan of the mystery hidden for ages in God who created all things; so that through the church the wisdom of God in its rich variety might now be made known to the rulers and authorities in the heavenly places.*

Could we describe our calling any better than this?

You see, my colleagues, we are little more than servants in God's kingdom, no matter what level of ministry degree we have.

And Paul identified himself as *the very least of all the saints*, so what does that make us? Few pastors, if any, are as educated as Paul was, as well versed on the law as Paul was, and as gifted for evangelism, teaching, and writing as Paul was.

But nevertheless, let us understand that we have, by God's doing, *become a servant according to the gift of God's grace that was given* [us] *by the working of his power*. We have been chosen to be a member of the "Epiphany team" to help reveal Christ to the world. This grace was given to us so that we might effectively bring the good *news of the boundless riches of Christ* to everyone we have opportunity to share it with. And the effect of this, according to Paul, is that *rulers and authorities in the heavenly places* will also have Epiphany experiences, whereby they will better understand the wisdom of God. Our mission and purpose of proclaiming the gospel is not to them, but to the spiritually lost in the world around us. As we do so, it is having a positive effect on heavenly beings to a degree that we will not fully understand until we get to heaven. That is a pretty awesome thought, when you think about it!

Paul then encouraged the Ephesian church with something that can serve to be an encouragement to us as well. What Paul had done by way of being a part of the Epiphany process; what the Ephesians were doing by way of being a part of the Epiphany process; and what we in the church today are doing by being involved with the ongoing Epiphany process of revealing Christ to the world, is *in accordance with the eternal purpose that he has carried out in Christ Jesus our Lord*. How exciting it is to be a part of something so huge and life changing!

A Pastor's Prayer:
Dear Lord,

Thank you for making me your servant and blessing me with your grace that I may be so privileged to be a part of this great Epiphany movement of revealing Christ, not only to Gentiles, but to all who do not know you. Amen.

The Baptism Of Our Lord/Epiphany 1

Mark 1:4-11

There are many events in the Bible that I wish I could have witnessed firsthand, and this is one of them! What an awesome scene! I'm sure it was a moving time for John, as he tried to grasp the significance of what was going on. Clearly he didn't fully understand it all, for we read in Matthew's Gospel that John thought it more appropriate for Jesus to baptize him rather than for him to baptize Jesus. However, Jesus insisted that John baptize him, *for it is proper for us in this way to fulfill all righteousness* (Matthew 4:15).

So this marvelous scene unfolded, where Jesus and John went down into the Jordan River where our Lord was baptized. As Jesus came up out of the water, *he saw the heavens torn apart and the Spirit descending like a dove on him.* It is not clear from the gospels whether anyone else saw this, but if others did, we can only imagine that it must have been a powerful experience! We have all seen some pretty amazing cloud formations, especially before or after a violent storm, but one can barely conceive what it would have looked like to see the *heavens torn apart!* To be sure, it was an awesome display of God's power being exercised over his creation.

Added to this magnificent scene was the descent of the Spirit of God upon Jesus in the likeness of a dove. Many artists have tried to capture this scene on canvas or paper, but the best imaginations and the most artistic abilities will always fall short of being able to capture the true awesomeness of this event.

Perhaps the most awesome part of this scene was when God spoke from heaven. What did that sound like? How would we have reacted to this? Would we have fallen on our faces, gotten chills down our spine, and goose bumps on our arms? Would we have understood the words or just heard a mighty sound? Perhaps I think too much, but I like to put myself in some of these situations, for it helps me get a better feel for what God might want me to hear, see, and experience from the text.

This much we can experience: to hear again what the Father said to the Son: *You are my Son, the Beloved; with you I am well pleased.* Wow! What powerful words of affirmation! Notice that this statement came at the beginning of Jesus' ministry, which means God was pleased as to how Jesus had conducted himself during the first thirty-some years of his life. His life had been largely private up to that point (at least private from the pages of scripture). God was also pleased, no doubt, that his Son was obediently and submissively beginning his ministry in accordance with God's timing, will, and plan for his life. And certainly God was pleased with his Son as he looked ahead to the future, knowing Jesus would carry out every detail of his will exactly the way he had planned it.

As ambassadors for Christ, God would certainly like to say the same of us as well. Could he say to you, "With you I am well pleased"? How have you lived your life up to this point? Did you go into active, parish ministry for the right reasons? Are you serving him, or self? Are you ministering according to his timing, will, and plan for your life? Are you determined (as best you are able) to carry out God's perfect will for your life in the future?

These are hard questions that remind us we fall short of God's will at times, and that we will never be as pleasing to God as Jesus was. But thank God for his grace that forgives our sins and enables us to be more and more like his perfect Son.

A Pastor's Prayer:
Dear Lord,

Thank you for sending your Son to carry out your good and perfect work of atonement on my behalf. Thank you, Jesus, for being well pleasing in your Father's eyes. Please forgive me for all the times I have fallen short of your perfect will for me. Help me, Lord, to more and more live my life, and carry out my ministry, in a way that is well pleasing to you. Thank you. Amen.

Acts 19:1-7

I think it would have been fascinating (yet exhausting!) to have traveled with the Apostle Paul on his missionary journeys.

Imagine spending day after day on foot, in the Middle Eastern and the Northern Mediterranean regions, trying to keep up with Paul! Or worse yet, sailing in the ships of his day in the midst of storms to the point of actual shipwreck, and still walking away from it without having lost our vision and purpose for what we were doing. That was Paul, a first-century missionary.

In this lesson we read that he had arrived in Ephesus where he found some followers of Christ. These people had not been converted by Paul, or by any of Christ's disciples who had been through the Pentecost experience that we read about in Acts 2. If they had come to faith in Christ through the teaching of one of them, they would have been fully aware of the Holy Spirit and been baptized in the name of Jesus. Instead, we read that they had been baptized into John's baptism and had no clue who, or what, the Holy Spirit was. So Paul brought them up to speed; explaining to them The Trinity and baptizing them *in the name of the Lord Jesus.*

What happened next makes many of us in the Christian church uneasy, as we more than likely don't practice this in our own church traditions and are often skeptical of those who do. Luke described the activity this way: *When Paul had laid his hands on them, the Holy Spirit came upon them, and they spoke in tongues and prophesied....*

What makes us uneasy is the part about these twelve people speaking in tongues and prophesying. I believe we need to be very careful not to develop formulas as to how God works in and through the lives of believers, whether they are new believers or people who have believed in Christ for a long time. Churches who have developed their theological positions, their doctrines, their traditions, and their rituals around formulas, end up implying (if not outright teaching) that everything has to happen a certain way (especially when it comes to the work of the Holy Spirit) or else one is not truly saved.

If we were to do a careful study of the book of Acts, we would find that the Holy Spirit came upon various individuals and groups of people in various ways, and the manifestation of his presence in that individual or group of people varied as well. In other words, is everyone who is baptized able to speak in tongues and prophesy?

If we can't do either, does that mean we have not truly received the Holy Spirit? Some would say, "Yes," but the Apostle Paul would say, "No," for he made it clear that speaking in tongues and prophesying are gifts that the Spirit gives to some people, but not everyone (see 1 Corinthians 12:4-11).

So why did the Holy Spirit come upon these people when Paul laid his hands on them? Because that is the way God chose to enter them at that time. Why did they speak in tongues and prophesy? Because that is the way God chose to manifest himself to them and to give them a visible sign of his invisible presence.

"But," we might wonder, "Why doesn't he do that today? Why doesn't he do that through me?" God seems to still choose when and how he is going to come upon those who believe. I have laid hands on people and prayed for them, whether at their baptism, or while anointing them with oil for healing, or for some other occasion of prayer, yet none of them ever spoke in tongues or prophesied. Does that mean that the Holy Spirit was not present or at work? No. It just means that he was doing his work in a different, yet equally effective, way.

If you believe in Jesus Christ for salvation and eternal life, know that the Holy Spirit is in you. We don't need an emotional experience with a special anointing or laying on of hands for that to be true.

A Pastor's Prayer:
Dear Lord,

Thank you for your Spirit who comes to us, not only in baptism, but in other ways and at other times, primarily through your word. Please manifest yourself to me, and through me, with the gifts you have given me now and those you reveal to me in the future. Amen.

Epiphany 2

John 1:43-51

The season of Epiphany is about revelation and coming to a better understanding of who Jesus is, as God's Son and the Savior of the world, for Jew and Gentile alike. However, as this Gospel Lesson points out, our quest to know who Jesus is can also result in us learning more about ourselves.

As Jesus went from town to town, calling men to follow him, not only was he revealing himself to them and the world, but he was also opening their eyes to themselves. Let's take Philip, for example. When Jesus called him, there was no hesitation on Philip's part. In fact, Philip's invitation to Nathanael revealed that he was not only expecting the Messiah, but he recognized and accepted Jesus as the fulfillment of Old Testament prophecy. He was so confident in his beliefs and convictions that he went immediately to his friend and told him about Jesus!

Nathanael, on the other hand, proved to be a skeptic. When he heard Philip's excited invitation to follow Jesus and recognized that Philip truly believed Jesus to be the fulfillment of prophecy, Nathanael blurted out: *Can anything good come out of Nazareth?* His reply revealed who he was and what he believed (or didn't believe). He seemed to believe that Nazareth was such a low-down community that nothing good could come from there, much less the Messiah! He had bought into the world's view of that community, and perhaps also the Judaist view of the Messiah. As the gospels unfold, it is very clear that the view and sentiments of the leading Jews were not all that different from that of Nathanael.

However, his negative comment didn't dampen Philip's enthusiasm, nor Christ's pursuit of Nathanael. Instead, it gave Jesus an opportunity to reveal to Nathanael more than he knew about himself. Jesus spoke of Nathanael as if he had known him before (which, of course, he had, for Jesus, being God, knows all things about all people). Nathanael responded with astonishment: *Where did you get to know me?* After hearing Jesus' answer, he then blurted out a whole new confession regarding Jesus: *Rabbi, you are the Son of God! You are the King of Israel!*

In the churches we serve, there are Philips who readily hear and respond to God's invitation to follow him. These people are exciting to minister to, for not only do they respond quickly and enthusiastically to the gospel, but they are also quick to share the gospel and invite others to Christ. The Philips in the world, not only grow God's kingdom, but they also grow the church!

But there are also Nathanaels in the church, who are skeptical of Christ, the gospel, and the church. As soon as we invite them to get more involved, they respond negatively, because they have an inaccurate and unbiblical view of the church. These people can discourage us and get us down. They are the ones who intimidate us to the point that we don't even want to witness for Christ, because the rejection hurts too much.

Even amongst clergy there are Philips and Nathanaels. The Philips have strong convictions, are confident in what they believe, are quick to invite others to come to Christ and to church, and are not intimidated by the sharp comebacks and skepticism of others. The Nathanaels, on the other hand, are easily discouraged and quick to be cynical, for people do not always measure up and the church often fails to meet their expectations.

The Nathanaels in our world, whether outside the church, in the pews, or in the pulpits, need to hear Christ's words when he said: *I saw you*. Christ sees us and knows us better than we know ourselves. In our quest to know him better, and to bolster our faith in him, he reveals to us those things that stand in the way of increased faith and a closer relationship with him. May we be quick to change our confession of faith, like Nathanael did, if it is lacking in understanding and weak in faith.

A Pastor's Prayer:
Dear Lord,

Please make me more like Philip, who was quick to follow you and witness to others. Replace my doubts with faith, my cynicism with love for you and others, and my fears with confidence and deep conviction. Thank you. Amen.

1 Corinthians 6:12-20

How well are you taking care of God's "house"? I'm not referring to the church building in which you serve, but the body in which you live. Every time I read this text I am convicted of one sin or another. Therefore, absolute honesty with ourselves and with God is essential if we are going to hear and be blessed by the full meaning and message of this text.

I fully trust what Paul wrote here, not only because it is the Word of God, but because Paul wrote it as a fellow clergyman. Paul was in ministry and understood the temptations we face, at least through the lens of his culture and period in history. The temptations he faced, though presented to him differently than ours are, were not all that different, in general, from what we face.

All too many people (pastors included) have taken the six-word phrase, *All things are lawful for me*, which is repeated twice in verse 12, and used it as justification for sin. They have convinced themselves that since they are saved by grace and not by works, they are above and immune to God's timeless, moral law. Therefore they can do whatever they want. WRONG!

How important that we read this in its complete context. There may be sins we commit that are permissible in our society, but that does not give us a license to sin. In fact, Paul said, what might be lawful may not be *beneficial* for us and others. With great boldness he stated: *I will not be dominated by anything.* Can you say that with all honesty, or is there something that is dominating your life? Paul identified one thing in particular that so many of us struggle with: sexual sin. However, there are many other things that we may say or do that are legal in our society but are not pleasing to God, and, in fact, are harmful to our body, such as working too hard and not getting enough rest. The mismanagement of stress in our lives is taking a huge toll on many pastors. Poor diet and a lack of exercise are other abuses of our bodies. The use of alcohol, tobacco, and other stimulating drugs, to help us function or as a way of coping with stress, are also harmful to our bodies and therefore displeasing to our Lord who desires to dwell in our bodies.

Paul went on to point out that *the body is meant not for fornication, but for the Lord, and the Lord for the body.* If you are struggling with sexual sin, or any other sin, remember that your body is not your own, to do with whatever you wish. It is a temple of the Holy Spirit — God's house. It is a place that he created, not only for your enjoyment, but for him to dwell in and, through that body, to bring honor and glory to him.

Temptation is a way of life for everyone. There is no way to fully avoid all temptations, but there are things we can do to minimize our vulnerability to them. I encourage you to get plenty of rest and work hard at nurturing and caring for your body. Nurture your relationships at home as well as in the church. Talk to someone you trust about your discouragements; find someone you trust to hold you accountable in areas of weakness. Set goals and priorities that include sufficient time for taking care of yourself and your loved ones. But most of all, remember what Paul wrote: *You were bought with a price; therefore glorify God in your body.*

The power to glorify God in our bodies is found in the resurrection; *God raised the Lord and will also raise us by his power.* We know he will raise us in the final resurrection, but let us be encouraged to know that he will also raise us out of times of temptation, out of bad habits, out of addictions, out of anything that is harmful to his temple — our body. As the old hymn of the church reminds us, there is "Victory in Jesus!"

A Pastor's Prayer:
Dear Lord,

You know my struggles and temptations, so please forgive me for all the times I have given in to temptation and sinned against you. Please send your resurrection power into my life to raise me to victory each time I am tempted to sin in thought, word, or deed. It is a great privilege to have you take up residency in my body. I want it to be a home you can be proud of, that will bring you much honor and glory. Thank you! Amen.

Epiphany 3

Mark 1:14-20

Last week's Gospel Lesson was about Christ's call to Philip and Nathanael to follow him. I pointed out how their first response to his call revealed a lot about who they were and what they believed. Today's lesson is similar: we find Jesus calling four more men to follow him. They are Simon, Andrew, James, and John. It's interesting to note that preceding their call, Jesus came to them, proclaiming *the good news of God,* which contained his purpose and his main message: *The time is fulfilled, and the kingdom of God has come near; repent, and believe in the good news.*

Jesus was there, in the fulfillment of time, to bring the kingdom of God to earth. If this message had not preceded their call, these men would have had no idea what they were being invited to join. So it is today, when we are called to serve God in his kingdom work. He clearly lays out for us in his word what his purpose and message is. Then he calls us to join him in *fishing* for men, women, and children who do not know him in a personal and intimate way for salvation and eternal life.

When was the last time you reflected upon God's call in your life to follow and serve him? Do you know why you were called? Do you know what you were called to do? Do you even know if you were called? Maybe you simply chose the ministry as a career choice because you like to help people, or you've always wanted to work in the church, or because you've had, for a long time, a curiosity in regards to spiritual matters. Dear friend, if you are in the ministry without a clear sense of call from God, you may be doing his church more harm than good.

Personally, I fought the call of God for a long time. It first came when I was eighteen years old, but I ignored it for thirteen years. Time and again God called me, in one way or another, but I ran from his call until I couldn't run anymore. Finally, in the midst of losing my dream — a beautiful dairy farm in west central Minnesota — I yielded my life to God and left everything, to follow him and *fish for people.* The thought of preaching and teaching was frightening, but I was willing to learn, for I now clearly understood God's will for me and my desire to listen to, and follow, his will. For all who hear and heed the call of God to follow him and fish for men, find it to be a life-changing experience and very rewarding. It's not always easy (in fact, it seldom is!), but God daily gives us everything we need to carry out this call.

I've often wondered what Zebedee must have thought as he watched his sons walk away, leaving him with the nets and boats. Maybe he was very understanding, but there is no way of knowing for sure. Unfortunately, many men and women follow the call of God into ministry, only to have their families show little or no support. Maybe that was your experience, and you still need some assurance from God that you really did hear his call and did the right thing.

Dear friend, if you understand and agree with God's purpose and mission here on earth, and if you have unmistakably sensed his call upon your life to serve him in parish ministry, then you can continue to serve him with confidence that you are in the center of his will for you. With that confidence before you, you don't have to worry about what others are thinking or saying about your decision to follow and serve God. It was hard work and often frightening for the disciples, too, but look at how God was able to use them to start and build the Christian church. In the same way, God is using you to grow his church and will continue to use you in ways that you can't even imagine at this time in your life.

A Pastor's Prayer:
Dear Lord,

If I am in the ministry for the wrong reasons, please forgive me and help me know what to do now. If you have called me, continue to give me reassurance of that and help me not to worry about what others think. Thank you that you can, and will, continue to use me to grow your church as I faithfully *fish for people*. Amen.

1 Corinthians 7:29-31

This is an interesting text for the season of Epiphany (or for any season of the church year, for that matter!). If taken all by itself, without understanding the context, it sounds like warped, legalistic advice from a pietist; but it isn't. Paul had a good reason for what he wrote, and although the specific advice may not apply directly to us today, at the heart of the text is a central truth that we would do well to take seriously and allow the Holy Spirit to apply to our hearts.

The larger context in which this passage is set, has to do with marriage, but there is another issue in the background that is driving Paul's advice. The issue is mentioned in verse 26 as an *impending crisis*. We are not told specifically what that crisis was, but it may well have been religious persecution, for that was an ongoing crisis for the first-century church. Due to the increasingly harsh treatment that Christians were receiving, it was commonly believed that the Lord might return at any time. We might laugh at that, but when you think about it, due to the fact that his return is imminent, we live with the same sense of expectancy as they did. The Lord could have returned at that time, if that had been God's will, just as he could return at any moment now. So they did not hold that belief due to ignorance, but due to the nature of the imminent return of Christ.

The danger for us, living 2,000 years later, is to slip into apathy, thinking, "They thought he would return very soon, but he didn't. It has now been 2,000 years and he still hasn't returned. Who knows, it could be a long time yet, so why get excited?" True, it could be a long time yet, but we don't know that for sure. Regardless of when he comes, it will be without warning and it will catch all people by some degree of surprise. For those who are ready and watching for his return, it will be a pleasant surprise! For those who are not prepared or watching for his return, it will be a horrific surprise!

So, due to persecution, Paul's advice to those living at that time was to avoid intimate relationships, if at all possible, and to not hold tightly to the things of this world, for such attachments — both to people and to things — can make faithfulness to Christ more difficult when facing death for that belief. For example, it would be easier for a man to face death for his faith in Christ if he were single, than if he had just gotten married; or worse yet, if he had children. The same held true for women and children.

We may not be facing an *impending crisis*, like that of the early church, but we may have a problem with holding too tightly to people and things. Unfaithfulness to Christ is a huge problem in the church today. People put others before Christ in terms of their love, time, and devotion. They put work and pleasure before serving Christ. They will spend money they don't have on things they don't need, which are things that won't last. Instead, they could be giving sacrificially to Christ out of gratefulness for all he has given them, thereby laying up treasures in heaven that can never be destroyed.

It is important for pastors to hear the heart of this text. The eyes of our congregations are upon us, watching our attachments to people and to things; they often pattern their attachments after ours. Are we setting a biblical example for them to follow? Are we living as if the Lord could return any day? Not in neglect of our loved ones, nor self-imposed poverty, nor even self-righteous celibacy for that matter, but in loose attachment to all that is temporal, and in an intimate, tight relationship with him who is eternal.

Neither Paul nor I am proposing a heavenly mindedness that makes us of no earthly good, but rather cautioning us from being so attached to people and things that it hinders our love for, loyalty to, and faith in, our Lord and Savior, Jesus Christ.

A Pastor's Prayer:
Dear Lord,

Please help me to see if any of my relationships with people, and my attachments to temporal things, are in any way hindering my love for, loyalty to, and faith in, you. I desire you above all else and ask that you forgive me for those times when I haven't put you first. Amen.

Epiphany 4

Mark 1:21-28

Do you find it difficult to preach with authority? If so, you are not alone. Many pastors do. Some are timid in their preaching because they are not fully convinced of what they are preaching. If we lack conviction and passion for what we are preaching, it will be evident to those who are listening.

Some pastors find it hard to preach with authority because they are afraid of people. They know there are issues that should be addressed, such as lying, gossip, adultery, and so on, but they are afraid of offending the big givers, or the visitors who could be potential members, or their church leaders who have cautioned them to avoid certain topics. How sad!

Some pastors find it hard to preach with authority because they've bought political correctness and relativism into it. They truly believe it is better to withhold the truth of God's Word than run the risk of offending any one individual or group of people. In some cases they believe that all truth is relative. Much of God's Word is true for them, but they don't want to offend those who disagree, so they avoid preaching it as universal truth for all people. Again, how sad, for in so doing, the authority of God's Word has been smothered and the proclamation of it has no power, rendering it basically useless. Perhaps this is why the thirty-minute sermon, which was more common in the past, has been reduced to a mere homily that often is little more than a nice story.

This Gospel Lesson helps us understand why Jesus spoke with authority, what the effect of that preaching was, and why it is so important for us to preach with authority as well.

First of all, notice that Jesus spoke with authority because he was (and is) the Son of God. It took a man with an unclean spirit to point that out! What a tragedy! Not even the scribes recognized who Jesus was, and they were regarded as the upholders of truth! Jesus also spoke with authority because nobody else did. The scribes were merely teaching people their traditions and passing on stories. They were telling the people what they wanted to hear instead of what they needed to hear. Jesus was not going to stand idly by when there were truths that needed to be spoken, and spoken with authority, lest the people perish.

The effect of his authoritative preaching was amazing! First of all, it stirred up an unclean spirit! This spirit was afraid, for suddenly someone posed a threat to him. Dear friends, think about it. What a sad state of spiritual affairs, when the preaching is so weak and pathetic in our churches that the unclean spirits are not even threatened or challenged! Could that be happening today? It surely could be!

In addition to the spirit's reaction, there was the reaction of the people who were listening. We read that the people were *astounded* and *amazed* at his teaching! When was the last time people filed out of your church astounded and amazed at the authority with which you spoke? If anything, some are amazed that more people didn't fall asleep! This goes for me, too. I grieve over my own failure to stir people's hearts with God's Word. Most certainly the stirring of the heart is a work of the Holy Spirit, and God can do that with a less-gifted preacher as well as he can with a dynamic one, for the Word of God has an authority all its own. However, when we preach it boldly, with conviction and passion that were first stirred deep within our own hearts, and preach it as well as we know how with the gifts God has given us, things are going to happen. Unclean spirits will be threatened, people will be amazed, some will come to faith in Christ, others might leave and never come back, but all in all, God will be glorified and people will be changed.

Remember, Jesus' *fame* wasn't all glorious popularity and backslapping. Some of it was outright hatred and death threats. Hopefully none of us experience that, but we shouldn't let the risk of unpopularity keep us from preaching with Christ's authority. So let's preach God's Word the best we can for his honor and glory.

A Pastor's Prayer:
Dear Lord,

You know what keeps me from preaching with authority. Please forgive me for when I have failed you in this way. Give me a deep conviction and passion for the truths of your word and boldness to preach them with authority to all who listen. Thank you. Amen.

1 Corinthians 8:1-13

Deep convictions, based on wrong or faulty information, have split many churches over the years. In this text, the Apostle Paul was addressing a very real issue for the Corinthian Christians, which was threatening to divide them. On one side of the issue were those people who were adamantly opposed to eating food that had been offered to idols. On the other side of the issue were those (including Paul) who believed it wasn't wrong to eat this food, for *no idol in the world really exists*, and therefore they believed the food was acceptable to eat.

However, Paul knew that simply defending his position was not going to make the issue go away. In addition to trying to help people be better informed about the reality of the issue, Paul knew that sensitivity toward the convictions of others must be exercised or they could be harmed spiritually.

In our churches today we face issues all the time that people strongly disagree on. We, as well, have our own convictions on some of these issues, like Paul did. To make matters worse, people often want us to pick sides, but this is dangerous and can severely damage our effectiveness as a pastor. I'm speaking now, of course, about those "gray" areas that Christians disagree on — issues that are *not* clearly spelled out in scripture.

During my childhood, I was raised in a pietistic home that had very strict guidelines about what could or could not be done, and what would or would not come into our home. The television was regarded to be about as pagan as food offered to idols. In other words, there would never be a television in our home, and we were seldom allowed to go to the homes of friends (or even cousins) that had televisions. Granted, there is little on television that is of much mental and spiritual value, but the programming of the sixties was a whole lot better than it is today!

When I came to the realization that I was *not* putting my salvation in jeopardy by having a television, I adopted a different set of convictions, based on new and, I believe, more accurate information. However, from time to time, I come across people who do not have a television in their home. Rather than criticize them for that or try to change their mind, I make sure I sympathize with their concerns and avoid putting them in an awkward position whereby they feel pressured to watch my television.

So the whole point of this text was not to settle, once and for all, what was right or wrong about eating food that had been offered to idols (or any other biblically unclear issue), but rather, what was the right way to relate to those who had different convictions. Paul pointed out one aspect of the answer in verse 1: *Knowledge puffs up, but love builds up.*

One of the mistakes many Christians make (pastors included) is to show off their knowledge and to insist that the knowledge they have, on any given controversial issue, is the best knowledge there is and therefore ought to be the final answer. I've been guilty of this, and when I have, I have pushed people away from me. I've seen others in the church do the same, and in so doing they have run people out of the church. It grieves me deeply, because these were issues that I (and others) could have held personally without imposing them on others. If we would have shown love and respect for them and their views, though they may have differed greatly from ours, we could have continued to worship and fellowship together. But because I, or someone else, insisted that we were right and everyone else was wrong, the "walls" went up and the relationships broke down.

Brothers and sisters in ministry, let us follow Paul's advice. *Love builds up*, so may we be quick to love and slow to judge. In addition to this, we will want to avoid eating, saying, or doing anything in the presence of others that would be a stumbling block to them, even though we are truly convinced God has given us freedom in that area.

A Pastor's Prayer:
Dear Lord,

Thank you for the freedom of the gospel that sets us free from legalism and observance to rules. Please show me if there is any area in my life where my thinking is wrong, due to faulty information, so that I may live fully in your freedom. Help me to be sensitive to what others believe and careful not to hinder their faith with my freedom. Amen.

Epiphany 5

Mark 1:29-39

One of the many things I appreciate so much about Jesus, due to his human nature, is that he understood fatigue and the need to withdraw from people. If he, being God, got tired and needed to get away from people, how much more do we? The sooner we admit this, the better, for our desperate attempts to be "Super Pastors" (most often driven by a desire to please people) will eventually burn us out.

Notice the intensity of Jesus' ministry on one given day, which resulted in his fatigue and need to get away. First of all, as we read in last week's text (which immediately precedes this one), Jesus was in the synagogue preaching with authority. I don't know about you, but I almost always had a headache by Sunday afternoon — especially when I was serving two congregations. Preaching is exhausting, especially when preaching with authority, because such preaching is intense, emotional, and spiritually draining. When Jesus spoke in the synagogue that day, he stirred up an unclean spirit. When we speak God's Word with his authority, we are going to stir up unclean spirits and that is exhausting!

From there, Jesus went to visit Peter's mother-in-law who was in bed with a fever. This would be similar to us going on a hospital visit on a Sunday afternoon. While there, Jesus healed her. I recall one Sunday, after preaching at two churches 25 miles apart, I grabbed a bite to eat. Then, with my wife along to do some of the driving, we traveled ninety miles to a larger city hospital to anoint with oil a seven-year-old boy who was dying of leukemia, and to also baptize his four-year-old sister. This was a high point in my day and an exhilarating experience that was very moving for all who were there, but it was also emotionally, physically, and, perhaps, spiritually draining for me. I can't imagine what it would be like to heal someone as Jesus did!

I don't know if Jesus got a nap in there somewhere or not, but notice verses 32-34. It was now evening, the sun was going down, and, when most pastors would probably be sitting down and relaxing with their families or a good book, Jesus was being surrounded by needy people. In fact we're told that *the whole city was gathered around the door*! Now, either it was a very small city or there was a large mob surrounding the house he was in. I tend to believe it was the latter. Jesus did not send them away, as many of us might have. Rather, *he cured many who were sick with various diseases, and cast out many demons*. What a long day that must have been! And if Jesus got tired from it and needed to get away, how much more do we!

We might assume that he got some sleep that night, but the text doesn't say for sure. He may well have healed people late into the evening and possibly all night. However, our text tells us that he *got up and went out* while it was still early in the morning and *there he prayed*. I am of the personal opinion that the early morning hours, when the sun is beginning to come up, are truly the best hours of the day. I often walk for an hour or so in the mornings and have come to appreciate that time alone with God. I'm not sure why, but it seems like it is easier for me to pray while out under the wide open sky.

It would be interesting to know what Jesus prayed about that morning. And consider this: If he needed quiet time alone with God, how much more do we? I have become firmly convinced of the absolute importance of this in our daily lives. Prayer helps us get our focus on what really matters and what is most important for that day. It is through prayer that our sins are confessed, strength is found, vision restored, and determination received from the Lord. Jesus needed all of this to carry out his ministry.

We, too, desperately need this if we are going to be effective in our ministries. I urge you, if you are not already in the habit, to begin a daily habit of getting away by yourself and praying. It will never hurt you and your ministry, but if anything, will improve you and your ministry.

A Pastor's Prayer:
Dear Lord,

Thank you for the example you have set for me; that it is okay, and even essential, to get away from people when I am tired, to rest and pray. Help me to make time in my busy schedule for this and to use the time alone with you wisely. Amen.

1 Corinthians 9:16-23

Often I've wondered what it would have been like to travel with the Apostle Paul and study under his leadership and example. This text gives us some idea, for it reveals some of his strategy, or methodology, for evangelism. One thing is clear, and that is what drove Paul. He wrote: *I do it all for the sake of the gospel, so that I may share in its blessings.*

Paul clearly was not in the ministry for money. In fact, to make sure everyone knew that, he refused to take any compensation, even though he was fully entitled to financial support by the Christian church. If you were no longer able to be paid for proclaiming the gospel of Jesus Christ, would you still do it? You see, a major difference between Paul and pastors of today, is that he proclaimed the gospel of his own will, free of charge, because that is what he wanted to do. No one (except the Lord, perhaps) was telling him that he had to get out there and preach. We might say that we proclaim the gospel free of charge and of our own will, but do we really? Is there not an offering taken at almost every service we preach at? Do we not serve under a board of some kind that dictates, to one degree or another, how we spend our time and (in some cases) even what we can preach on? Do not many of our church traditions dictate the form and style our worship will take, the texts we shall preach on, and the doctrines we are to be loyal to? What if all that was gone? What if you were free to travel and preach the gospel to any one you wanted, from any text you wanted, in any style and format you wanted, for only one reason and one reason only: that you *might by all means save some*? Do you see now the big difference between Paul's ministry and ours today? I don't know about you, but I find Paul's ministry quite intriguing and refreshing!

Paul's ministry approach, as spelled out in verses 19-23, was flexibility. He didn't compromise with sin, but he was willing, so far as it didn't conflict with God's will for his life, to do whatever it took to help someone come to faith in Christ. Can we say the same of our ministries? Are we willing to share Christ with anyone, or just those who come within the doors of our church? Are we willing to build relationships with anyone, or just those who have something to give back to our church by way of money, time, talents, and leadership? Are we willing to become *a slave to all* so that we might *win more of them*, for no other reason but for *the sake of the gospel*?

Paul's greatest passion seemed to be that of saving souls. Paul wasn't a "sheep" counter, nor did he allow himself to be consumed with matters of money, politics, and social concerns. I'm not saying he didn't write about those issues, for he did. However, his greatest concern was for the spiritual well-being of Jews and Gentiles alike.

Fellow colleague, what is your greatest passion in ministry? Is it that souls are saved, or that attendance is up? Is it that people grow up in Christ, or that the budget balances? Is it for the spiritual well-being of everyone you come in contact with, or is it to make yourself look good in the eyes of others?

What consumes your time? Is it administration? Is it people-pleasing? Is it social concerns?

May God have mercy on us and help us to make some quick changes if our passion is not that of saving souls. God help us, if the majority of our time is spent on anything but that.

Dear friend, follow the example of Paul by sharing the gospel freely, not because you are paid to, but because you want to. I also urge you to exercise flexibility in how you share it, so that *by all means you might save some*.

A Pastor's Prayer:
Dear Lord,

Please examine the attitude of my heart. Where it is wrong, forgive me. Please show me what needs to change and help me to make the right adjustments so I might serve you as faithfully as the Apostle Paul. Even though I am paid for what I do, may I not proclaim your word for the purpose of money, but for the purpose of growing your kingdom. Thank you. Amen.

Epiphany 6

Mark 1:40-45

This passage is a beautiful word picture of Christ's compassion. As we picture the man with leprosy kneeling and begging, we get a real sense for the desperation of his situation. The man's life was being consumed by an illness that no one had been able to cure. It ruled his life, his relationships, and his future. It robbed him of most everything that was near and dear to him, including his hope.

As the picture of this scene unfolds in our mind's imagination, "watch" the face of Jesus as he looks intently at the pitiful, unclean, leprous beggar. Can you see the emotion? Can you see the compassion in his eyes, moistened by what could easily become tears?

Our text goes on to say that Jesus was *moved with pity*. The pity he felt throughout his very being moved him to do something shocking: He reached out to the man and *touched him*! That was unthinkable! The risk of Jesus getting leprosy, at that time, was like one of us deliberately exposing ourselves to an HIV infection. But that's what makes this word picture so powerful. Pity for others means nothing unless we are willing to touch them.

I see two powerful truths in this text for those of us who are actively ministering to broken people. First of all, remember that Jesus has taken pity on us. We will never, truly, sincerely have compassion and pity on others until we realize just how much compassion and pity Jesus has for us. And we will not know the full extent of that, until we agree with him on the full extent of our sinfulness. It doesn't matter how good a life we have lived up to this point, or how faithfully we have served our Lord; the truth of the matter is, we are all (as the Apostle Paul put it so bluntly in his letter to the Romans) *under the power of sin, as it is written*:

There is no one who is righteous, not even one and *all have sinned and fall short of the glory of God* (Romans 3:9, 10, 23).

Apart from the grace and mercy of God through Christ Jesus, we are all as damned and spiritually lost as the worst imaginable sinner who has ever lived. That neither sounds good nor feels good, but is true. Like the man with leprosy, apart from Christ, we are in a desperate situation — bound by a sin problem that no one but Christ can cure. It rules our life, our relationships, and our future. It robs us of most everything that is near and dear to us, including our hope. When we see who we are in this light, it helps us better comprehend the tremendous compassion and pity that Christ has had on us. May we rejoice in this, as the man did, when he realized he was not only healed, but declared *clean* in the eyes of everyone! May we respond to this as he did by going out and proclaiming *freely* the good news of the gospel so others might experience this same compassion and pity from Christ.

The other truth, which this text subtly brings out, is the example which Jesus set for those of us in ministry. Let's be quick to notice the "lepers" around us, who, like the man in our text, are desperate for the help that only Jesus can give. I'm not referring to those who come to our office desperate for financial help, or desperate for some favor, or desperately ashamed because they were caught in sin but are not sorry for it. I'm referring to those who have hit bottom spiritually, have lost all hope, and are desperate for what Jesus has to offer them. Maybe they know of Jesus, but just need someone to clearly explain the way of salvation to them and give them God's word of absolution after genuine confession of sin. Or, as is sometimes the case, maybe they don't know a thing about Jesus and we have to start from the beginning.

Bringing the healing of Christ to the "lepers" in our life is one of the most fulfilling things a pastor can do in his or her ministry. Pray that, by God's power, you can "heal" a leper today.

A Pastor's Prayer:
Dear Jesus,

I thank you and praise you for touching me and making me clean from sin! Lord, I ask that you would, through me, touch others, that they, too, might be clean from sin and know the joy of having you in their heart and life. Thank you. Amen.

1 Corinthians 9:24-27

In ministry, we often feel more like we are running a "rat race" than the race that Paul described in this text. Paul was a master of illustration. Good preachers and teachers know the power of illustrations to communicate truth, so we can appreciate this illustration from Paul.

In the preceding verses, which were last week's Epistle Lesson, Paul wrote about how his approach to spreading the gospel was in becoming all things to all people. He saw similarities between his ministry and that of the sport of competitive racing. His emphasis, however, was not on competition, for there is far too much of that in the church already. Pastors are guilty of this, too, as we often feel pressure to do better than other pastors in the area, or better than the pastor who served before us, or better than other pastors in our district. The more competitive we are by nature, the more likely we are to fall to this temptation. So, Paul was not encouraging churches to compete with each other, but calling Christians to be disciplined and self-controlled.

First of all, he urged us to *run in such a way that* [we] *may win* [the] *race*. This race is different from competitive races. In competition, only one runner wins and it is the one who finishes first. In the race that God would have us run, everyone who runs in a disciplined, self-controlled way, and crosses the finish line, is a winner! Are you running your race this way, so that you will be a winner?

Secondly, Paul emphasized the importance of self-control. In his letter to the Galatian church, he identified self-control as a fruit of the Spirit. Without self-control, we will never win the race. We need it for our tempers, our tongue, our thoughts, the use of our time, and our appetites. If we don't practice self-control we will get distracted and seriously hinder our ability to *run the race*.

Paul went on to point out that a competitive racer practices self-control in order to receive a *wreath* that perishes. Seems pointless, doesn't it? However, in our ministries, we are running for a prize that is imperishable! We are not running for salvation, for that comes through faith in Christ, who ran the race perfectly for us. Instead, we run the race with self-control; for in doing so, we will receive imperishable prizes in heaven that we cannot even begin to imagine. And trust me, we will not be disappointed!

Last of all, Paul urged us, by way of his own example, to not *run aimlessly, nor ... box as though beating the air.* All too often I have been guilty of this in ministry, either because I was so busy I didn't know where to turn next, or because I did not have a plan or a set of goals. Blessed is the pastor who has leaders who work with him or her on this. Planning and goal setting is a wise, strategic way to bring direction and focus into our lives and ministries. If a competitive runner had no plan as to where to run and how to get to the finish line, or worse yet, if they did not set the finish line as their goal, they would never win the race, much less cross the finish line. So, too, if we in Christian ministry have no plan as to what we are going to accomplish for Christ or how we are going to accomplish it, we will get little or nothing done for his kingdom.

Therefore, Paul's approach was to *punish* [his] *body and enslave it,* so that he might effectively proclaim the good news of Jesus Christ, and avoid, at all cost, being disqualified in this race which God had called him to run. We ought not hear *punish* and *enslave* in a negative sense of self-abuse, but rather in the context of discipline. Paul would not let himself be distracted and dragged away by any sins that would hinder him from running the best race he possibly could. May it be our daily prayer and desire to run the same kind of race that Paul so faithfully ran; so that we, too, might win the imperishable prize that God has reserved for all who do so.

A Pastor's Prayer:
Dear Lord,

Please help me run the race you've called me to run with discipline and self-control. Forgive me for all the times I have run *aimlessly* and have merely been *beating the air.* Help me to make plans and goals for today that are in accordance with your will for me and my ministry. Thank you for the imperishable prizes that await me in glory for faithfully running and finishing the race. Amen.

Epiphany 7

Mark 2:1-12

Every time I read this text, I find myself dreaming and thinking, "Wouldn't it be great if we had this problem in our churches?" Can you imagine if your church was packed to the door, not for a funeral or wedding, but because people wanted to listen to your preaching? And to top it off, some would be so desperate to reach you; they would tear a hole in the roof and lower themselves down in front of the pulpit! We laugh, perhaps, at imagining a scene such as this in our own ministry. But this is what happened that day in Jesus' ministry.

There is a big difference, of course, between our ministries and that of Christ's. There was something about Jesus that drew people to him. In part, it was the message of the words he spoke and the authority with which he spoke them, but in large part, it was the miracles he was doing. Oh, if only we could preach like Jesus! If only we could do miracles like Jesus! Then people would flood into our churches and tear holes in the roof to get to us!

But wait a minute; is there really that much difference between our ministries? Granted, we will never be the Son of God, but by faith in him we are sons and daughters of God. True, we can't forgive people their sins on the basis of our blood and righteousness, but we can declare to people that their sins are forgiven on the basis of Christ's blood and righteousness. Maybe we can't tell people to rise up and walk, as Jesus could, but we can pray for them to receive healing, in the powerful name of Jesus, and the outcome of that prayer is ultimately in God's control.

So, this text is about more than a day in the life of Christ's ministry, and is not something to merely covet from a distance and wish we could see something similar in our church. This text is about the power of God's Word to change people's lives. The Epiphany portion of this text is the revealing of Christ's identity as God and having the same power as God to forgive sins and heal the sick.

Coming through the doors of our churches are people who need the forgiveness of sins. Maybe they have been worshiping there for years and are regarded as dear old saints in the church, but they still need to hear the good news of the gospel that their sins are, indeed, forgiven by faith in Christ.

In addition to this need for forgiveness, maybe there is overwhelming pain that exists in the lives of those who consider your church to be their church. There are unhappy and broken marriages, there are strained relationships between parents and children, there are those who are struggling through a health crisis, some are dealing with financial crisis, some are living with a secret sin that is troubling their conscience, others are living under the oppressive load of bitterness and unforgiveness. The list goes on and on. Do we have anything to offer them? Can we hold out hope of healing for them? Most certainly!

He who has the authority to forgive sins also has the authority to heal broken lives and take away the pain. This healing comes to our parishioners the same way forgiveness comes to them — through God's timeless, living, powerful word. As we faithfully proclaim God's Word to these hurting people, week after week, God creates faith within them. He opens the eyes of their hearts to see the meaning of his word and how it applies to their situation. He gives them ideas of things to say or do differently that might take away the pain in their particular situation. He comforts them in the midst of their hardship, so even if things don't get better, they get stronger and they put their hope more fully in the promises of God for this life and for all eternity.

Some of the greatest miracles in the church today are those of changed lives. Not only changed lives in terms of inward change, when people come to faith in Christ for salvation, but also in terms of outward change, when they start thinking, talking, and acting more and more like Christ. Don't ignore or downplay these miracles, for they are often the greatest evidence of God's power at work in your church.

A Pastor's Prayer:
Dear Lord,

Thank you for the power and authority of your word that not only changes my life, but the lives of those I minister to. Please continue to do your powerful work in and through me. Amen.

2 Corinthians 1:18-22

Have you ever been accused of not keeping a promise? I'm sure we all have. I recall one incident in my own ministry where a parishioner had felt strongly that I had promised to be their pastor for a long, long time. They were extremely hurt and angry when I resigned from their church, after seven years of successful ministry, to accept a call to serve a congregation in another state.

In this text, the Apostle Paul was addressing a similar issue that had arisen in the church at Corinth. Apparently some had felt that he had broken a promise in regards to visiting them. As a result, they assumed that perhaps his preaching shouldn't be trusted either, since that was coming out of the same mouth! A ridiculous assumption, perhaps, but it was what Paul faced.

Dealing with broken promises is a difficult issue for pastors, especially for those of us who don't want people to be upset with us. I personally hate it when I have to break a promise to my wife, one of my children, a parishioner, or an entire congregation, but we don't have as much control over things as we, and others, would like.

If we are to have an effective ministry, I believe we must do as Paul did to help people distinguish the difference (and there is a huge difference!) between the human promises that we make, but have to break from time to time, and the divine promises of God, which we preach and teach from the same mouth, but which can never be broken. Oh, how we wish our word could be as good as that of God's Word, but it can't, for we are ministering on the basis of a human, finite mind where we cannot see and know all the possible scenarios of the future as God can.

So we turn our attention to God's promises, as Paul did. Notice what he said in the opening verse: *As surely as God is faithful....* Paul's appeal was not on the basis of his faithfulness, but on that of the most faithful person that exists — God himself. Then, in verse 20, he went on to write: *For in him every one of God's promises is a "Yes."* That is a powerful truth for us and our parishioners! First of all it is powerful for us, because we desperately need all of God's promises to back us up in our ministries. Without them, we would be a mess and so would our churches. I urge you to take a moment and list some of God's promises to you as a pastor. I'll give you one for starters from the Great Commission: *Remember, I am with you always, to the end of the age* (Matthew 28:20). Oh, how we need that promise in order to keep going from day to day and week to week! After listing some of his great and precious promises to you, take a few minutes and thank him for each one.

Secondly, the fact that every one of God's promises are *"Yes" in him*, is a wonderful message to give to our parishioners. They need to know that we, as their pastors, are human and finite. We can't possibly measure up to God in terms of keeping all our promises, but that in no way weakens the certainty of God's Divine promises. Help them to know how significant it is for them that God's promises are always *"Yes"* and what that means for their everyday lives.

Paul summed up this issue by writing: *For this reason it is through him that we say the "Amen," to the glory of God.* "Amen" basically means "so be it." It is a term of acceptance and a statement of trust. When coming at the end of a prayer, it indicates that we want to leave all that we have prayed about in God's hands on the basis of his grace and promises to us. When using "Amen" as a statement of agreement with something that someone has just said (for example, saying "Amen" to something we just heard in a sermon or Bible study), we are indicating that we believe that what was said is true. We agree with it and want it to continue to be that way.

May that be our attitude, to God's promises to us; and may we set an example for our parishioners in this too, to fully trust in God's promises to them and say *"Amen"* to all of them!

A Pastor's Prayer:
Dear Lord,

Thank you for your great and precious promises to me, and that they are always "Yes" in Christ! Help me to be, as best I'm able, a promise keeper to my loved ones and parishioners. May my "Amens" to your promises set an example for those who watch and listen to me, that they, too, will agree that all your promises deserve a hearty "Amen!"

The Transfiguration Of Our Lord
(Last Sunday After The Epiphany)

Mark 9:2-9

I can't begin to imagine what it must have been like to be Jesus' disciples: at one moment to be growing leaps and bounds in one's knowledge and faith from sitting under his teaching, and at other times be totally confused and full of doubts. Even harder to imagine is to have been one of his inner core of disciples — Peter, James, or John — and be taken on this privileged, mountaintop experience where they witnessed the transfiguration of their Lord. Is it any wonder they were *terrified*?

I find Peter's response to this wonder-filled experience typical of so many people, pastors included. Perhaps you've experienced what I'm referring to. You went to a pastor's conference, or a spiritual growth retreat, or some similar event, which proved to be a mountaintop experience for you. You came back home all fired up to do great things for Jesus in your church. You couldn't stop talking about it to anyone who would listen. You had wonderful ideas and plans that were going to turn your ministry around to be more dynamic and effective than ever before. And then it seemed a heavy, black cloud settled over all your grand ideas. You blamed it on a lack of vision or apathy on the part of the people around you, but if the truth be known, it may well have been God who was slowing you down that you might listen to him. I know, for this has happened to me.

I see some important truths in this text for us, as clergy, to consider when it comes to mountaintop experiences. First of all, we need them. Jesus pulled these three guys away from the other nine disciples and away from the crowds of people for a reason. It may well have been to prepare them for the huge mission that lay ahead of them; that of building Christ's church. These three men needed to know, without a doubt, that they were following the Son of God. They needed to know that his words were true, were worth listening to, worth passing on, and worth dying for (which they would).

So too, we need mountaintop experiences, whether at a major pastor's conference or a private retreat alone with God. We need to be renewed in our calling and be reminded that Jesus is the Son of God, that his words are true, that they are worth listening to, they are worth passing on, and they are (if necessary) worth dying for. We may not be starting a new church, but we need this as much as the disciples did in order to keep growing Christ's church.

Secondly, in these mountaintop experiences, whether with thousands of people or alone with God, we need to be silent and listen; as James would later advise his readers, *be quick to listen, slow to speak* (James 1:19). How often we need to hear these same words which the Father spoke from the cloud that day on the mountain, *This is my Son, the Beloved; listen to him!* Spiritual growth and maturity seldom happen when we are talking. Nor do new ideas and insights, whether for ourselves or our church, come while we are talking. That's why God told the Psalmist: *Be still and know that I am God* (Psalm 46:10).

Last of all, it is important to come down off our mountain. Oh how hard that can be, as we love to be on the mountain! Mountaintop experiences are fun! They often give us more joy and energy than the experiences and the people in the valley. However, while it is on the mountain where we get a peek into the kingdom of God with all its glory, it is in the valley where God reflects his glory through us and does his kingdom work. He wants us to go back down to our people, and when we do, he goes with us, even as Jesus did with the disciples.

I hope you will plan into your schedule, mountaintop experiences where you can get a peek into God's kingdom and glory in a new and fresh way. And while you are there, be sure to listen carefully to him. When it is all over, let the experience propel you back to your people rather than keep you away from them.

A Pastor's Prayer:
Dear Lord,

Thank you for providing mountaintop experiences for me. Help me to make good use of them and to listen carefully to you in those times. Show yourself to me, Lord, in new and renewing ways that I may be better prepared and strengthened to serve you in the future. Thank you for the people in the valley. Help me to want to return to them and to share your glory and grace with them for your sake. Amen.

2 Corinthians 4:3-6

In this passage, the Apostle Paul used an illustration that Jesus often used, of light and dark, or sight and blindness, when referring to the truth of the gospel versus the lies of the world. Paul wrote that it is *the god of this world* [which] *has blinded the minds of the unbelievers, to keep them from seeing the light of the gospel of the glory of Christ.* Few things are more frustrating and heartbreaking for a pastor than when people don't respond to the preaching and teaching of God's Word. However, there is more to the equation of belief and spiritual growth than our preaching. There is also the listener and what they do with what they hear.

Without a doubt, we have a responsibility to prepare the best we can and preach and teach the best we know how, but the results of that preaching and teaching do not lie completely in how well we do this. They also lie, in part, in how well our parishioners listen, and beyond that, how well they apply what they have heard to their personal lives. How well they do this has a lot to do with which god they are yielding their lives to. Are they yielding to the God of the Bible or the god of this world? The best preacher in the world can't save anyone, or cause them to mature spiritually, if their listeners are yielding their life to the god of this world.

Just as the glory of Jesus was veiled to most of the people around him, with the exception of those who yielded their lives to him and followed him faithfully, so too, his word (and especially the gospel) is veiled from those who refuse to believe it, live it, and faithfully follow it.

What then are we to do? Paul urged us to keep proclaiming the truth of God's Word, for we are not proclaiming ourselves, but Christ Jesus. This makes all the difference in the world, for if we are proclaiming ourselves and trying to gain a following for us and our ministry, then we will get discouraged (unless, of course, you are one of those charismatic types who seem to be able to get a huge following just by your personality). But if we are proclaiming Christ, we've done all that God asks of us. We don't preach Christ so that we can have a bigger church or look better in the eyes of others. We preach Christ because he commanded us, in The Great Commission, to do so. The end result of that proclamation is in God's hands, not ours.

How freeing this is as we step before a group of people week after week, faithfully proclaiming God's Word the best we know how, after having studied and grasped it the best we can. God merely asks of us, like the Nike commercial, to "Just do it." He will take it from there. There will always be those who resist the proclamation of the gospel, but remember, they have rejected Christ Jesus, not you. We will not be held accountable for those who do not believe, but we will be held accountable if we do not preach the word in truth whenever we have the opportunity.

Whatever we do, let us follow closely Paul's stern advice in verse 2, which precedes our text: *refuse to practice cunning or to falsify God's word; but by the open statement of the truth we commend ourselves to the conscience of everyone in the sight of God.*

Far too many pastors are buckling under the pressure of the world around them, and the people in their church, to merely tell them what they want to hear, for fear of offending anyone. The end result of that fear is an inevitable use of cunning words and a falsifying of God's Word. This is a grave sin and we will be held accountable for it. Let us pray, every time we are to preach and teach, that God will help us to proclaim his word in truth and leave the results up to him.

A Pastor's Prayer:
Dear Lord,

Thank you for your word, that it is truth, and that through it people are saved and grow in their knowledge and faith in you. Please help me to proclaim this word, without ever falsifying it, and to preach and teach it the best I can with the knowledge and gifts you have given me. Help me, Lord, to leave the results in your hands and not take it personally when people to do not respond positively to it. Yet, dear Lord, I pray that many will hear and believe before it is too late. Thank you. Amen.

Lent 1

Mark 1:9-15

This Gospel Lesson overlaps the Gospel Lessons for the first and third Sundays after the Epiphany, so for the purpose of this devotional we will look only at those verses that are unique to this text — verses 12 and 13.

Mark wasted no words on the account of Christ's temptation. He simply gave us the facts. The first fact was that *the Spirit immediately drove him* (Jesus) *out into the wilderness*. There certainly is no question what God's will was for his Son at that point. This time of temptation was to prove to the devil that Jesus was both God and man, and therefore more powerful than Satan. It was also for our benefit, to assure us that Jesus is able to fully identify with us when we are tempted.

It's interesting to note that the Spirit led Jesus into this wilderness test immediately prior to the start of his ministry. How many of us may well have had a "wilderness" experience prior to the beginning of our ministry? This can be God's way of testing us, to see of what we are really made. There's no doubt that times of intense temptation truly test our character. We may also experience a season of temptations, because God is about to use us to accomplish great things for his kingdom. This was certainly true in Jesus' case. People, who have undergone severe trials and testing and experienced victory through their relationship with Christ, are purified through the "heat" of those trials and often proven to be more mature and fit for ministry than those who have not.

"Wilderness" experiences don't only come at the beginning of our ministries though, as seen in how the devil would revisit Jesus from time to time throughout his ministry. Those times of severe testing and temptation are hard. Often they come immediately following, or prior to, spiritual growth in our life or revival in the church. Satan hates it when pastors grow spiritually, for it rubs off on their parishioners. He doesn't want us to be effective in our ministries, for then he loses some of his "slaves to sin." We shouldn't be surprised when seasons of temptations come, whether they are for forty minutes, forty days, or forty weeks! But when they come, let us be quick to flee to him who is without sin and is more than able to deliver us from evil.

I'm not sure what Mark's point was, in regard to the second fact that Jesus *was with the wild beasts*, but maybe it was to emphasize the fact that this was a lonely, remote, unsafe region that Jesus was in. Was he in danger of being harmed by the very creatures he created? The divine nature of Jesus would enjoy being with the wild beasts he had made. The human nature of Jesus might possibly be afraid of them. John wrote in his first epistle that, *There is no fear in love, but perfect love casts out fear; for fear has to do with punishment, and whoever fears has not reached perfection in love* (1 John 4:18). Maybe this aspect of Christ's character was being tested.

It is the last point that is most worthy of comment: *and the angels waited on him.* What a beautiful picture! The Father wanted the Son to go through this intense time of testing, but not alone nor unattended. I don't know what the angels did for him, but we can be sure they did whatever the Father asked them to do, and that it was exactly what Jesus needed at the time. May we find great comfort in this as we couple this fact with that of Hebrews 1:14: *Are not all angels spirits in the divine service, sent to serve for the sake of those who are to inherit salvation?* The answer is, of course, "Yes, they are!"

Has God's Spirit led you into a *wilderness* for a period of time? Know that it is for a good reason, and that good will come of it. Perhaps something better than you can imagine is about to happen through you! Find great hope in knowing that God would not put you in a wilderness without sending angels to care for you.

A Pastor's Prayer:
Dear Lord,

May this Lenten season be a time of victory for me, where I am not only reassured that all my sins are forgiven, but can also experience the working of your Spirit, and the care of your angels to deliver me from all evil. Thank you that you are more powerful than Satan and are constantly preparing me for ministry. Amen.

1 Peter 3:18-22

To get a more complete understanding of this text, it is better to start reading at verse 13. When we set verses 13-17 alongside our Gospel Lesson, we see the greatest threat we face is the devil himself. It is he who wants to *harm* us for doing *good*. It is he who wants us to *suffer* for *doing what is right*. It is he who wants us to be afraid and *intimidated*. It is he who demands an *accounting* of us *for the hope that is in* us. It is he who sets out to *malign* us and to *abuse* us for our *good conduct in Christ*. However, he most often does this through people. This was certainly the case for the first-century church that Peter was writing to, because the Romans and the Orthodox Jews were dead set on making life miserable for the followers of Christ.

Verse 17 takes this issue and transitions it into the truths in our text, as Peter wrote: *It is better to suffer for doing good, if suffering should be God's will, than to suffer for doing evil.* While in the wilderness for forty days, Christ suffered for doing good; that suffering was God's will for him. However, far too many Christians, pastors included, suffer for doing evil. This is what Peter was warning his readers about, and we do well to heed the same warning.

With this as a backdrop to our text, the marvel of God's abundant grace and mercy, as brought out in verse 18, is all the more beautiful and humbling. What we deserve is to suffer for doing evil, for we have been (and maybe are at this moment) in the "wilderness" and have failed big time. But listen to this: *Christ also suffered for sins once for all, the righteous for the unrighteous, in order to bring you to God.* Wow! Who of us deserves that?

What we deserve is to suffer for doing evil. It is honorable to suffer for doing good (provided we take the suffering in an honorable way). But how do we describe willing and deliberate suffering for the sins of others? We call it grace. We call it generous. We call it loving. We call it sacrifice. But do those words really do justice to what was happening on the cross? Do they stir us to have a deep, passionate, humble attitude of gratefulness that causes us to fall on our faces before our Savior and weep?

Peter summed this up by pointing out that we are able to make *an appeal to God for a good conscience*, because of Christ's death and resurrection. Since we all know how awful it feels to have a guilty conscience, we then know what a tremendous gift it is to be able to stand before the Father and appeal for a good conscience.

My friend, is the devil out to get you? Without a doubt he is, if you are faithfully serving your Lord and Savior and wanting to live a life that pleases him. Sometimes, though, we are more aware of Satan's efforts to harm, attack, intimidate, malign, and abuse us than at other times. Maybe it is because he actually turns the "heat" up more at some times than at others. Maybe it is because we are doing some particular good for God that the devil has noticed, and he is upset. Maybe it is because of willful sin in our lives and the natural consequence of sin is suffering; whether physically, mentally, emotionally, spiritually, or any combination of all four.

In those times when our conscience is troubled, let us be quick to turn to God, and appeal to him for a good conscience on the basis of the shed blood of Christ and the power of his resurrection to make all things new. Having felt the load of that guilt lifted, we are in better shape to help others find the same release from the burden of guilt. And, may we be quick to point out to others, as a result of our experience, how the devil operates and what they can do to resist him with the power of God and the help of his angels.

Notice how Peter ended this as a way of encouraging us with the truth of who it is that is defending us: [Jesus] *has gone into heaven and is at the right hand of God, with angels, authorities, and powers made subject to him.* Thank God for that!

A Pastor's Prayer:
Dear Lord,

Thank you for paying the enormous price for my sins so that I can stand before the Father and appeal for a good conscience. I am overwhelmed by your grace and mercy, which I do not deserve at all. Help me to proclaim these truths in a way that many might be drawn to you and find release from sin. Amen.

Lent 2

Mark 8:31-38

What a difference there is between the early Peter, in this Gospel Lesson, and the later, more mature Peter, who wrote last week's Epistle Lesson. Early Peter saw no need for suffering — at least no need for Christ to suffer. The later, mature Peter, saw value in suffering — and especially Christ's suffering for our sins. What a difference the cross and the resurrection can make in a person's outlook on life!

Since the Lenten season is intended to be a time for personal reflection and sorrow for sin, let's look at two statements in this text that can be helpful in this process. In so doing, perhaps we can tell if we are more like early Peter, or late Peter.

The first statement, which had to have pierced Peter's very being, is that of verse 33: *Get behind me, Satan! For you are setting your mind not on divine things but on human things.* On the surface, it looked as if Peter meant well by what he said and maybe he did. Perhaps any of us, put in the same situation, would have said the same things in reaction to Christ's words about his future suffering and death. Who can blame Peter for getting upset with Jesus for talking this way? Peter knew full well that Jesus could avoid such experiences and deliver himself from any peril. Therefore, Peter assumed the role of authoritarian and tried to put Christ in his place. But it didn't work, did it?

What Peter failed to take into account was the fact that he was dealing with the Son of God who has ultimate authority over everything. Peter did not look at the big picture. He only saw the here and now and what impact Christ's words were having, and would have, on Peter's life. All too often we are guilty of the same, narrow-minded approach to looking at life. We see the here and now and don't like the way God is seemingly dealing with things (or failing to deal with things, as we might sometimes imply). So we assume the role of authoritarian and try to tell God what to do. Big mistake! For in times like that, we have failed to consider who we are dealing with, and that he has ultimate authority over all things. Is Jesus saying to you, today: *Get behind me, Satan! For you are setting your mind not on divine things but on human things?* If so, humbly confess your arrogance and step out of the way so God can carry out his perfect plan in your life and in the ministry of your church.

The other statement for consideration is that of verse 38 and is closely related to verse 33: *Those who are ashamed of me and of my words in this adulterous and sinful generation, of them the Son of Man will also be ashamed when he comes in the glory of his Father with the holy angels.* Peter's rebuke came out of embarrassment over his Lord's words. He couldn't accept what Jesus was saying, for it was foolishness to him, so he tried to stop Jesus from saying anything further about suffering and death.

At times, we too find our Lord's words difficult. Sometimes they just don't make sense. Other times they seem too harsh. We would probably deny it, but if the truth be known, we are, at times, ashamed of him and his words. We want to assume the role of authoritarian and tell God the way things are going to be, whether in our own personal life or in the life and ministry of our church (or the church at large).

May God have mercy on us in these times, even as he had with Peter. Jesus saw through Peter and recognized that it was really Satan who was trying to hinder God's will from being carried out in his suffering and death. He also sees through us and probably finds the same to be true. Let us thank him for his patience with us and ask for his forgiveness of our arrogance, for help to *deny* ourselves, and for a willingness to *lose* our life, so that in Christ's will we may *find* our life, even as Peter did.

A Pastor's Prayer:
Dear Lord,

Please forgive me for those times when I have tried to tell you what to do. Please be patient with me and help me to die to my selfish desires and ideals. Lord, as I lose my life in you, thank you that you help me to find it. May I never again be ashamed of you or your words, but boldly proclaim them for your honor and glory. Thank you! Amen.

Romans 4:13-25

Whenever I read about the faith of Abraham, I am ashamed of my own lack of faith. What an incredible man of God he was, to simply take God at his word, as unbelievable as that word was to human reason. As a result of that faith, God credited to him righteousness far in advance of (yet in view of) the cross. How does your faith compare to that of Abraham?

How important it is for us to keep in mind that Abraham's faith was in relation to God's Word. It wasn't faith in a miracle, or merely faith in an invisible God, but faith in the *words* of an invisible God who could perform miracles. Let us never lose sight of the fact that our ministry is, first and foremost, a ministry built around the Word of God and faith in that word. If we don't have his word, our churches are little more than social clubs. If we have his word, but have no faith in that word, our worship and ministries in the church are little more than the meaningless activities of a dead religion. How is your faith in God's Word?

I love verse 13: ... *the promise that he would inherit the world did not come to Abraham or to his descendants through the law but through the righteousness of faith.* What an outlandish promise! If any of us told a farmer in our congregation that he was going to inherit the world, he might think the stress of ministry had fried our brains! However, God's promises never have to make sense to us. They are God's promises, not ours. Therefore, they are God-sized promises that we can't even begin to comprehend. And, because they are God-sized, only God can fulfill them, meaning we will have no clue as to how he will do it.

What made this promise to Abraham even better was that it came not through the law (such as, "If you do everything I tell you, then, and only then, will you inherit the world"). No, the promise came to Abraham *through the righteousness of faith.* In other words, "Just believe and the promise will come to pass."

We know the significance of this for our salvation, which is, of course, Paul's main point in this text. The promise of salvation and all it contains (forgiveness of sins, removal of the debt of guilt, eternal life, and the like) does not come to us through the law (such as, "If you obey me perfectly I will give you all these things"), *but through the righteousness of faith!* In other words, *believe on the Lord Jesus and you will be saved!* (Acts 16:33). Salvation does not come through faith in miracles, or merely faith in an invisible God, but faith in the WORDS of an invisible God who works such a marvelous miracle in the life of every believer in Christ.

Faith is not limited to the realm of salvation only, however. There is also the realm of God's provision, which calls for faith as well, and is where Abraham's faith began. I don't know about you, but I find it a lot easier to trust God for salvation, than to trust him to provide for me. Don't get me wrong, I know he cares, for his word promises that; but it is easier for me to doubt his promises of provision than it is for me to doubt his promise of salvation.

Abraham's righteousness did not come out of faith in God's Word with regards to a cross and a resurrection. He didn't have a clue about those things, which are essential for our saving faith today. Abraham's righteousness came out of faith in God's Word about descendants, land, nations, kings, and a son — all of them being temporal things that God cared very much about. Now we are not saved by believing that God can provide for us financially, but since we are saved through faith in Christ (the greatest miracle we will ever experience!) can we not believe that he will provide for us financially? Oh, how I pray that God will strengthen my faith in this area and that he will do the same for you, if you too are struggling with doubts over his promises to provide for your temporal needs.

A Pastor's Prayer:
Dear Lord,

Thank you for your powerful word that is full of one great and precious promise after another! I thank you that my life, my purpose, my calling, and my ministry all revolve around your word. Lord, I believe, but help my unbelief, especially in the area of your promises to provide for me. Give me a faith like that of Abraham that I might experience the fulfillment of your promises in your perfect timing. Thank you. Amen.

Lent 3

John 2:13-22

Here's a question for all of you experts in practical theology: Is it biblically wrong to hold bazaars and bake sales in the church?

I ask this question somewhat tongue-in-cheek, for countless churches have struggled with this issue down through the years and this Gospel Lesson has often been used as "proof" that it is wrong.

As we watch the action in our text, there is no question that Jesus was upset. The temple, which had been built as God's house and a place for people to worship him, had been turned into a marketplace. The intensity, with which Jesus threw the merchants and money changers out, indicates that the economic aspect of the sacrificial system had gotten way out of hand. The merchants were no longer merely providing a service to Jewish pilgrims who had come to worship, but rather had found the whole sacrificial system (and the fact that people found it more convenient to purchase their animals there rather than bring them from home) to be a lucrative trade. The primary emphasis on worship had been lost, and this upset Jesus greatly.

Pastors seem to have, more or less, the responsibility of overseeing the use of the church facilities today. We still refer to it, from time to time, as "God's house." What the building is used for can be controversial at times. I have had to deal with this on more than one occasion. Making this issue even more complicated has been the increase in popularity of what is known as "multi-purpose facilities." The same room that is used for worship on Sunday morning, may be used for a Christian rock concert that evening (with music that some generations in your church would adamantly argue is *not* worshipful!). Later in the week the same room is used for lively games (maybe even basketball) by the youth ministries department. Is this a misuse of God's house? The answers to that question might be about as varied as the people you ask.

To get a proper perspective on this text, I think we need to look closely at how the doctrine of the temple evolved throughout the New Testament. The temple had, up to this point, been understood as a building — a beautiful building at that, which had taken *46 years* to construct! But Jesus introduced a new concept of the temple, and that was his body. He charged that the people would destroy this *temple*, but he would *raise it up in three days*. Those listening that day could not grasp what he was talking about. Neither did his disciples until after the resurrection. Then it made sense to them.

The Apostle Paul knew well the original temple building. He also had, on the road to Damascus, encountered the risen, glorified temple of Jesus Christ. Yet, writing some years after our text was written, he described another "temple": that of every believer in Christ. Every one of these temples — the building, the body of Christ, and every believer in Christ — is a dwelling place for God. Only one of them cannot be defiled by humanity, and that is Jesus.

When determining whether we are using our church building in a way that glorifies God or not, I think one has to keep all three "temples" in mind and ask: Is the activity God honoring? Would Jesus be pleased to be there? Will this activity serve to strengthen the faith of others and possibly result in people coming to faith in Christ for the first time?

What was going on in the temple that day was fattening the pockets of cunning merchants. It brought no glory to God, angered Jesus, and strengthened no one's faith. Many of the fund-raisers that are held in our churches today are for the purpose of funding the ministry of the church and not for someone's personal profit. Whenever facing this issue, ask God to give you wisdom as to what is appropriate for your church, and the words to share with your people that will give them a greater understanding of, and appreciation for, God's house and its proper use.

A Pastor's Prayer:

Dear Lord,

Your house is a precious place, and I don't, in any way, want to be guilty of bringing shame upon it or angering you for how we use it. Help me to know how to lead my congregation in the proper use of it, and how to teach them to bring honor and glory to you through the use of your church. Thank you. Amen.

1 Corinthians 1:18-25

In ministry, we live and minister in a delicate balance between the *foolishness* of God and the *wisdom* of the world. At times, perhaps, we resent the tension that the two create, wishing that it would just go away. Many pastors are under tremendous pressure, by individuals and congregations, to harmonize and unite the two. It never works. It's like trying to mix oil with water. Just as oil and water corrupt each other, so too, the *foolishness* of God and the *wisdom* of the world will corrupt each other's goals and ideals if forced to co-exist in ways they are not meant to.

Paul made it clear that the *wisdom* of the world is subservient to the *foolishness* of God. This is clarified in the verses following our text, especially verse 25, which reads: *For God's foolishness is wiser than human wisdom, and God's weakness is stronger than human strength.* But what does the world teach us that many in the church have bought into? It teaches that humanity's wisdom is superior to God's wisdom. So when great minds from any particular age have developed a theory that is contrary to the timeless truths of God's Word, God's Word has been forced to bow to this new "revelation" and be silent.

Paul specifically referred to the message of the cross as that which is *foolishness* to the world. One does not have to delve too deeply into a study of world religions to see that this is exactly how many people regard the cross. Every non-Christian religion that exists was established (knowingly or unknowingly) in an effort to find a better way to believe in God (or a god) and gain entrance into some form of an eternal paradise.

We all know that many people regard the message of the cross as foolishness, for it is mocked, ridiculed, slandered, and ignored. But notice who Paul said these people are and what their end will be if they don't change their thinking and beliefs; *the message about the cross is foolishness to those who are perishing.* So those who laugh at, or deny, the cross are perishing.

But what about those who believe in the foolishness of the cross? To them *it is the power of God* which saves them. This is a marvelous truth about how God relates to his creation. He allows humanity to think that they are smart and have all the answers, but in the end their "wisdom" will destroy them.

Those who admit to their foolishness and weaknesses, and believe in Christ's death on the cross as essential for their salvation, are the ones who experience the power of God to rise to new life for all eternity!

You see, as Paul pointed out, it is a part of God's wise plan for humanity that they would never be able to find him through human wisdom. In other words, the wisest person in the world could never conceive of God and find salvation apart from God's help to do so. Instead, God chose, *through the foolishness of our proclamation, to save those who believe.* Isn't that awesome? You don't need a master's degree or a Ph.D., to find salvation! Those with a degree of M.Div. have no advantage over those who don't, when it comes to being saved. Salvation is found, not in universities and institutions of higher learning, but in Sunday schools and Bible camps. It is found, not when people are at the top of their intellectual game, but when they have hit bottom and don't know where else to turn.

The quest for knowledge is good, as long as it doesn't undermine and destroy the childlike faith that is a prerequisite for salvation in Christ. But saving faith is not a "no-brainer," either; for it does involve the mind. The mind is essential for reflecting on who we are and the predicament we were born into — a lost and condemned sinner. The mind is essential to process the truths of God's Word on how to be saved. The mind is essential in weighing the pros and cons of belief versus unbelief, and to go one way or the other. So wisdom is a vital part of salvation, but there always comes a point where the seeker stops pursuing truth through wisdom alone, and, with the faith of a child, believes and is saved.

A Pastor's Prayer
Dear Lord,
   Please help me find that delicate balance between the *wisdom* of the world and the *foolishness* of God. No matter how much education I have now, or should gain in the future, help me to always hold, with the faith of a child, to what is most important — the *foolishness* of the cross and its tremendous *power of God* to save me and all who will believe. Amen.

Lent 4

John 3:14-21

This text is perhaps one of the most familiar texts to the church since it contains the oft quoted verse, John 3:16. The context of this passage is so important to consider, for it helps us understand the importance and truth of Jesus' words. He was speaking with Nicodemus, a Pharisee and *leader of the Jews*. Nicodemus represents all intelligent seekers of truth, for he was no dummy. He was trying to figure out who Jesus was and whether the things he taught were true, for the Pharisees were adamantly opposed to Jesus.

In helping Nicodemus understand who he was and his purpose for coming to earth, Jesus compared his future crucifixion to the bronze serpent that Moses raised up in the wilderness. Just as all who looked at the bronze snake would be spared the judgment of death, so too, all who look to the cross will be spared the judgment of eternal death in hell.

I can't emphasize enough how important it is for us to communicate this truth over and over again, for there are many Nicodemus' in our world who are trying to figure out who Jesus was (and is, if they believe he still exists). Many people question the truth of what he spoke in this text. Many others bristle at the exclusive nature of this text, where Jesus clearly stated that those who believe are saved and those who do not will perish.

In our age of relativism and political correctness, there is much pressure to imply (if not outright preach and teach) that Jesus is one of several ways to heaven. Popular reason goes something like this: "It's not so important what (or who) you have faith in, just as long as you have faith in something." Now if this human reasoning were true, then Jesus was either a fool, a liar, or deluded, for this passage leaves no room for such reasoning. There is only one explanation for why some in the Christian church would teach and preach anything but Christ alone for salvation and eternal life, and it is this: *the light has come into the world, and people loved darkness rather than light because their deeds were evil.*

Anyone who will not preach that Jesus is the only way to be saved clearly *loves darkness rather than light* (whether they are aware of it or not) and this is *because their deeds are evil*. Such people feel condemned by Christ, for they have missed the point of his grace and are focused on rebelling against his law. If they do consider his grace at all, it is to take advantage of it.

Dear friends, if we find it hard, like Nicodemus, to believe that Jesus is the only way to be saved, then we need to do a thorough inventory of our life to see if there is sin that we are trying to hide in *darkness* for fear that our *deeds may be exposed*. Having then confessed any such sin, and accepting by faith that Jesus came, not to condemn us but to save us from our sin, it is a lot easier to see why he is the only way for salvation.

If you believe that Jesus is the Son of God and that he is not a fool, a liar, or deluded, then there is only one truth to preach: Jesus is the only way to be saved. In the days of Moses, there were no alternative ways to be spared death from the deadly snake bite. Either look at the bronze snake and live, or ignore it and die. Jesus said it is the same way with him. Look at the cross as our only hope for salvation and live, or ignore it and perish for all eternity. This holds true for us and everyone to whom we minister.

Pray that God will help you to receive these truths by faith, even if it goes against reason and popular thought. Pray for courage to preach and teach these truths without any compromise or allowance for other ideas of how to be saved. If you are condemned for preaching and teaching this way, don't be surprised, for so were Jesus and the apostles. Maybe you will have to do what Jesus and his followers did in those situations. They shook the dust out of their clothes and went somewhere else where people would listen to the truth.

A Pastor's Prayer:
Dear Lord,
Your word is truth, and simple to believe. Forgive me for those times when I have let reason and popular thought get in the way of simply receiving these truths by faith. Help me to preach them boldly so that your word can call people into a saving relationship with you. Thank you for dying for my sins; and that simply by looking to the cross and what you did for me there, I am saved! Amen.

Ephesians 2:1-10

This is one of my favorite passages of scripture, for it is rich with mercy and grace! *But God, who is rich in mercy, out of the great love with which he loved us even when we were dead through our trespasses, made us alive together with Christ — by grace you have been saved —* Isn't that awesome?

This is also a great text because it is the great leveler. By that I mean it brings everyone down (or up) to the same level. How important this is for us to remember, especially during those times when we, or others, tend to elevate pastors to a level higher than others. I have listened to more people than I want to count, who have told me of bad experiences with pastors who portrayed themselves as better than their parishioners. How sad, for that couldn't be further from the truth.

The truth is, we were once *dead through the trespasses and sins in which* [we] *once lived ... following the desires of flesh and senses, and we were by nature children of wrath, like everyone else.* Some pastors have lived a portion of their life apart from Christ and have come into a saving relationship with him later. They don't have a problem understanding this passage. Their challenge is to not forget where they came from. Other pastors, like myself, grew up in a Christian home where we were "good" kids who grew up to be "good" adults. Therefore, we find it more difficult to identify with those who have lived a portion of their life apart from Christ — *following the desires of flesh and senses.* For us, we need to hear (and let it truly sink in) that we too *were by nature children of wrath, like everyone else.* In spite of our "good" past, at the core of our being we are no better than anyone else, due to the sinful nature we were born with and need to be set free from.

But the good news, for us and for all whom we share the gospel with, is that *God ... raised us up with him* (Christ) *and seated us with him in the heavenly places in Christ Jesus.* What wonderful, good news that is! Again, we don't deserve that, but this is the nature of our gracious and merciful God.

If you have been thinking rather highly of yourself, allow the law in this passage to bring you down to the level of the worst sinner you know; but then let the grace of Jesus bring you up to the same level as him. When you think of those to whom you minister, try to avoid thinking of them in terms of the "bad" people and the "good" people, but rather in terms of the lost and the found — the perishing and the saved. When I started seeing people in this way, I didn't see anyone (myself included) as better or worse than another. Instead, I started seeing people as either those who were saved by grace, or those who needed to be saved by grace.

Be very careful to avoid teaching, or implying, any form of salvation, or elevation in God's kingdom, by works. Paul made it clear to the Ephesians that it is *by grace you have been saved through faith, and this is not your own doing; it is the gift of God — not the result of works, so that no one may boast.* When it comes to salvation and our place in God's kingdom, none of us have anything to boast about, other than Christ Jesus. We are members of God's kingdom only because of the atoning work of Christ. We are "good" people in God's kingdom (when we are good) only because of the sanctifying work of God's Holy Spirit. All glory and boasting about who we are, always goes to God.

How do you see yourself? Do you see yourself as a good person and look down on those who are not? Do you see yourself as superior to those to whom you minister? May God, through this text, give each of us a reality check, and allow the law and grace to put us in our place — the place where Christ has seated us. And may we never forget, as Paul pointed out at the end of this text, that *we are what he has made us, created in Christ Jesus for good works, which God prepared beforehand to be our way of life.* Good works are never *for* salvation, but *because* of salvation.

A Pastor's Prayer:

Dear Lord,

I thank and praise you for your rich grace and mercy to me. Thank you for saving me from the old nature I was born with and seating me in heavenly places with you, now and for all eternity. Help me to do the work you have called me to, not *for* salvation, but *because* of salvation, and to never boast in self, but always in Christ Jesus. Thank you. Amen.

Lent 5

John 12:20-33

This text contains a hard truth — hard in the sense that it goes against our human nature. Few people want to die, and especially not to their selfish desires and self-interests. But that is what Jesus challenged his disciples and us to do.

May I ask: What was your attitude when you went into the ministry? Had you hoped it would make you feel more alive, more spiritual, more worthwhile? Jesus portrayed service to him as being quite different from what we might think. Certainly it was different from what the disciples had in mind.

Some Greeks had come to them, wanting to see Jesus, but Jesus seemed to be warning the disciples about what they would really end up seeing. If they had come wanting to see someone glorious, the glory might not look like what they were expecting. Jesus acknowledged that he would be glorified; in fact the time had come for that. But the glorification would come by way of the ugliness of suffering and death. In the latter part of this text, Jesus foretold his death and the kind of death it would be. Nothing too appealing to look at there! But Jesus used an illustration to help the disciples (and us) understand what glorification through death really is: *unless a grain of wheat falls into the earth and dies, it remains just a single grain; but if it dies, it bears much fruit.*

Unless Jesus died and rose again, he would remain a single, solitary man (albeit the God/man who could do miracles). However, he would not have been able to pay the required price for our sins, if he had not died. The Holy Spirit would not have come to earth, and would not move and work throughout it today, if Jesus had not died, risen again, and ascended into heaven. The *fruit* of his death, which became his ultimate glorification, would never have come to pass without his death.

Now Jesus was not only talking about the importance of his own death, but he wove through this passage the sobering truth about the necessity of our own death. This truth applied to the disciples, the Greeks, and you and me today. *Whoever serves me must follow me, and where I am, there will my servant be also.*

If we truly want to *serve* Jesus and experience his glory, it must involve death. To *follow* Jesus involves following him to the cross. It means suffering for his name. It means undergoing ridicule and persecution, as Jesus experienced. The disciples learned this truth firsthand. We, too, must be willing to face the same scenario of dying, like wheat, if there is going to be any fruit.

What are we to die to? We are to die to any grandiose ideas of being great and famous. We are to die to the desire to be rich and comfortable. We are to die to insisting that things always go our way. We are to die to the habit of giving our time and emotions only to people we like or feel comfortable with, or who seem to have something to offer us in return. We are to die to anything and everything that would stand in the way of us being effective for Christ in his kingdom work. The apostles did this, and out of it grew the Christian church.

We, in America, have little idea of what it means to suffer. We are far too comfortable; and we do as much as we can, and dare to keep it that way. I'm appalled by pastors who, due to pride and a selfish agenda, destroy one congregation after another. I'm disgusted with pastors who don't want to go out of their way to minister to, and be inconvenienced by, broken people.

Who did these Greeks think they had come to see — someone glorious? They were about to see his death, which would give way to something more glorious than they could ever have imagined.

Who did you go into the ministry to be — someone glorious? If so (and if you haven't been through this yet), you are about to face death — death of selfish desires and self-interests. But in the process, if you obediently submit to that death, you will find that God will glorify you and honor you in the eyes of people and himself.

A Pastor's Prayer:
Dear Lord,

Help me to grasp and accept these truths by faith. I desire to die to my selfish desires and self-interests, like a grain of wheat that is planted; that out of that death, you might bear much fruit through me. I ask this, not so I can receive honor and glory, but that you might be honored and glorified through my life of service for you. Thank you. Amen.

Hebrews 5:5-10

This text is a wonderful companion text to the gospel for this Sunday. I have already stressed the importance of death for true glorification, and I touched on the importance of being willing to suffer as Christ suffered. However, it is good for us to hear these themes again from the perspective of another author who wrote a commentary, of sorts, on the life of Christ, that we might understand the significance of that life better.

There are at least three points in this text that I feel are very significant for us as pastors to notice. The first is that Jesus was *appointed by* and *designated by God* to be a *high priest*. God had his finger on Jesus from the beginning to carry out this high priestly work of not only interceding on our behalf, but actually being the sacrifice as well, which no other high priest ever did. Christ came and did the work that he was appointed and designated to do, and then returned to the Father. We, however, have been left with the commission to be "priests" in Christ's place. We will never function in the exact same way, but we do have a very vital ministry which God has *appointed* and *designated* us to do. May we never underestimate or downplay this high calling that God has laid upon the hearts of each of us. It is a great honor to serve him in the ministry.

Secondly, notice what was an important aspect of Christ's earthly ministry: *In the days of his flesh, Jesus offered up prayers and supplications, with loud cries and tears, to the one who was able to save him from death, and he was heard because of his reverent submission.* Immediately the scene from Gethsemane comes to mind, but I think there is more to this than just that night. When Lazarus died, Jesus wept. When he rode into Jerusalem that first Palm Sunday, Jesus wept over Jerusalem. We are not given the details of most of his prayers, whether those prayed publicly or privately, but it is safe to assume that many of those prayers may well have been offered with *loud cries and tears.*

Such prayers are the prayers of someone who feels deeply and passionately, not only about life and death, but about their ministry and the people to whom they minister. This was certainly true of Jesus, but is it true of us? How deeply and passionately do we feel about the life we live and what we accomplish in this life? How deeply and passionately do we feel about our ministry and the people to whom we minister? When was the last time you cried out in a loud voice and in tears, whether publicly or privately, about anything? I believe we are called to a passionate ministry, where we are moved to tears, both in our preaching and in our praying, due to the great needs around us. The alternative is to become callous and cynical. All too many seasoned pastors have become this, for the pain of feeling deeply and passionately for others can be more than we can bear at times, especially if we have a history of being hurt by people and seemingly ignored by God.

Last of all, Jesus *learned obedience through what he suffered; and having been made perfect, he became the source of eternal salvation for all who obey him.* Clearly, when applying this to us, I'm in no way implying that we will be made perfect in this life or become the source of salvation for all who obey us! However, please consider this with me: Since we do suffer, as I pointed out in the devotional on the Gospel Lesson, we have multiple opportunities to learn obedience through what we suffer. When we learn obedience, we will not become perfect, but we will mature in faith, character, and wisdom. When we do mature in this way, we will become more effective in our ministries for Christ's sake. We will increasingly become a source, not of eternal salvation, but of wisdom and knowledge about how to live the Christian life. People will have greater respect for us (provided we share this wisdom and knowledge humbly) and the outcome will be a ripple of spiritual growth and maturity in the church that may not have happened in any other way.

A Pastor's Prayer:

Dear Lord,

Thank you for appointing and designating me to proclaim the good news of Jesus Christ. Please give me a love for my people and a passion for their souls. Lord, when you permit me to suffer, may I suffer graciously, and through that suffering learn obedience which will have a positive influence on others. Amen.

Sunday Of The Passion/Palm Sunday

Mark 11:1-11

Have you ever felt led by the Lord to do something for him that others (and maybe even yourself) thought was ridiculous, and in the end basically flopped? This is how one might characterize the scene in our text. Imagine being one of the disciples who were asked to get this colt. First, getting the colt had the potential of being an embarrassing experience, for they would be asked why they were taking it. Then, when they brought it to Jesus, he got on the colt and rode it in to Jerusalem! What was that all about? He had always walked wherever he went before (unless it was to take a boat across the lake). And the crowds, what was their spontaneous excitement all about? If this all was leading up to something big and important, then why did the week end with the same crowd shouting, "Crucify him!" and Jesus being killed? This whole event seemed pointless.

I wonder how many pastors could identify with this? Perhaps they felt led by God to start a church, or some form of ministry, and others thought they were crazy. They put everything they had into this project and maybe for a while it went well, but then the whole thing fell apart and died. Has this happened to you? If so, did you find yourself asking: "What was the point of that?"

This event in our text stands at the beginning of a week we often refer to as "Passion Week," and passionate it was! On this particular day Jesus was passionate about setting his face toward Jerusalem, where he knew he would die within the week. It was with passion that he set out to do his Father's will.

With passion, the people stripped branches from the trees and waved them at Jesus — declaring him their newfound "king." As the days went by other passions arose, such as Jesus cleansing the temple and the Jew's determination to arrest and kill him. What was the whole point of this royal entrance into Jerusalem?

I've struggled with this often, for nothing good seems to have come of it. When one looks at how the week ended, it seems like an absolutely embarrassing beginning to a frightening and hopelessly discouraging week. I'm speaking, of course, completely from the perspective of a finite person who might be watching all of this unfold. These could have been some of the thoughts the disciples had on that depressing sabbath before the resurrection.

My point is this: From time to time in ministry, we feel strongly that God is calling us to do something that few (if any) will agree with. There will be those who will come alongside us to support and help, out of loyalty to us, but not necessarily because they agree with what we are doing. For a time it seems like everything is going well and people might be shouting our praises and others joining our cause, only to later have the whole thing seemingly blow up in our face. And we find our self asking: "What was the purpose of all that? Was God really in this?" Yes, he was!

That day in Jerusalem, God was revealing things about the crowd that would later speak volumes about humanity. When people hear only what they want to hear, they misunderstand and misinterpret the words of others. The crowd that day thought Jesus was going to become their earthly king, like David had been for their forefathers, but Jesus never said that. He would become a king of another kind, but that truth was really hidden from the eyes of everyone that day.

Maybe God has you doing something today that doesn't make sense to anyone, including you, for his purpose is hidden. Don't give up or quit, if you are fully convinced that this is what he has called you to do, for someday there will be a "resurrection." Someday it will all make sense and you will see the purpose of this mission God had for you. You see, when we are in the center of God's will, it doesn't matter what other people think. It only matters whether or not we are passionate about doing this thing for the Lord and willing to leave the results up to God.

A Pastor's Prayer:
Dear Lord,

Please help me to be passionate about serving you, even when no one else understands or joins me. Help me to avoid doing anything wild and crazy that would not be your will. On the other hand, please help me to do, with passion, those things that might seem wild and crazy to others, but are really your perfect will for me. Thank you. Amen.

Philippians 2:5-11

Whenever I get off track from thinking the way God would want me to think, both as a believer in Christ and as a minister of the gospel, I come back to this passage. It is a powerful directive as to what the thoughts and attitudes of every believer should be and how that will affect their words and actions. Let's apply these truths to ourselves as we consider the significance of letting *the same mind be in* [us] *that was in Christ Jesus.*

Though Jesus *was in the form of God,* [he] *did not regard equality with God as something to be exploited.* We are not *in the form of God,* but often people look up to us and think highly of us, either out of respect for the office of pastor or because they respect us as a person. Christ's example for us is to *not* exploit this position which God has given us. Sadly, many pastors have, and it has ruined their reputations and ministries. One thing I am convinced of is that a good reputation is a gift from God. Anything we say or do that causes people to look up to us and respect us is only by the grace of God, for we are not, by nature, good people. Cherish and protect a good reputation. If you don't have one, ask God to help you begin to develop one right now.

Jesus *emptied himself, taking the form of a slave.* How important that we do the same if we want a long and effective ministry for Christ. Pastors who communicate that they have come to be served rather than serve, will end up destroying the very flock they were called to serve. This grieves our Lord greatly! His example for us is to empty ourselves of selfish ambitions and desires, pride, and anything else that is not of him. He would have us do as he did, which is to serve rather than be served. In so doing, many will come to faith in Christ and grow under our preaching and teaching.

Jesus also *humbled himself and became obedient to the point of death.* Can that be said of us? I've always maintained that if I don't humble myself, someone else will, and usually it is God who does it. If we wait for God to do it, generally the process is much more painful. This humbling of self is not putting ourselves down or thinking less of self than God does, but is the act of being like Christ. Study his life, his words, his behavior, his attitude toward others, and if you prayerfully apply those truths to your own character and behavior, you will become a truly Christlike, humble pastor.

Obedience is also crucial. How hard it is to obey our Heavenly Father at times, but Jesus is, again, our model and inspiration in this area, not to mention our source of power and strength to be obedient. We read that he was obedient to the point of death. Could we do that? Would we die for God if he asked us to? That should not be a hard question to answer, but one that we would immediately say, "Yes" to.

Last of all, I want us to notice what God the Father did, as a result of his Son's obedience: *Therefore, God also highly exalted him and gave him the name that is above every name.* What an awesome reward that would be! Christ certainly deserved it. But did you know that God wants to exalt us as well, not only in heaven, but while we are yet on this earth? He wants to exalt us in the eyes of our spouse and children. He wants to exalt us in the eyes of our parishioners. He wants to exalt us in the eyes of those in our community who know us. Why? Because that is how others see Christ in us. If we think like Christ, we will speak and act like Christ, which is very attractive and will exalt in us a wonderful reputation for God's honor and glory.

A Pastor's Prayer:
Dear Lord,

Please help me to have the same mind as you. Help me to think about my ministry as you do and to think about the people you have brought to this ministry in the same way you think about them. Please forgive me when I have tried to exalt myself, for I desire to humble myself and allow you to exalt me in the eyes of others, in whatever way and at whatever time you desire. Thank you. Amen.

The Resurrection Of Our Lord/Easter Day

John 20:1-18

One thing that strikes me in this text is the different reactions of each character to the resurrection. The *other disciple* (whom we might safely assume was John) stopped outside the tomb and looked in, cautiously surveying the scene from a distance. Peter rushed right in, wanting to get a close-up look at the situation. The other disciple then entered the tomb after Peter, and when *he saw*, he *believed*.

The two disciples *returned to their homes*, where they no doubt pondered the situation, but didn't seem to actively pursue any answers to their questions. Mary, on the other hand, who had been there first and ran back to town for the disciples, returned to the site of the resurrection and *stood weeping outside the tomb*. Not only did she show her grief through emotion, but she was insistent on finding answers.

Notice what the two disciples missed out on by returning to their homes. First, they missed out on seeing and conversing with two angels. Maybe it wasn't that big of a deal, but then again, it wasn't every day that angels appeared to people! Secondly, they missed out on seeing and conversing with Jesus, which would have been an awesome experience!

The point I want us to consider is that often it is those who hang around the "empty tomb" who get their questions answered. Now, granted, the disciples finally got their questions answered, too, but how much richer the experience might have been if they had stayed at the tomb (provided that the angels and Jesus would have shown up if the disciples had been there).

The tendency of many people is to walk away from the empty tomb, shaking their heads, and denying that the resurrection ever took place. Like the two disciples, they go off to their homes and ponder the whole thing over and over again, but never come to any solid conclusions. If they do, it is very likely denial, for no one can figure out the resurrection on their own. It just goes against our ability to fully comprehend and explain.

Unfortunately, there are some pastors who have done this, too. They've left the empty tomb and quit talking about the resurrection as a possibility. Since it goes against the laws of nature and doesn't seem logical to them, they call it a myth.

I would much rather be like Mary — and I urge you to be the same — for even though Mary wept with grief and confusion, she hung in there. She stayed by the tomb and the Lord rewarded her with some answers and an exciting experience of joy and comfort! First, the angels helped bring some clarification to the situation, then the presence and words of Jesus brought the joy and comfort she desperately needed even more than the answers to her questions.

How important it is that we, as students of the word, when encountering difficult truths and mysteries in God's Word, do not "walk away" from them, but stay and wait for an answer. Certainly, God will not reveal all his mysteries to us until we get to heaven, but, like Mary, if we wait and insist on knowing what it is that he wants us to know, he will reveal his truths to us, little by little, as we are ready for them. He didn't tell Mary everything, nor did he tell the disciples everything, but once they encountered their risen and living Lord, Jesus Christ, they believed.

The main way we encounter this risen and living Jesus today, is through his word. This is why time alone with him, in Bible reading and prayer — apart from sermon and Bible study preparation — is so important. It is when we are quiet before him, without any distractions, that he seems to speak to us in that still, small voice that brings joy and comfort to the heart of every believer. It is in these times that he might reveal truths to us that we never saw in scripture before: he'll give us peace to accept by faith the things we cannot fully know; and he will give us great joy in those things that we do know and believe strongly in, just as he did for Mary.

A Pastor's Prayer:
Dear Lord,

Please give me patience to wait at your word for you to speak to me. Teach me your truths, O Lord, and give me peace to accept by faith those things that I can never know in this lifetime. Thank you for rising from the dead — guaranteeing that my sins are forgiven and that I will enjoy a resurrection to eternal life, just like yours, when I leave this body some day. Amen.

1 Corinthians 15:1-11

All of scripture should be read as if it were the very words of God speaking directly to us, for it is. However, this text is one of those passages that, if read as a letter specifically to us, causes us to sit up and really think about what it is saying.

The Apostle Paul was emphasizing to the Corinthian church how important it was that they believe in the death and resurrection of Christ. Of all the doctrines of the church, Paul considered this to be *of first importance*. He then cited a list of witnesses who could vouch for the truth of this essential doctrine. It is this doctrine which makes the gospel *good news*. Without it, we have no hope of salvation and eternal life.

Now I'm going to help you hear this text as a letter directly to you by asking you a series of questions.

When was the gospel first *proclaimed* to you? Was it as a child? Was it later in life? For me, it was from birth. There was never a time in my life that I wasn't exposed to the gospel.

When did you first *receive* it? Was it at the first moment it was proclaimed to you? Was it at your baptism? Was it in Sunday school, at a Bible camp, or Bible college? Perhaps it was at an evangelistic crusade where you fought it off for some time, but finally couldn't any longer, and you received this good news into your heart and life.

Are you currently *standing* in this good news? In other words, are you relying solely on the death and resurrection of Christ for the forgiveness of your sins and the hope of eternal life in heaven?

Are you holding *firmly* to this gospel, or have you *come to believe in vain*? To believe in vain is to no longer hold firmly to this gospel as the only way to be saved. If we no longer believe in the death and the resurrection of Christ, then what about Christ is there to believe? I suppose one could believe that he was a good man — a historical figure — who had a big ego and believed he was the Son of God, but with no effect on the rest of humanity. Many people believe similar ideas about Jesus, but to do so is to believe in him in vain; for there is no point in believing in Jesus if we don't believe the whole package exactly as scripture has spelled it out for us. Paul was very concerned about this for his readers, and I am very concerned about this for those who read his letters today. If we downplay the death and resurrection of Christ, we end up with a gospel that is no longer good news. To preach such a "gospel" to people is to do a great injustice to God's Word and is leading people astray. We are, in effect, causing them to *believe in vain*.

Our calling, as pastors, is to hand on as *first importance* what we have *received* from God's Word: the truth of the gospel, as witnessed by many, that Jesus was indeed put to death, buried, and on the third day rose from the dead. May we not forget that our situation in life is not all that different from that of Paul's, where we, too, can say, *But by the grace of God I am what I am, and his grace toward me has not been in vain.*

If it were not for the grace of God, you and I would not be believers. If it were not for the grace of God, you and I would not be ministers of the gospel. If it were not for the grace of God, we would have no good news to share with those we minister to. Can we honestly say: *his grace toward me has not been in vain*? I pray that we can, and that it may stir us to believe and hold firmly to the central teaching of the gospel that Christ Jesus was indeed raised from the dead.

The only way we can proclaim the Easter story in all its power and glory is if it truly dwells in our hearts in all its power and glory. Pray for faith to believe it. Pray for boldness to proclaim it. Pray that others will receive it by faith as well.

A Pastor's Prayer:

Dear Lord,

If I have believed in vain, please forgive me. Correct my thinking and strengthen my faith. May I hold firmly to that which I have received and am, in fact, standing in — the truth of the gospel that you were indeed put to death and on the third day rose from the dead. May I proclaim this truth in all its power and glory, that many others might hear and receive it for their salvation and no longer believe in vain. Thank you. Amen.

Easter 2

John 20:19-31

We minister to people who have been heavily influenced by a faithless world, which says, "Seeing is believing." Oh how often I have wished that Jesus would show up, whether during a sermon, a Bible study, or while witnessing to a skeptic. But he doesn't, for it isn't necessary. Weak is the faith of those who always need something tangible to see or touch before they will believe.

Jesus made a powerful case for the value and importance of God's Word when he said, *Blessed are those who have not seen and yet have come to believe.* Our calling is not to give people things to see, so they might believe, but to clearly proclaim the good news of Jesus Christ so that those who will, might believe.

The issue being doubted in our text was the resurrection: Thomas refused to believe it until he saw Jesus for himself. I'm sure it was disappointing and frustrating for the other disciples that Thomas would not take their word for it. Why would they make up a story like that? Did he really think they were pulling his leg?

Why do people doubt what we tell them? Do they really think that we, or someone who has gone before us, made all this up about Jesus' death and resurrection? Why don't they trust us? Do they really think we're pulling their leg for some personal gain?

People doubt for many reasons. Perhaps it might be because what we are telling them is such good news they can't believe it. That might have been Thomas' reason for doubting. He no doubt loved his Lord greatly and grieved as much as any of the disciples when Jesus died. But being somewhat of a pessimist, he would be slower to embrace good news.

Other people doubt because they are logical thinkers. If something is outside the laws of nature and science, then it is not to be believed, according to them. Others doubt, not because they don't want to believe, but because they have weighed the pros and cons of believing a given thing, and the negatives won out. For example, if believing in the death and resurrection of Christ means having to acknowledge one's sin and need for Christ's forgiveness, then they would rather doubt all of it so they don't have to deal with their sin. These doubters, and others like them, are what we are up against when proclaiming the good news of Jesus Christ. It is not always fun, or easy, to share what we fully believe is good news. The disciples experienced that with Thomas.

But there are great rewards for believing in Jesus! First of all, Jesus said, *Blessed are those who have ... come to believe.* What are the blessings associated with belief in the resurrection? The list could be long, but the main ones are: the forgiveness of sins, a guilt-free conscience, a personal and intimate relationship with God, and the hope of eternal life. Those blessings far outweigh any advantages to not believing (if there are any).

In addition to the blessings, John made an editorial comment at the end of this text which reads: *these are written so that ... through believing you may have life in his name.* John saw the value and importance of the word in regard to belief and salvation. He didn't draw pictures or create statues for people to look at and worship, nor did he make little crosses that people could carry in their pockets to help them believe. Don't get me wrong, these all have their place to help us visualize the word which they represent. However, the primary means of grace is the Word of God, as compiled in the Bible, and it is only through believing in what has been written that we will have life.

Unfortunately, there will always be those who doubt this and therefore will not believe. We are not responsible for them. What we are responsible for, is to hold up God's Word as the only true means by which people can come to faith in Christ for life.

A Pastor's Prayer:
Dear Lord,

Thank you for your word that tells us everything we need to know for salvation and eternal life. Thank you for making it so simple that even a child can believe and be saved. Please forgive me for any time I have complicated the basic gospel message with my doubts and faulty human logic. Thank you for the gift of life! Amen.

1 John 1:1—2:2

I've heard it said that pastors often have favorite themes that they like to preach on. This is certainly true of John when it comes to his writing. The opening lines to this epistle have a familiar ring to them as we think back to the opening lines of his gospel. There are also familiar themes that show up through the text, such as: *the word, life, light, darkness, sin,* and so on. John did not write on these themes simply because they were his favorites, though. No doubt the Holy Spirit was laying these issues heavily on his heart to share with his readers, for they are extremely important for all of us.

Notice what it was that John declared to his readers: *We declare to you what was from the beginning, what we have heard, what we have seen with our eyes, what we have looked at and touched with our hands, concerning the word of life.* John declared that which was real and what he and others had experienced.

In our preaching, we ought to declare that which is real and that which we have experienced personally. If we only share nice, emotional stories; or our philosophies on life and spirituality; or the stories from the lives of others, people will not encounter the true and powerful Word of God which changes lives.

Notice that John declared these truths *so that you also may have fellowship with us.* Why do you declare the things you do? Is it because that is what is expected of you? Do you prepare for your weekly sermon thinking, "Well, I suppose I better come up with something to share this week." Or do you, like John, prepare and declare the Word of God so that others might hopefully *have fellowship with us* in God's kingdom? The attitude with which we go into our sermon preparation will often be reflected in our sermon. Even if we can fake it and give the impression that we really enjoy preaching, yet have no real vision for why we are doing it, we will probably fail to communicate God's Word in a way that allows the Holy Spirit to speak and change hearts and lives.

A pastor once told me that he never prepared for a sermon other than to read through the text early in the week and pray and reflect on it all week. Then on Sunday he would get in the pulpit and start preaching, believing the Holy Spirit would give him the words to say. If he had been a seasoned, disciplined preacher, I would have felt better about his style, but he wasn't. In fact, he was a poor speaker. He believed that whatever he said was from the Holy Spirit. I believe that is a dangerous way to think about preaching, for it can be an excuse for sloppy and careless sermon preparation and preaching. Without a doubt, the Holy Spirit helps us preach, but he doesn't take up residency in the pulpit only. He also resides in our study and desires to help us prepare a well-thought-out and prayed over sermon that will declare the truths of God in a way that is easily understood by all who listen.

There is so much in this text that we could meditate on, but for the sake of space, I will draw your attention to one last point in verse 4: *We are writing these things so that our (your) joy may be complete.* Does the reading of God's Word give you joy? That is God's intent. When it doesn't, it is probably due to sin, and John devoted the rest of the text to that issue. You see, from the very beginning God desired that his words to humanity would bring joy! It grieved the heart of God greatly when Adam and Eve hid from him when he spoke to them. That had never been an issue before, but when sin came into the garden, they became afraid of his voice and defensive over his words.

When we become afraid of God's "voice" and defensive when reading his Word, we have a sin problem; and it needs to be dealt with if we want to effectively declare his Word. I pray that you find great joy in his Word today! And keep this in mind when preaching: Not everyone is going to receive God's Word with joy. Only those who have sincerely confessed their sins and are living in grace are going to receive the truths of God with joy.

A Pastor's Prayer:
Dear Lord,

Please help me to prepare my sermons for the right reasons, and to do it with much care and prayer. Please forgive me for my sins and restore to me the joy of your salvation. I want to proclaim your truths from a heart that is clean, and do it in such a way that many are drawn into *fellowship with us*. Thank you. Amen.

Easter 3

Luke 24:36b-48

Do you think our reaction to Jesus' sudden appearance would have been the same as that of the disciples? How terrifying it was for them to suddenly see Jesus standing in their room! This was, no doubt, also a marvelous time for them as Jesus assured them that he was indeed alive. He invited them to touch him, and he ate some fish as evidence that he was physically present and not a ghost as they first thought.

The second half of the text was extremely significant for the disciples and still is for the church today, as Jesus said, *These are my words that I spoke to you while I was still with you — that everything written about me in the law of Moses, the prophets, and the psalms must be fulfilled.*

The way that the Old and New Testaments harmonize with each other gives the whole of scripture much credibility. Not only was it encouraging for the disciples that their scriptures were being fulfilled in Christ, but it ought to be a great encouragement to us as well. For we are not working with two totally unrelated stories — that of God's Old Covenant with Israel and his New Covenant with the church — but rather with one total story that had its beginning in the Old Covenant relationship and has its fulfillment in the New Covenant relationship.

Jesus then *opened their minds to understand the scriptures.* Oh how we need our minds *opened* each week as we prepare to preach his word. No matter how many times we have spoken on a particular passage, there is always something more we can learn. For example: We can always gain a better understanding of how Christ fulfilled the Old Testament. We have a constant need for Christ to help us understand how to apply the same, timeless truths of God's Word to the ever-changing and increasingly challenging issues in our world today.

There was a particular message that Jesus told his disciples to proclaim. It was *that repentance and forgiveness of sins* is possible through faith in Christ Jesus. This message is to be proclaimed in the name of Jesus *to all nations, beginning from Jerusalem.* Jesus repeated this missionary mandate on more than one occasion. It was not just for the disciples, however; it is a universal mandate for all who believe in him. Everyone who believes is to be a missionary, proclaiming the importance of repentance and the forgiveness of sins.

More and more, various voices throughout the world are telling the church that we should NOT be engaged in missionary work. We are to let people believe what they want. Who are we to say that Christianity is the only way to God and eternal life? They bristle at such exclusive "narrow-mindedness and arrogance." The Muslims and the Jews refuse to accept that Christianity is the only way to be saved, and now many Christians, including some pastors, are questioning that, too.

However, we must remember that the exclusive claims of Christianity were not made up by Christians, but spoken by Christ Jesus himself. It is the exclusiveness of Christ's message that makes it an urgent one. Since he is the only way to be saved, then that message needs to get out to as many people as possible. It's as if a cure had been found for cancer. That would be good news and one would want to spread that good news far and wide. However, if it were one of many ways to be cured, then the urgency decreases. Many Christians have bought into the lie that the claims of Christ are one of many ways to God, and have therefore minimized the urgency of proclaiming this message to all nations. In so doing, they have stripped the gospel of its good news.

Pray for courage to uphold this truth and to preach the message of Christ for what it is: the only way to God and eternal life with him.

A Pastor's Prayer:
Dear Lord,

You know that many people claim there are multiple paths that lead to you. However, your word clearly claims that there is only one. Please give me the faith to hold to that truth and to preach it with the same unwavering boldness as that of the first witnesses, so that many might be saved and find life in you. Amen.

1 John 3:1-7

This text has a clearly discernable law/grace balance to it. In the first half, John describes the wonderful relationship we have with God and what this means for us. Notice what John used as a way of measuring the love that God has given us: *See what love the Father has given us, that we should be called children of God.* The fact that we — small, insignificant people in comparison to God's vast, infinite universe — are called children of God is marvelous! It shows the extent of his love for us, that a pure and holy God wants to be a Father to this fallen human race that we are a part of. That is grace at its best!

But John didn't stop at making an observation about God's love. He went on to state that, by faith in Christ, we *are* children of God. There is no question about it and there should be no doubt in our minds: we are *children of God!* We don't deserve it, but such is the beauty of God's grace and mercy. What a wonderful truth! But there's more.

John went on to point out that the Father/child relationship gets better: *We are God's children now; what we will be has not yet been revealed. What we do know is this: when he is revealed, we will be like him, for we will see him as he is.* There is a sense where there can be a partial fulfillment of this in our lifetime, but its ultimate fulfillment is when we get to heaven. We will see, in the second half of our text, that there ought to be changes in the child of God that make us look more like the Father; but we will never be fully *like* him in this life, nor will we ever fully *see* him in this life. Here again, there is a partial fulfillment now, in that we can see some things about God through his word and by looking at his creation; but we will never fully *see him as he is.* That privilege and pleasure has been reserved for our arrival in heaven.

Part of what gives every child of God joy is the expectancy of what awaits us in heaven. We will not be disappointed, that's for sure! And John had this to say as he transitioned from his grace portion of the text to the law portion: *All who have this hope in him purify themselves, just as he is pure.* We know that this purity comes, not by works, but by faith. So all who have hope in Christ purify themselves, not by anything they have done, but by faith in what God has done for them and declared them to be: pure!

The law portion of our text is hard to read, for it makes us uncomfortable in regards to our relationship with God, and has become a point of controversy in the Christian church. We can't argue with verses 4 and 5. They are very clear. We are all guilty of sin and therefore of lawlessness. We ought never water down sin and call it mistakes or flaws of character. Sin is a breaking of God's Laws and it comes out of sheer rebellion against God. But thank God that Jesus came to take away our sins, for in him there is no sin.

The next verses are more difficult, for if taken at face value, they dump huge amounts of guilt upon us and shake our assurance of salvation. Since we all sin daily in thought, word, and deed, this passage can leave us thinking, "Apparently, I'm not abiding in him and I've neither *seen him* [nor] *known him.*" Such a statement is troubling, for we know we are abiding in him, that we have seen him through the eyes of faith, and that we know him. How are we to understand this?

It is important that we hear this in terms of ongoing attitude and relationship. The more we fellowship with Christ, the less we sin. The less we fellowship with Christ, the more we sin. The better we get to know God, and the more we see of him in his word and his working in our lives, the less we will sin (or even want to sin, for that matter). The more we hang around our Father, the more we will be like our Father.

A Pastor's Prayer:
Dear Lord,

Thank you for making me your child and wanting to be my Father. Forgive me for when I have taken that relationship for granted. Forgive me, too, for all my sins. Lord, I desire to know you better and to allow you to live your righteousness through me. Amen.

Easter 4

John 10:11-18

If we read this text from the perspective of a *sheep*, it is very comforting. Pastors, who are often perceived as "The Shepherd of the Flock," need to remember that they are as much sheep as those to whom they minister and care for spiritually.

The statement, *I am the good shepherd*, is such wonderful imagery, as sheep are, by design, very vulnerable. Whether talking about the farm animal or the believer in Christ, we are all vulnerable and rather helpless when it comes to protecting ourselves and delivering ourselves from evil. The farm animal requires the protection of its shepherd to defend it in times of physical danger. So too, believers in Christ require the protection of their *shepherd* not only in times of physical danger, but also in times of spiritual danger. How good it is to curl up in his "arms" at those times and be reminded that our sins are forgiven, that his great and precious promises will never change or fail, and to feel the strength of his protection as he carries us through times of danger.

Pastors fool themselves if they think they are any less vulnerable to Satan's attacks than the *sheep* they care for. If anything, we are more vulnerable, because we are out in front of the flock, proclaiming the word and trying to not only bring people into the flock, but also protect those who are already there. Because of this, we desperately need the *good shepherd*!

To be reminded of the fact that he willingly laid down his life for us is also very comforting and humbling. Without this *shepherd*, we would have no hope, no joy, nothing to live for, and no purpose in ministry. Let us be sure to thank him often for being not only a *good* shepherd, but the best there is!

If we read this text from the perspective of the *hired hand*, it is very convicting. At times, we fit this description more closely than that of a shepherd. Consider with me these two questions: Do you have a sense of ownership for the sheep that God has put in your care? Do you care intensely for them? Some pastors may say, "Yes" to both questions. Others may say, "Yes," to one and, "No," to the other.

Sadly, there are those pastors who would answer "No" to both questions. It's frightening to think that someone could serve a congregation and not *care* for the *sheep*. Sometimes it is difficult to have a sense of ownership of the sheep, either because we don't want to control them (and that's a good thing!) or we don't want to get attached to them. Granted, we will never take ownership of the flock in the same way our Lord does, but I believe we are called to *care* intensely for those who are under our spiritual care.

When we are no longer able to properly care for the sheep we are responsible for, then it is best we move on to other sheep or take a break from ministry. I've had to do this. I cared intensely for the sheep in three congregations and it exhausted me — physically, mentally, emotionally, and spiritually. I came to a point where I needed to be cared for more than I was able to care for others. I firmly believe that if we do not step back at that point, we run a serious risk of being the hired man who, when he sees the wolf coming (which is the devil seeking to destroy an individual or a congregation), he flees the scene. The pastor in that case may not physically leave, but might leave emotionally and mentally. They detach themselves from the problems at hand by avoiding certain people, ignoring issues that need to be dealt with, and not preaching on sins that need to be addressed.

In some cases, burnt-out pastors may do just the opposite. Instead of withdrawing from the sheep, they start beating them with the law and withholding God's grace. In this case, the *hired hand* has basically invited the *wolf* to mingle with the *sheep*.

If you are no longer able to care intensely for God's sheep, then I urge you to take a break. Do something different where you will have more time to be alone with the *good shepherd* and receive the care and nurture you need, so one day you can go back and care for his sheep.

A Pastor's Prayer:
Dear Lord,
Thank you that you are the best shepherd we could ever have. Thank you for laying down your life for me. Give me the strength I need to care for your sheep in the same tender way that you do.

Help me to recognize when I need a break and to allow you to nurture me according to my needs. Amen.

1 John 3:16-24

Pastors who want to be effective and successful in ministry will make sure that they possess two things, first and foremost: love for God, and love for people. Without these two, as the Apostle Paul wrote to the Corinthians, we are little more than a *noisy gong or a clanging cymbal* (1 Corinthians 13:1). Both of those instruments, when out of beat and harmony with the rest of the band, are really annoying. So, too, a pastor without love for God or people, or both, is going to be really annoying!

Notice how John defined love. It is brief and to the point, but yet a powerful definition: *We know love by this, that he laid down his life for us.* Our world's attempt to define love is pathetic. It is emotionally charged, all about feelings, and often involves some form of physical intimacy. Not so with God's definition. In fact, God's definition of love is not all that pretty. It involves sacrifice, blood, sweat, tears, pain, punishment, and finally death. There is nothing pretty or romantic about one person laying down their life for another. Our world has mixed that up to think true love is lying down with another. Two totally different definitions with two totally different outcomes!

In the same breath as his definition of love and with one stroke of the pen, John bluntly wrote: *and we ought to lay down our lives for one another.* Do you find that hard to do? It's not so hard to do that for our loved ones or people in the church whom we really appreciate and care about, but what about a homeless person? What about those in jails and prisons? What about those who keep coming to the office, taking so much of our time, yet never getting their act together? These are much harder to love.

But John challenges us to look deep within at the core attitudes of our hearts when he asks: *How does God's love abide in anyone who has the world's goods and sees a brother or sister in need and yet refuses help?* Good point. So the love that John described manifests itself in what we do for others, especially those who have done nothing to deserve our love and can do nothing to pay it back — such as people like you and me in our relationship with Christ.

John re-emphasized this point with verse 18: *Let us love, not in word or speech, but in truth and action.* Our words about loving God and others are empty and meaningless if they are not backed up by true, genuine, loving actions toward others and particularly the unlovely. That is what is so powerful about God's love towards us as expressed through the death and resurrection of Christ. God didn't just tell us how much he loves us; he actively loved us in truth and action. We are to do no less.

As we do so, John identified at least one blessing that will come back to us. *And by this we will know that we are from the truth and will reassure our hearts before him whenever our hearts condemn us.* Does your heart ever condemn you? I know mine does, and it is the devil who is behind that. The condemnation sounds something like this: "Are you sure you are a Christian? You know, Christians wouldn't think, say, or do the things you do. What if God doesn't really exist? What if the Bible is just a myth?" If we entertain and dwell on such condemnations, it can get really overwhelming. So, if we see God's love being extended to others through us, it shows that God is truth and that he does indeed dwell in us.

In addition, John wrote that we *know that he abides in us, by the Spirit that he has given us.* Do you see the Holy Spirit at work in you, convicting you of sin, teaching you things from God's Word that you didn't know, enabling you to live out the fruits of the Spirit? Sure you do. And that is additional assurance that God does, indeed, abide in us and we in him.

A Pastor's Prayer:
Dear Lord,

Thank you for the love you have for me, and for showing me what true love is. Help me to love others in the same way you love me. Whenever my heart condemns me, remind me, by how you love others through me and by the indwelling presence of the Holy Spirit, that you do indeed dwell in me and I in you. Thank you. Amen.

Easter 5

John 15:1-8

I have come to appreciate the concept of *abiding*, which Jesus teaches in this text. I appreciate it, first and foremost, in my relationship with him; but it is a concept that can be applied to our earthly relationships with loved ones and friends as well. Both relationships (whether with God, or with loved ones and friends) help us better understand what *abiding* looks and feels like.

For example, notice what begins the abiding relationship: *You have already been cleansed by the word that I have spoken to you.* The Word of God that is received by faith cleanses us from all unrighteousness, and grafts us into the *vine* and an abiding relationship with him. This relationship is only possible due to the grace and mercy of God that he first extended to us. It's similar to parents who desire to adopt a child. It is the desire of the parents, expressed in words to an adoption agency and later to the adopted child, which makes it possible for that child to be adopted and grafted into an abiding relationship with them.

Now it is important for pastors to be reminded of this, for if we want to bear fruit for Christ we must abide in him. Have you been *cleansed by the word* that Jesus has spoken to you? Have you been grafted into his family? If so, then you will bear fruit for him. If not, then you will be fruitless and eventually cut off from the vine. That is a chilling thought, for no believer in Christ wants to be cut off from the vine.

Jesus went on to say that *every branch that bears fruit he prunes*. If it is bearing fruit, why prune it? Why not leave good enough alone? Because Jesus wants *to make it bear more fruit.* The only way to be truly fruitful is to experience the cutting and trimming of God's pruning shears. Another word for this might be "discipline." The author of Hebrews wrote: *discipline always seems painful rather than pleasant at the time, but later it yields the peaceful fruit of righteousness to those who have been trained by it* (Hebrews 12:11). Are you experiencing the pruning of God? Try to see it for what it is, God's way of preparing you to produce more fruit. Yes, it can hurt at times, but in the end it's worth it.

It's also good for us to be reminded that *apart from me* (Jesus) *you can do nothing*. It doesn't matter how gifted and talented we are, or how well trained and dedicated we are, or how big of a church staff and budget we have, the same truth remains — apart from God we can do nothing (nothing that counts for eternity, that is). If we want to bear fruit, we will want ourselves and our congregation to abide in him and allow him to abide in us.

The abiding, like any good relationship, takes time. If we want our marriage to flourish, we will take time to abide with our spouse in quality conversation, playfulness, nurture, and intimacy. If we want a strong, healthy relationship with our children we will take time to abide with them by playing with them, reading the Bible and praying with them, and taking time to listen to them. So it is in our relationship with God. Make time for him every day.

This *abiding* in Christ always involves the word. It is not enough to just be quiet before the Lord. It is not enough to attend worship one hour a week. It is not enough to have prayed to him. Abiding in Christ involves the reading of, meditating upon, praying about, and the application of God's Word. As we do this, Jesus said, *ask for whatever you wish, and it will be done for you.* Really? We can ask for whatever we wish and it will be done for us? That's right, but keep in mind that the wishes of someone who is abiding in Christ, compared to those of someone who is not, may be very different. The difference in having those prayers answered is also directly related to the abiding relationship. When we abide in him, and he in us, we will have a much better understanding of what to ask for, and a greater confidence that he agrees with our request and will do what we have asked of him.

A Pastor's Prayer:
Dear Lord,

Thank you for grafting me into your vine. Thank you for pruning me, even when it is painful. Lord, teach me how to abide in you and to allow you to abide in me. Grow me and make me fruitful. I ask these things with confidence, for I know they are your will for me and you will do this for me. Thank you. Amen.

1 John 4:7-21

This text continues the theme of *love* from last week's Epistle Lesson and expands on the theme of *abiding* from this week's Gospel Lesson. These seem to be some of John's favorite themes in his writings. Since we have touched on both of them, I don't want to belabor the points in this reading, but rather look at some truths that we may not have looked at yet.

The first is from verse 12: *No one has ever seen God; if we love one another, God lives in us, and his love is perfected in us.* One of many things that amaze me about God is why he chooses to reveal himself to the world through the church. Christ, of course, was perfect at revealing the Father to the world, but in spite of the fact that he was perfect, most people did not believe he was God. After Jesus ascended into heaven, the responsibility of revealing God and his qualities to the world has fallen on the church. Granted, revelation is a work of the Holy Spirit, but if the word is not proclaimed in truth and its entirety, or if any part of it is pulled out of context, the world ends up with an incomplete and inaccurate view of God. This is no fault of the Holy Spirit, but completely the fault of the church.

If the church is lazy, hypocritical, self-righteous, proud, greedy for money, or just fails as a whole to live out Christ's qualities for the world to see, the world gets a poor impression about Christianity and wants no part of it. Granted, the ability to live out the fruits of the Spirit is something that the Holy Spirit enables us to do, but when we don't do it, that is not his fault. Once again, it is the fault of individuals in the church.

John's point is this: *No one has ever seen God*, for no one needs to. They ought to be able to "see" God through the attitudes, words, and behaviors of the church. All that anyone needs to know about God can be found in his word. Much of what anyone needs to experience from God can be experienced in and through the church. But for the most part, it's not happening. The church, as a whole, is failing to reflect God's righteous qualities due to compromise. The church is a weakening institution because many are not taking a stand for absolute truth. Therefore, the church is tossed to and fro, for it has nothing solid to stand on. In addition, we have failed to take seriously the fact that the world is watching us and trying to learn something about God. What are people learning about God through your words, attitudes, and actions? What is your community learning about Christ through watching your congregation? This is a frightening thought and is one reason this text is to be taken so seriously by us and our people.

Speaking of frightening, that is another issue that John lightly touched on in this text. In verse 18, he wrote: *There is no fear in love, but perfect love casts out fear; for fear has to do with punishment, and whoever fears has not reached perfection in love.*

A pastor's fears are generally twofold: a fear of God and a fear of people. When it comes to fear of God, it is usually related to sin. Guilt makes us afraid — afraid of God's punishment and discipline, afraid of being found out, afraid that we are failing him, and so on. Expectations also create fear, whether they are God's expectations or that of ourselves or others. We are afraid that our sermons aren't good enough, or that we haven't visited enough people. Such fears can paralyze us and lead to depression.

We also fear the people. We are afraid that they won't like us, afraid that they will criticize us for something, and afraid that they might leave the church — affecting numbers in terms of worshipers and the budget.

The antidote for fear though, according to John, is *perfect love*. Where do we find this perfect love that casts out fear? We find it in our relationship with Christ. He doesn't want us to live in fear, but instead to hear and believe the words of assurance that *God abides in those who confess that Jesus is the Son of God, and they abide in God.*

A Pastor's Prayer:
Dear Lord,

I ask that you live your qualities through me so that others might "see" you and get to know you through me. I confess, and ask forgiveness for, all that stands in the way of that happening. Lord, please replace my fears with your peace. Thank you. Amen.

Easter 6

John 15:9-17

John brings out two attitudes in this text that are so important for us to have in ministry. The first is *joy*. Few things are sadder than a pastor who has lost his joy. I know, for I was one of them. Now I'm not referring to feeling unhappy, or having a down day, or the Monday "blues." I'm talking about the absence of that deep-down joy that only comes from being a child of God and working for him. Do you remember a time when you were really excited about being a Christian and could hardly contain your joy? Can you remember when you were so excited and full of joy over your calling to be a pastor? That's the joy I'm talking about.

The devil is constantly trying to rob us of that joy. He does it with sin, with guilt, with self-condemnation, through wrong priorities, and he can do it through people (even our church leaders). He tries to wear us down until there is nothing left but cynicism, a bad attitude, and depression. The devil knows that if he can take away our joy — both that which comes from our position in Christ and our position in the church — then he has basically defeated us and our ministry. I know, for he did it to me.

The key to maintaining and sustaining our joy is in *abiding* and *obeying*. Whenever we fall out of close, intimate fellowship with God, we cease to abide in him to the degree that he wants with us. Not that we have fallen out of grace, but we have fallen out of his arms, so to speak. That nurturing, Father/child relationship just isn't happening and we know it, for we have not been abiding in him. All it takes to restore this joy is to get right with him and spend more time with him in Bible reading, quiet reflection, and prayer.

A failure to obey his commands is another thing that saps us of our joy. It might be secret sins that we refuse to deal with. It might be a root of bitterness toward a church leader, or some other member, whom we refuse to forgive. It might be materialism, pornography, selfishness, a need for control, or lying. All of it robs us of joy. David knew this. That is why in his famous confession, as recorded in Psalm 51, he asked the Lord to *restore* to him *the joy* of his *salvation* (Psalm 51:12). Only the Lord can restore our joy, but he's only going to do it after we truly repent of our sins and ask him for forgiveness.

The other attitude has to do with how we see ourselves in relation to God. Not only does he want us to be filled with his joy, but he wants us to be his friends! Notice again what Jesus said, as recorded by John, *I do not call you servants any longer, because the servant does not know what the master is doing; but I have called you friends, because I have made known to you everything that I have heard from my Father.*

Pastors aren't merely servants of God who are slaving away in some church somewhere, barely noticed by our Master. No! We are his friends! We are working together on a huge kingdom-building project. Servants don't know what the master is up to. They just do the work he requires, often begrudgingly. Sadly, all too many pastors view their ministry with this attitude, for either they have never sensed the friendship relationship with God, or they feel abandoned by their friend. I have felt the latter, and it was really lonely and depressing. The truth of the matter is my best friend had not abandoned me. I had lost sight of the reality of our relationship and, coupled with my lack of joy, it became overwhelming for me.

When we revisit the tremendous privilege of having been let in on *everything* that Jesus heard from the Father, we realize that we are not servants who have been left with all the dirty work. We are in a partnership with our best friend. We are co-equals (to some degree) in this task of bringing the good news of Jesus to a lost and dying world. May that truth give us renewed vision, energy, and joy!

A Pastor's Prayer:
Dear Lord,

I confess to you all that I have allowed to come into my life and rob me of the wonderful joy you have given me. Please restore that joy to its fullest extent in my life, so that it overflows to all who come in contact with me. And Lord, thank you for the wonderful friendship! Again, forgive me when I have accused you of abandoning me and treating me like an ignorant slave. That was my fault due to my ignorance. We are a team, and I want to work alongside of you like the best friends we are. Thank you. Amen.

1 John 5:1-6

Do you ever feel defeated? Do you have those days where you feel like evil is controlling our nation and our world? I know I do. In this text, John gives us the key to avoiding such feelings of defeat — our faith. Now it is not faith, in and of itself, but what (or who) we have put our faith in. If we put our faith in the economy, we will feel defeated when it takes a downturn. If we put our faith in our leaders, we will feel defeated when they fail. If we put our faith in worldwide peace, we will feel defeated when it doesn't materialize. If we put our faith in our congregation, we will feel defeated when they fall short of our expectations. So our faith needs to be in something infinitely greater than those things. It needs to be in something (or someone) that can't fail or disappoint. Clearly, it needs to be in God himself.

John pointed out that *whatever is born of God conquers the world*. Clearly that refers to Christ, for he was *born of God* and single-handedly *conquered the world*. But we too are born of God, by faith in Christ, and can therefore conquer the world as well.

The *world* is all that is under Satan's temporary control. God has ultimate authority and control over everything and everyone, but he is allowing the devil temporary, free reign and control over the whole earth. That is why it appears at times that evil is prevailing, because in a sense it is. As one looks back over history, there have been many times that evil seemed to have had the upper hand, but God was not defeated. He allows evil in the world to go only so far and then he seems to stop it, often by causing it to self-destruct.

Is there any way that we can conquer evil? Yes there is, but it is often a slow, painful process where, day by day, we battle against the potential for evil that lies within our sinful nature and lurks in our own homes and churches. It is here that we fight the devil, the world, and our own flesh. It is here that we can conquer and experience victory.

The good news, though, is that we do not fight this battle alone! We have the armor of God, as Paul wrote the Ephesian church: *Take up the whole armor of God, so that you may be able to withstand on that evil day ... fasten the belt of truth around your waist, and put on the breastplate of righteousness. As shoes for your feet put on whatever will make you ready to proclaim the gospel of peace. With all of these, take the shield of faith, with which you will be able to quench all the flaming arrows of the evil one. Take the helmet of salvation, and the sword of the Spirit, which is the word of God* (Ephesians 6:13-17).

God has thoroughly equipped us for battle against the evil in our world, but keep in mind that the battle first begins in our own hearts and minds. It is tempting to rush off and fight some great evil in the world as a warrior for God's kingdom work. However, when we have not first dealt with our own personal struggles with evil, we will be going off to do battle with our armor poorly fitted and, in many ways, not even in place. This, of course, makes us vulnerable to serious injury and a menace to the cause of Christ. When Christians go off to fight the evils of the world half-cocked and unprepared, they most often prove to be hypocrites and their poor witness turns into an object of scorn and embarrassment.

Jesus is our perfect example of how to fight evil in our world. He did it humbly, fully prepared, and with the proper use of God's Word. It was costly for him, but very effective. For when the battle was over, Satan, death, and the grave had all been defeated. What a capable warrior we have on our side! And all who put their faith in him will experience victory in this life and for all eternity.

A Pastor's Prayer:
Dear Lord,

Thank you for conquering evil once and for all. Help me to remember your victory whenever I feel personally defeated by sin or discouraged with the evil in the world around me. Teach me how to fight these battles, both the ones within me and the ones around me. Protect me and empower me to fight as you fought, that I too may share in your victory. Thank you. Amen.

Easter 7

John 17:6-19

I urge you, while reading this text, to pretend you are sitting in a pastor's conference and Jesus is at the podium praying this prayer for you and all the other pastors. I have found this to be a powerful way to hear this prayer, so I'm including it in this devotional and will make brief comments throughout it. Imagine now that Jesus is praying for you.

[Dear Father], I have made your name known to those whom you gave me from the world. They were yours, and you gave them to me, and they have kept your word.

The key point of this prayer, especially when prayed for pastors, is that we receive and keep the word that God has given us, as found in the Bible. It is through this word that God has been made known to us. To stray from this word and no longer keep it, is to stray from the truth about who God is.

Now they know that everything you have given me is from you; for the words that you gave to me I have given to them, and they have received them and know in truth that I came from you; and they have believed that you sent me.

Faith in God's Word is essential, if we are to preserve its truths and proclaim it accurately. Jesus desires that we move from a head-knowledge of the facts to embracing them by faith. Without faith in God's Word, we are merely passing on information versus passionately proclaiming truth. There's a huge difference, both in the preaching and in the end results.

I am asking on their behalf; I am not asking on behalf of the world, but on behalf of those whom you gave me, because they are yours. All mine are yours, and yours are mine; and I have been glorified in them.

We do well to ask ourselves, from time to time: Is God being glorified in me and through my ministry? Are people hearing the whole truth about God through my preaching, teaching, and pastoral care? If we just talk about the good news of Jesus and don't tell people the bad news about sin, they will not have a complete knowledge of God and he will not be *glorified in them*. We need to preach the whole package — law and grace.

> *And now I am no longer in the world, but they are in the world, and I am coming to you. Holy Father, protect them in your name that you have given me, so that they may be one, as we are one. While I was with them, I protected them in your name that you have given me. I guarded them, and not one of them was lost except the one destined to be lost, so that the scripture might be fulfilled. But now I am coming to you, and I speak these things in the world so that they may have my joy made complete in themselves. I have given them your word, and the world has hated them because they do not belong to the world, just as I do not belong to the world. I am not asking you to take them out of the world, but I ask you to protect them from the evil one. They do not belong to the world, just as I do not belong to the world.*

This is a tremendously comforting portion of Christ's prayer. He was (and still is) praying this for us, as he knows how dangerous this world is for those who believe in him. It was extremely dangerous for the apostles and the first-century church, for persecution broke out quickly. It is still dangerous for many Christians around the world today for the same reason. But it is dangerous for those of us in a free, wealthy, pluralistic society as well. If we boldly proclaim scripture as the living word of God to a fallen humanity we will feel the "heat." Some people might get angry with us and either leave the church or try to throw us out. If we preach the word of God for what it is, absolute truth for salvation, eternal life, and how to live the Christian life, we will be labeled, by some people, as "narrow-minded" and "intolerant." Oh, how we need his protection.

Sanctify them in the truth; your word is truth. As you have sent me into the world, so I have sent them into the world. And for their sakes I sanctify myself, so that they also may be sanctified in truth.

To be sanctified is to be made more and more in the image of God. We won't become a god or like God in this life, but we will reflect his character. Sanctification can never happen with halftruths, or a law/gospel imbalance, or when truth is reduced to mythology or the relative ideals of only a few. Sanctification only happens on the basis of absolute truths. God's Word gives us those truths and Jesus prayed that we and the church would be sanctified in those truths. Are we? Is the church?

A Pastor's Prayer:
Dear Lord,

Thank you for praying for me and the whole Christian church. Lord, help me to hear this prayer and respond to the working of your Spirit in and through me as a result of it. Help me to uphold your word as absolute truth. Thank you. Amen.

1 John 5:9-13

There are many important aspects to pastoral ministry, but I think the most important is that of proclaiming the good news of Jesus Christ. Along with this is the important role of assuring people that they do, indeed, have eternal life simply by believing in him. Few things grieve me more than when people profess to believe in Jesus for salvation and eternal life, but have no certain assurance that they will indeed go to heaven. Perhaps you have ministered to people who struggle with this.

Do you have absolute assurance of salvation? John wrote that his whole purpose in writing (whether he was referring to the whole epistle or vv. 9-12 is debated) was so that *you who believe in the name of the Son of God ... may know that you have eternal life.* We can know that we are going to heaven when we die! How sad that there are Christians who do not know this. The fault of that lies, to some degree, with those who are proclaiming God's Word. Are we preaching and teaching our people that if they believe in the name of the Son of God they will go to heaven?

There are Christian denominations who teach some form of eternal security, but the assurance rests, in part, in what the individual has done. The emphasis is put on rituals, or traditions, or activities, all of which may have good, biblical basis, but nonetheless are men's activities that in and of themselves can save no one and serve only to give false assurance. Here then, is the huge danger of the church and pastors preaching and teaching assurance of salvation and eternal life in anything other than the name of Jesus. False assurance is nothing more than that — false assurance. It is a grievous sin to lead people to believe that they will have eternal life in any other way, and by any other means, than by grace alone, through faith alone, in Christ alone, as revealed in God's Word alone.

If you have been trusting in an event, or a ritual, or a prayer, or some tradition, or anything other than Christ, I beg you to listen carefully to what John so emphatically wrote to us in this text: *If we receive human testimony, the testimony of God is greater; for this is the testimony of God that he has testified to his Son.*

There is no testimony greater than God's. However, the pride and ego of mankind (which is fed by the lies and deceptions of Satan) has convinced them that their testimony is more reliable than God's testimony, which is the Bible. This is why we have people standing in authority over the Bible and telling God what is true and what is not. They determine truth based on science, or pop culture, or what feels right and good at any given moment. This testimony is false testimony, and when connected to salvation and eternal life, gives people false assurance. There is only one testimony to be trusted and for us to pin our eternal hopes on — the testimony of God which he testified to (and through) his Son.

I'm bad at remembering the words to songs, but I vaguely recall a phrase from a song that I sang as a child. It went something like this: "God said it, I believe it, that settles it."

Could that be said of us? Whose testimony is greater to us, that of human doctrines, traditions, rituals, and so forth (even if they have some biblical basis), or that of God himself through his Son, Jesus Christ? I pray that for all of us it is the latter and that we will preach and teach that truth as if our very existence, now and for all eternity, depends on it — for it does!

A Pastor's Prayer:
Dear Lord,
 Thank you that your word is a certain and trustworthy testimony for us to stake our lives on — now and for all eternity. If I have been depending, in part or in whole, on anything other than your word for assurance of eternal life, please forgive me and help me to trust in you alone. Help me to know how to preach and teach this assurance to those in my care so they are not given false assurance. Thank you. Amen.

The Day Of Pentecost

John 15:26-27; 16:4b-15

The setting in which the words of our text were spoken was a difficult one for the disciples. Perhaps something we could compare it to would be a pastor's announcement of his or her resignation or new appointment. So far, in my years of ministry, I have had to announce my resignation to three separate congregations. I'm blessed that in each case the reaction was sadness and grief — indicating that they didn't want me to go. I'm always humbled and honored by that.

But what those congregations lost and what the disciples lost can't even be compared. I'm nothing compared to Christ. Can we even begin to imagine what the disciples were facing? Our congregations can find replacement pastors. They might even find someone who is more gifted and talented than we are! But who would replace Jesus? Who could do better than he did? How would they possibly get by without him? Obviously, no human could replace him and they certainly wouldn't get along without him, so he promised to send them someone who would be as good as him; in fact better, for he would never leave them. I'm referring, of course, to the Holy Spirit.

How thankful we can be for this wise arrangement that God planned from the beginning. How thankful we can be that Jesus is no longer on this earth in the form of the God/man who, though being infinite in his divine nature was finite in his human nature. While ministering on earth, Jesus was always located in one place at any given time. He could not be everywhere at once, as he now is through the power of the Holy Spirit. How much greater it is for the church that Jesus now locates himself in our hearts rather than in the Middle East. How thankful we can be that he shares his wisdom with each of us individually as we read and prayerfully reflect on his word. We don't have to take a pilgrimage to Jerusalem to sit under his teaching in the temple.

In this text, see at least two things which the Spirit does that ought to take some pressure off of us as we preach the Word of

God week after week. First, it is the Holy Spirit who *will prove the world wrong about sin and righteousness and judgment.* It is our role to preach about sin, righteousness, and judgment, but it is not our role to prove the world wrong. I think some pastors feel it is their mission and calling in life to prove the world wrong. If that is our approach, we will unnecessarily agitate people and make enemies. Our role is to faithfully proclaim God's Law and grace, and then allow the Spirit space and freedom to do the convicting (or *proving*) about sin.

Secondly, it is not ultimately up to us to guide people into all truth. Again, we have the God-given responsibility to faithfully preach and teach his word, but it is ultimately the Holy Spirit who — through the word — guides people into all truth. Don't both of these truths remove a lot of pressure from us? Not so we can be lazy and careless in our sermon preparation and delivery, but so we keep in mind that the actual moving of people to act upon God's truths and to bring them to salvation and spiritual maturity is a work of the Holy Spirit.

Our text began with these words of Jesus in the end of chapter 15: *When the Advocate comes, whom I will send to you from the Father, the Spirit of truth who comes from the Father, he will testify on my behalf. You also are to testify because you have been with me from the beginning.*

In Pentecost, we celebrate the good news of God's mercy and grace toward us in the sending of his Holy Spirit. It is he who ultimately testifies on Christ's behalf, but notice how we are drawn into this mission: *You also are to testify.* For whatever reason, God has chosen to involve us in the process of testifying. The Holy Spirit could show up on earth visibly and speak to people on his own, but he doesn't. He speaks to and through us. May we take that responsibility seriously and serve him faithfully as his mouthpiece.

A Pastor's Prayer:
Dear Lord,

Thank you for sending your Holy Spirit. Thank you that it is his work to prove people *wrong about sin* and to guide them into all truth. Since you have called me to be a part of this process, by being your mouthpiece, please help me to do it faithfully and effectively for your honor and glory. Amen.

Acts 2:1-21

I'm so thankful that this account of the Holy Spirit coming upon the apostles is not the "formula" for how he comes upon the church and individual believers today. There are elements of Christianity which believe that. They feel this is a model of what the experience of every Christian and every church should be when the Holy Spirit comes upon them and their places of worship. I recently heard a song in a church that was basically begging for this to happen. The plea was made over and over again. That is *not* what the apostles had to do to receive the Holy Spirit. They simply waited, in obedience to their Lord's command, until the promised gift arrived in his time and in his way.

We cannot conjure up the Holy Spirit in songs and incantations, as may be the case with spirits of darkness and evil. I believe that to be completely obsessed with what happened to the disciples, and to try replicate that today, is to miss the point of the text. What we should take note of is the reactions of the bystanders.

Some of them were amazed and perplexed. It doesn't matter if an unbeliever sees fire coming down on the head of a believer and hears them speaking in a different language, or if they see that believer loving and forgiving others, selfless and self-controlled, the reaction is going to be about the same. They will be amazed and perplexed. You see, it is as much a miracle and evidence of the indwelling Holy Spirit if someone lives out one or more fruits of the Spirit, as it is if they speak in tongues. In fact it may well be easier to speak in tongues than to forgive someone who has sinned against you repeatedly, for you can fake speaking in tongues and fool some people for a long time, but it is really hard to fake forgiveness for any amount of time and have people believe it is genuine.

Another reaction was that of asking questions. When unbelievers see and experience pastors and parishioners living a genuine, Christ-like life, that prompts questions, such as: "How come you always seem so happy? How are you able to be so patient with that obnoxious person? I don't see how or why you forgave that individual who has hurt you repeatedly and still does." The life of a Christian ought to stand out in stark contrast to that of the world around us; not in odd, offensive ways, but in ways that grab people's attention so they ask questions.

Last of all, if we are going to replicate anything at all in this text, it would be what Peter did. He didn't brush off what had happened to them, nor did he ignore the criticism. He stood up and proclaimed the Word of God and pointed out the fulfillment of scripture.

When God is at work in us and our congregations, we ought to be the first to stand up and explain what is happening. And we should not be ignorant of what is happening. How sad if God were working mightily in your church, but you hadn't studied his word well enough to recognize his activity. This has happened in more than one church, to be sure; and what was really the activity of God, was labeled as fanaticism, obsession with experience, or emotional foolishness. The work of God's Spirit was stifled, possibly by the one person who above all should have known what was going on.

Do you have a grasp of how the Holy Spirit works? Is he being allowed to manifest himself and his fruits through you? Would you be able to recognize the activity of the Spirit of God if it were suddenly at work in one or more individuals in your church? If you are not sure, don't start buying and reading books on the Holy Spirit, but rather pick up and study intently the best source of information there is on the Holy Spirit — the Bible. For he authored it, helps us understand it, reveals himself and his work in it, and does his marvelous work of convicting and saving people through it.

A Pastor's Prayer:
Dear Lord,
 Thank you for the gift of your Holy Spirit. Help me, Lord, to better understand how you are at work in me and my church. May I readily recognize your work, and be able to not only explain it but give you all the credit and glory for it. Thank you. Amen.

The Holy Trinity

John 3:1-17

Nicodemus was certainly in a tough spot. He seemed to be struggling with the tension between faithfulness to the doctrines, traditions, and teachings of the Jewish religion, and a growing sense that Jesus might be speaking God's truth. How troubling it is to have our beliefs turned upside down and proven false.

Nicodemus, along with the rest of the Pharisees, had been watching Jesus. They had witnessed his miracles, they heard him teach, they saw how the crowds of people who were following him were growing by the day. Perhaps he wondered out loud with others, "Is this just another false prophet? Will his following last? Does he even know what he is talking about?" But where other Pharisees had written Jesus off as a fraud who need to be silenced, Nicodemus went secretly to him and encouraged conversation. He wanted to know more about what Jesus was teaching, for he seemed to be wondering if it was true. The quandary he faced was, if Jesus was right, then he and his colleagues were wrong; and that was a serious situation, not only for themselves, but for the countless people they were misleading.

Have you ever been in a similar situation? Perhaps your denomination was (or is) taking positions on things that conflict with the teachings of Christ or other portions of scripture. Maybe you even voted for some of the new resolutions, amendments, or by-laws, but now, like Nicodemus, you are having second thoughts. You are wondering if possibly your church body, which you have been with for years and have trusted, appreciated, and supported, is in the wrong.

To be in such a situation is enough to make a person physically sick. You don't dare to talk about it with other pastors in your church body, for fear of what they will say or think of you. You surely don't dare to talk to the church leaders, for you fear that they certainly won't understand. Perhaps you fear that your ministry could be in jeopardy if people knew to what extent you are questioning and doubting. If you could, you would go to Jesus at night to see what he thinks about the whole situation. But you can't, so what do you do? You go to Jesus in the privacy of your study.

Jesus wants us to ask him hard questions. He doesn't want us to be blindly led by others without thinking about what we believe. He gave all of us a brain to think with, a heart to believe with, and a tongue with which to discuss hard issues with him and those we trust. I urge you, if you are currently finding yourself in a similar situation to that of Nicodemus, to run to Jesus and start asking some hard questions. Where will the answers come from and how will they come? They come primarily through his word, and they are revealed to us as we read it, ponder it, pray over it, and sit quietly before him so that he can "speak" to us in the stillness of time alone with him. He will make Bible passages suddenly stand out to you like never before. He will help you see things in the context of scripture that you've never seen before. He will help you wrestle with difficult texts that you have avoided in the past for fear of controversy. He will help you make adjustments to beliefs and convictions that you thought were just fine until you were challenged in some way about those convictions. He may prompt you to develop new convictions on issues and doctrines that you never thought of before.

This work of the Holy Spirit was happening in Nicodemus' life and he didn't even know it. He was just asking the hard questions and listening to Jesus' answers.

Allow those to whom you minister to also ask hard questions. Don't shoot them down because you are concerned about what they believe, or you don't understand where they are coming from, or you are trying to avoid a conflict. Let them ask and, together, study God's Word to see if he will provide the answers.

A Pastor's Prayer:
Dear Lord,

If I'm more like Nicodemus than I am like a disciple, please be patient with me and help me understand your word. Where the things your word says differ with what my church believes, help me to know what to do. Thank you. Amen.

Romans 8:12-17

Our text is from a larger passage comprised of verses 1-17. In this larger passage, Paul distinguished between the person who *lives according to the flesh* and the person who *lives according to the Spirit* of God. There is a huge difference between the two.

Those who live according to the flesh are *hostile to God*; they do not *submit to God's law* — nor can they do so. In addition, those who live according the flesh *cannot please God*. Paul pointed out that such people have *their minds set on the things of the flesh* and their end result is *death*.

On the other hand, those who live according to the Spirit do so because the *Spirit of Christ dwells* in them. Due to the redeeming work of Christ, *the just requirement*[s] *of the law* [are] *fulfilled in* those who have the Spirit. Such people have *set their minds on the Spirit*, and in so doing they experience *life and peace*, now and for all eternity.

The question we all need to ask ourselves is: "Upon what am I setting my mind?" In the daily routine of ministry, the one thing that pastors use the most is their minds. We spend hours thinking upon God's Word in preparation for Bible studies, sermons, devotionals, homilies, and so on. We sit at our desks, thinking about people — both those who are a joy to us and those who are a grief to us. We think about how to minister to them, how to comfort them, how to counsel them, and, in some cases, how to discipline them. In addition to this, we are required to devote hours every week to thinking on administrative details and making decisions.

Our thoughts are not limited to ministry, however. There are the emotionally draining thoughts about ourselves and our loved ones. When we think of ourselves, we often think of our sins, our failures, and our shortcomings — and that brings sorrow. Yet we also think about who God made us to be and how he redeemed us through the blood of Jesus — that gives us joy! When we think of our loved ones, we think of their love for us and how much we love them; that also brings us joy. On the other hand, we think about their unhappiness with our long days of ministry and the tensions that can develop between us, and that brings sorrow.

We ask, "Upon what am I setting my mind?" How we think makes all the difference in the world as to our attitudes, our words, our actions, and our overall reputation. Our thinking shapes the kind of spouses we are, the kind of parents we are, and the kind of pastors we are. It determines our effectiveness in and out of the pulpit, for the pastor who thinks upon, and lives according to the flesh, will be fighting an uphill battle with God and people. They will not be able to please God and their ministries will die. But the pastor who thinks upon, and lives according to, the Spirit of God, will be in harmony with God and his people. They will have good consciences and speak the Word of God boldly. They will be experiencing *life and peace*, and it will be evident to all to whom they minister.

Having considered all this, we read again what Paul wrote in verse 12: *So then, brothers and sisters, we are debtors, not to the flesh*, [but to the Spirit, to live according to it]. We owe an enormous debt to Christ for what he has done for us and, consequently, who he has made us to be; *children of God*. God would have us live out that indebtedness through an obedient life that reflects his character. To do so, we must begin by setting our minds on the Spirit. May that become a daily discipline for each of us at the start of our day, before we say or do anything else.

A Pastor's Prayer:
Dear Lord,

Thank you for fulfilling the just requirements of the law through the sacrifice of your Son and his indwelling Holy Spirit. Help me today to set my mind on you; that all I say and do would be of you and reflect your righteous character, for your honor and glory. Amen.

Proper 6

Mark 4:26-34

We live and minister in one of the greatest mysteries known to humankind; the kingdom of God. One of the tendencies of the modern church has been to think of itself more and more in terms of marketing strategies. What once were considered "sheep" to be cared for have become consumers to cater to. What once were places of worship have become places of entertainment. What once brought people together in intergenerational fellowship now divides them into age-appropriate ministries. What once was considered evangelism has now become slick and competitive advertising. What once was regarded as building the kingdom of God has now become the building of a human institution. When we remove the element of mystery from kingdom work, all we have left is purposeless busywork.

Many in the church today want proven strategies, successful programs, "five easy steps to growth," and so on. We want a way of bringing people into God's kingdom that will work every time. We want to know exactly how to get people into the church and how to keep them. We want *control!* Now that I think of it that is not only a modern-day phenomenon. This institution called the church has tried to control people and manipulate God for centuries, and it has resulted in just the opposite of what the church fathers had hoped for. People have fallen away from the church. Many have become disillusioned and want nothing further to do with it. Others have felt used, having thought that the only thing the church wanted from them was their money. In some cases, this may be closer to the truth than we would like to admit.

Jesus, in our Gospel Lesson, clearly pointed out that there exists in God's kingdom an element of mystery that the church is a part of, when he said, *the seed would sprout and grow, he does not know how.* When we preach and teach God's Word, which is the most essential element for kingdom growth, we are *scatter*[ing] *seed on the ground.* Oh, how we wish we knew exactly when and how it was going to sprout, but we don't. This is something that has perplexed me for years; for I can share God's Word faithfully, in one form or another, yet it can seem as if very little comes of it. Then one day, out of the blue, someone to whom I've been ministering comes to faith in Christ. I wasn't there when it happened! How can this be? Doesn't God need me to be there when kingdom work is happening? No, he doesn't.

Notice what Jesus said in verse 28: *The earth produces of itself, first the stalk, then the head, then the full grain in the head.* We scatter the seed, which is God's Word. It falls on the earth, which is human hearts. Then the farmer (which is us) sits back and watches what happens. There is nothing more we can do for the seed at that point other than to pray that it will sprout, grow, and yield a harvest. We cannot force people into the church, for we cannot force them into God's kingdom. We cannot force them to be saved and to grow up in Christ, for if we try, we will damage them spiritually.

Equally a mystery is that which Jesus describes in verses 30-32. How does such a small seed grow to be such a large plant? The potential just doesn't seem to be there. So, too, how is it that some little churches have grown up to be such large churches? The potential just didn't seem to be there. How much of it was due to the hard work of gifted pastors and lay people, and how much of it was the mysterious working of the Holy Spirit? Attempts to find satisfying answers to these questions can result in the mistake of removing the mystery that God intended to exist in his kingdom work. The role of pastors is to faithfully *scatter the seed*, and leave the results up to the mysterious working of God's Spirit in his kingdom.

A Pastor's Prayer:
Dear Lord,

Thank you for involving me in your kingdom work. Help me to accept the element of mystery and to live with that tension. Please forgive me for when I have fallen too deeply for methods and strategies in an effort to produce predictable results. Lord, I want to faithfully *scatter seed* and leave the results to you. Amen.

2 Corinthians 5:6-10 (11-13) 14-17

How important is this life to you? The real answer to that question is evident in how we live this life. We might say that this life is not all that important, but if we are materialistic and live as if it is the most important thing to us, our words mean nothing.

In the opening verse of this chapter, Paul put it all in perspective when he wrote: *For we know that if the earthly tent we live in is destroyed, we have a building from God, a house not made with hands, eternal in the heavens.* Paul went on to explain that this certainty comes from God's Spirit who dwells in us and serves *as a guarantee* of eternal life.

One characteristic of a child of God, who has this proper perspective, is to say as Paul did, *we would rather be away from the body and at home with the Lord.* Some think that is morbid and depressing to say, but what is morbid and depressing about wanting our new, glorified, eternal, heavenly body? What is morbid and depressing about wanting to be in the presence of God? It is only morbid and depressing if we view this life as more important than the life to come, and that view is only possible by having a false and inadequate understanding of heaven.

The believer in Christ does not walk through this life like unbelievers do. *We walk by faith, not by sight.* That doesn't mean we are blind to reality or ignorant about this life. It means that we are fully aware of a greater reality that exists beyond this real, physical life that we are currently experiencing. The mistaken conclusion that faithless people arrive at is that this reality is all there is or, if there is more beyond this life, it is not as good as what we now know and experience.

For those of us who believe in Christ, for this life and all eternity, we would do well to follow Paul's example in verse 9: *we make it our aim to please him.* This aim to please God comes in response to what God has already done and given to the believer. It is not, as some professing Christians believe, an effort to please him so that he will let us into heaven. Many people are growing up in the church believing, either due to an absence of complete, biblical teaching or due to outright false teaching, that they must try to please God in order to get to heaven. That is heresy, and absolutely misleading, to the detriment of their souls!

We, and all to whom we minister, need the truth of the gospel as laid out in verses 14, 15, and 17: *For the love of Christ urges us on, because we are convinced that one has died for all; therefore all have died. And he died for all, so that those who live might live no longer for themselves, but for him who died and was raised for them.*

So if anyone is in Christ, there is a new creation: everything old has passed away; see, everything has become new!

That glorious hope is ours, and we get to pass it on to others! If we believe in Christ, we are a new creation. Everything that is going to happen to us in eternity is as good as done. Even though we have not fully changed and become what we will be there, it is as good as ours, for the guarantee of that is given to us in this life. This guarantee comes through faith in Christ and is made sure through his word and his indwelling Holy Spirit. Thank God its certainty has absolutely nothing to do with us or our performance.

A troubling statement which Paul made in verse 10, is: *all of us must appear before the judgment seat of Christ, so that each may receive recompense for what has been done in the body, whether good or evil.* Apart from Christ, this statement would fill our hearts with terrifying fear and dread. But thank God for our "defense attorney" who will stand before the Father on our behalf and declare all our evil deeds forgiven and all our good deeds for what they are: *our aim to please him.*

A Pastor's Prayer:
Dear Lord,

Thank you for the certainty of heaven and eternal life. Thank you for the gift of your Holy Spirit that is a guarantee to us that our new, heavenly body is as good as ours, even while we are still in this body. Lord, help me to walk by faith, and not by sight. May I, today, aim to please you and no one else. Amen.

Proper 7

Mark 4:35-41

Who's "calling the shots" in your ministry? Is it you? Is it your spouse? Is it your church council, your district president, or your bishop? Or, is it the Lord? We would all like to believe it is the Lord, but is it really? One way to determine that is to re-evaluate how you and your church make decisions. Are decisions made on the basis of long meetings with people in debate, or long meetings with God in prayer? Do the decisions generally fit your comfort level and serve you, or do they stretch you and serve God?

Notice how Jesus addressed his plans with the disciples that evening, as they ended another day of ministry: *Let us go across to the other side.* God never tell us to do something on our own. His plans are always about *us*. "*Let us* go and visit that shut-in or inmate at the jail. *Let us* preach on this or that difficult subject or text. *Let us* deal with this particularly difficult person in the church. *Let us* go into this congregational meeting together. *Let us* pick up from here and move to another congregation. *Let us* do something other than parish ministry for a while. *Never* does he send us into his work alone. It's always *us*. When we feel alone, it is either because of sin in our life or we have run ahead of him into something that is not his will or plan for us. Jesus is always inviting us to join him in his plans. Are we listening?

Sometimes his call to join him involves leaving our comfort zone. It might be to leave the people we feel most comfortable around. It might be a call to go to a dangerous mission field. It might be to minister to someone who makes us really uncomfortable. It might be a call to preach on a text or subject that makes us nervous. The call might come in the evening, when we are tired and would just as soon call it a day. What will you do? How will you respond? The disciples got in the boat. Will you?

It is always risky to go with Jesus. Seldom are we given the details of the mission. Seldom do we see the "storms" on the horizon. So why does he lead us into danger? Why does he call us to churches that have the potential to "chew us up and spit us out"? Why does he send people to us who cause us stress and fatigue?

Have you ever asked the question the disciples asked: *Teacher, do you not care that we are perishing?*

What was one thing in particular that the disciples learned that evening? It was about the power and authority of Jesus to calm storms. How would they have known this about him if he had not taken them into a storm? The next time Jesus takes you into a "storm," ask yourself, "What can I learn about him through this experience?" There is so much about Jesus we will never know first hand if we never go with him into a "storm."

May we also remember that it is only Jesus who can calm the storm. Only Jesus can bring peace into the marriage of that couple you are counseling. Have you been counseling them as if it were up to you? It's exhausting, isn't it? Only Jesus can bring peace between the members of your church who are feuding over a building program, or some other element of the church's ministry. Have you been trying to bring a peaceful resolution on your own? Don't do it, for without Christ's help you are bound to get hurt. If the disciples had tried to calm the storm by themselves, what are the chances that at least a few of them might have drowned?

Jesus asks us: *Why are you afraid? Have you still no faith?* What is your answer? I know what mine is: "Lord, I'm sorry, but my faith is so weak." Only Jesus can grow and strengthen our faith. The greatest growth in faith usually takes place in a storm.

If you are going through a "storm" of some kind in your ministry right now (or maybe it is in your personal life), be assured that Jesus is with you. Cry out to him for courage and faith. Perhaps you are about to be *filled with great awe!*

A Pastor's Prayer:
Dear Lord,

You know the storm that I am in right now. Please protect me and grow my faith in you through this storm. Thank you that you will bring peace and calm at just the right time. Thank you for not sending me into ministry alone, but that everything you call me to do is about *us*. Lord, I stand in awe of your power and authority over the storms of life. May I rest in you and follow only your plans for me. Thank you. Amen.

2 Corinthians 6:1-13

In our Gospel Lesson we took note of how our Lord invites us to join him in his plans for us. In this lesson, Paul was encouraging the Corinthian church to *work together with him* (or Christ). Immediately preceding this text, in chapter 5, Paul wrote that *we are ambassadors for Christ* (2 Corinthians 5:20). In other words, we are to represent him before others, whether in our own community, our nation, or around the world. Pastors are certainly *ambassadors for Christ.* The very nature of our call, along with the Great Commission, is to *work together with him.*

As the church works together with Christ, it is urged *not to accept the grace of God in vain.* People receive God's grace in vain when they hear it but refuse to respond to it by faith. Perhaps we also receive God's grace in vain when we take it lightly. I have noticed that people who have lived a life of gross sin and evil, but come to faith in Christ later in life, are deeply appreciative and moved by the grace of God toward them. Those of us who have grown up in Christian homes, have heard about God's grace since we were children, and have lived relatively "good" lives, don't nearly appreciate God's grace as we ought, for we haven't regarded ourselves as all that sinful. That is outright arrogant and proud! We are just as damned under God's Holy Law as the worst sinner imaginable. We need God's grace as much as they do. His grace ought to be just as precious to us as it is to a new believer in Christ.

How critical it is that we agree with Paul when he wrote: *now is the day of salvation!* The significance of that statement for us is twofold. First, *now is the day of salvation* for us! Now is the day for us to get right with God, if there is sin standing between him and us. Now is the day to make sure we are in a right, saving relationship with him. Being a pastor does not guarantee us eternal life in heaven. It give us no advantage over anyone else in terms of salvation. We, too, must come to that point of humble repentance, confession of faith, and personal belief in Christ alone for salvation and eternal life. So I urge you to take time right now to get right with God if there is any possibility that you are not.

Secondly, the statement, *now is the day of salvation,* has significance for us in terms of what we ought to be proclaiming. Some may feel this is alarmist theology and say something to this effect: "Why press people to believe? It's been 2,000 years since Christ left this earth; apparently he is in no hurry to come back. We have more urgent things to think about and preach on." Due to the fact that the return of Christ has always been imminent, this message has always been urgent. This imminence and urgency hasn't diminished one bit in God's eyes, nor should it in ours. But there is also the reality that anyone could die at any moment. Who sat in your worship service last Sunday that will not be there this Sunday, due to death? Were they ready to die? Who might be there this Sunday, but pass away before next Sunday? Are they ready to die?

Granted, salvation is a work of the Holy Spirit. We can't make people believe and be saved, but we have been given the awesome responsibility of proclaiming God's Word faithfully and with authority so that people are without excuse for not believing.

The faithful proclamation of God's Word is no picnic, as Paul pointed out. Can you identify with any of what he had experienced, when he mentioned afflictions, hardships, and sleepless nights for proclaiming the gospel? If not, maybe you are not preaching a balanced law/grace message. For when we do, we are going to prick people's consciences and many will rebel against that — taking out their anger on us for the guilt we stirred up within them.

Paul certainly knew how to fight the good fight of faith and faithfully proclaim the gospel without getting discouraged and giving up. May we be known for doing the same.

A Pastor's Prayer:
Dear Lord,

I desire that there be nothing standing between you and me. Please forgive me my sins. Thank you for saving my soul, Lord. Help me to proclaim your word in a law/grace balance, and as urgently as if this were the last Sunday that people will hear your word. May many come to faith in you before it is too late. Amen.

Proper 8

Mark 5:21-43

The activity in our text revolves primarily around two people who demonstrated an extraordinary faith in Jesus. The first is Jairus, a leader of the synagogue. It is surprising to read how he came up to Jesus, fell on his knees and begged Jesus for help. As a synagogue ruler, he was most likely a devout Jew whom we would expect to have been as skeptical of Jesus as many of his colleagues were. But desperation seemed to drive him to Jesus for healing for his dying daughter. We don't know what was bringing her to the edge of death, nor do we know how long she had been in that condition. What we do know is that it was a grave situation.

Now notice Jairus' expression of faith: *Come and lay your hands on her, so that she may be made well, and live.* He believed that if Jesus would just come and lay his hands on his daughter, she would *be made well, and live.* He believed there was something about Jesus' touch that would bring about these results. Perhaps he had seen it done to others. So putting aside any prejudices or criticisms he might have had toward Jesus, he begged from a heart of faith, that Jesus restore his daughter to health.

We know, from the text, that there was a delay in arriving at Jairus' home and, during that delay, his daughter passed away. When they received word of this, Jesus spoke these reassuring words to Jairus: *Do not fear, only believe.* Jairus did exactly that, and the end result was getting his daughter back, alive and well.

The woman who interrupted Jesus on the way to Jairus' home was also an interesting individual and demonstrated an extraordinary faith in Jesus. She had wormed her way through the crowd thinking: *If I but touch his clothes, I will be made well.* How did she know that? Our text does not say, but it might have been due to her faith beforehand; believing that this could be true even if no one else had tried it. The end result, of course, is that she was healed simply by touching the hem of Jesus' garment; and Jesus not only healed her, but commended her for her faith. *Daughter, your faith has made you well; go in peace, and be healed of your disease.*

When we consider these two individuals, may we be reminded that faith does not always look or express itself in the same, predictable ways. All too often we look at certain people and draw the conclusion that they will never believe in Jesus. Or, we might look at someone's faith and think, "That's not right. They did not come to faith in the way our church teaches they should."

As you carry out your ministry, keep in mind that people are watching and listening to you. They might not come to faith in Christ at the time you had wanted them to, nor in the way you had hoped they would. Faith is something that, as Paul wrote to the Roman church, *comes from what is heard, and what is heard comes through the word of Christ* (Romans 10:17). I'm sure these two people had heard Jesus preach many times. Faith came to them through what they heard, and that faith gave them the courage to approach Jesus face-to-face for a miracle of healing.

When you get down and discouraged, thinking that no one is listening to you and no one is coming to faith or growing in faith, keep in mind that there is a lot going on that you cannot yet see. Someday, if not in this life, certainly in heaven, we will see the impact that our preaching and teaching had. We will meet, face-to-face, the people who came to faith in Christ because of our faithfulness to proclaim the Word of God.

Be encouraged, knowing that God is at work through you, and thank him often for that.

A Pastor's Prayer:
Dear Lord,

Thank you for creating faith in me. I ask that you would keep enlarging and growing my faith. Thank you that, as I proclaim your word, you are creating faith in the hearts of those who will listen. May I be overcome with amazement at what you are able to do, simply through the life-changing power of your word. Amen.

2 Corinthians 8:7-15

If we look at verses 1-6, it seems as if Paul was using a motivational approach that parents sometimes use on their children when they ask: "Why can't you be more like so and so?"

The issue at the heart of this text is generosity in giving. Apparently, the Corinthians had begun a collection a year earlier to help some needy people, possibly the Christians in Jerusalem. For some reason their efforts had fallen off and the collection was never completed. Paul didn't shame the Corinthians into giving, but rather used the churches in Macedonia as an example of what sincere, enthusiastic, sacrificial giving looks like.

Few things are more disappointing to a pastor than a church that doesn't give. All too often we know more about people's lives than we would like. If we have some idea what they might be giving to the church, then we know who is giving generously and who is not. As we face issues of stewardship in the church, we often become fearful of what people will think, say, or do if we preach on the subject. This text can give us courage in this area, as we see how Paul faced the issue head-on with no apologies.

Notice the tact with which Paul addressed the issue. First he complimented them: *you excel in everything — in faith, in speech, in knowledge, in utmost eagerness, and in our love for you,* or *your love for us.* This is a wise approach, for if we just whack people over the head with a fiery sermon on stewardship, we will ruffle some feathers and maybe even lose some people. It's okay to build people up and affirm them in areas they are strong. That not only encourages them to do as well as (if not better than) before, but it also prepares them to more readily receive the harder truths they need to hear. In the case of the Corinthians, the harder truth was; *we want you to excel also in this generous undertaking.* It was time for them to grow in their attitude toward giving.

Generosity does not come naturally for most, because it is contrary to the selfish, human nature we were born with. Like all good qualities, we need to be trained through confrontation, correction, and practice. Paul was doing the first two and Titus would help them with the third. But genuine generosity is preceded and motivated by genuine love for God and others. There is a perfect standard of that love and the natural generosity that flows out of it. Paul reminded them that the standard is Christ. However, the Macedonians had demonstrated great maturity and Christlikeness in their giving, and Paul felt it appropriate to hold them up as a less-than-perfect, yet worthy example as well. Therefore he wrote: *I am testing the genuineness of your love against the earnestness of others.*

That's quite a statement for us to consider as well. Just how does the genuineness of our love stack up against the earnestness of others? I've never liked comparing humans to other humans, whether when dealing with my children or my parishioners, for we are then measuring them by an imperfect example. I feel it is much better to test the *genuineness* of our love (or that of others) against the *earnestness* of Christ. No one has been more eager to give to us than Christ has. No one has made a greater sacrifice on behalf of others than Christ has. No one has ever expressed their love more fully through generosity than Christ has.

Not only do we need a reality check on this issue, but so do our parishioners. It is not an easy topic to preach on, but a very important one. If we fail to preach and teach this issue to our people, they will continue (due to ignorance) to be selfish and stingy in their giving — the very thing that frustrates us so much in our relationship with them. We have a responsibility, as Paul had, to point these things out to people for their own good and the glory of God.

A Pastor's Prayer:
Dear Lord,

Thank you for your overwhelming generosity to me. Lord, you are the perfect standard by which I should measure my own attitude toward, and discipline of, grace giving. Help me to recognize the valid needs around me, to make a commitment to giving toward those needs, and to set a Macedonian example for others to follow. Please give me courage to preach on this issue and wisdom in what to say and how to say it. Thank you. Amen.

Proper 9

Mark 6:1-13

Just as last week's Gospel Lesson was about great faith, this week's lesson is about great unbelief. So great was the unbelief, that even Jesus was amazed! Right away we see what the outcome of the unbelief in Nazareth was: *he could do no deed of power there, except that he laid his hands on a few sick people and cured them.* What a tragedy, that this community who had raised the Son of God could not swallow their pride and unbelief so they might see and enjoy the blessings of faith in Christ Jesus.

I shudder at the thought of how much of this goes on in Christian churches across America. Our so-called "Christian nation," with its thousands of Christian churches, has become so accustomed to Christ and the gospel that we actually mock and scorn it through our complacency and compromise. Is it any wonder that Christ can *do no deed of power* in many of our churches?

I'm intrigued by how vulnerable God made himself to our unbelief. He, who is omnipotent and can do anything he wants, anytime he wants, with anyone he wants, designed his relationship with us in such a way that our unbelief actually hinders the working of his power in our individual lives and churches. What a sobering reality that is.

Is there unbelief in your relationship with God? I'm not talking about those nagging doubts that serious Bible students wrestle with from time to time. I'm talking about outright unbelief of God's Word. Are there portions of scripture you refuse to believe, because they seem unbelievable as you filter them through the popular thought processes of modern philosophy and science? Dear friend, if God seems to have quit working powerfully in and through you, this may well be the reason.

Paul wasn't kidding when he wrote to the Corinthians about this: *For since, in the wisdom of God, the world did not know God through wisdom, God decided, through the foolishness of our proclamation, to save those who believe* (1 Corinthians 1:21). How do people experience the saving power of God? It is not through the wisdom of our world, but rather through the *foolishness of our proclamation.* We greatly hinder the "wonder working power" of God in our churches when we force his word to be subservient to the so-called wisdom of humanity. Is that not what happened in Nazareth that day? Since Jesus did not fit into the thinking processes of his hometown people, they would not listen to him or receive his miracles. They wanted it all to make sense before they would believe in him. When it didn't, they turned their back on it (and him). May we, and our churches, not be guilty of what the people of Nazareth were condemned for.

The second half of our text gives us some great advice for dealing with difficult people — specifically those who refuse to believe our message and would rather argue with us. Jesus' advice to the disciples (and I believe all ministers of the gospel) is this: *If any place will not welcome you and they refuse to hear you, as you leave, shake off the dust that is on your feet as a testimony against them.*

How freeing this is! It is not our responsibility to force people to believe. It is our responsibility to proclaim the good news of God's kingdom, but what people do with it is up to them. I have used this approach often in ministry, and it has helped me avoid unnecessarily beating myself up over people who refuse to believe. Unbelief is a real issue in ministry. There is no way to avoid it and no simple solution to it. There are no formulas and easy steps to faith. It comes through the proclamation of God's Word, and what people do with it determines the outcome. Make sure that, in your personal life and the spiritual life of the church you serve, unbelief is not a problem; otherwise it will greatly hinder (maybe even paralyze) your ministry.

A Pastor's Prayer:
Dear Lord,

Forgive me for times of unbelief. Help me to recognize areas in my relationship with you and your word where I'm refusing to believe what I should. Lord, may I, and the people in my church, not be counted amongst those who refuse to believe, but rather make us people of faith, so you are free to work your deeds of power amongst us. Thank you. Amen.

2 Corinthians 12:2-10

If one were to read this text without any prior knowledge of Paul, we might come to the conclusion that he had a big ego and was a bit eccentric. He wrote verses 7-10 almost in the form of a riddle, in which he enthusiastically tried to share the high points of an experience that he could not adequately describe.

It must have been incredible, for Paul seems to have been greatly impacted by it. As a result, he felt such intense elation that he believed: *a thorn was given me in the flesh, a messenger of Satan to torment me, to keep me from being too elated.* That's quite a humbling thing to admit.

I wonder how many of God's children actually have similar incredible experiences? I don't recall that I have, but if it were this exciting I think I would have remembered it! However, whether we have some incredible out-of-body experience like Paul or not, one thing we all have in common is the problem of pride. I've come to the conclusion that Christians seem to have a greater problem with this than the average unbeliever. Maybe I'm wrong and hopefully I am. Yet, it seems that many Christians become proud of who they are, what they have, what they believe in, and so on. But pride is repulsive. Like all sins, it is grossly offensive to our Heavenly Father.

Perhaps what more of us need is a *thorn in the flesh* to *torment* us. I know from personal experience that they are very effective in humbling us. For a number of years I have lived with what has proven to be an untreatable back pain. In addition, I'm highly susceptible to depression. For years I complained to God about these *thorns in the flesh* that torment me daily. Often I would reflect upon the fact that Paul asked the Lord only three times to take his *thorn* away, but I must have asked 3,000 times or more! It wasn't until one day, as I was taking my usual early morning walk and trying to count my blessings, that I realized how good these "thorns" have been for me. Not only have they kept me humble at times when I most likely would have been proud, but through them I have learned so much more about God's *grace* [which] *is sufficient for* [me], *for power is made perfect in weakness.* From that point on, I have never asked God again to take the pain and the depression away. Instead, I have developed the habit of thanking him for both the "thorns" and the things he has taught me about himself through those "thorns."

I still have much room for growth and maturity in this area, for I still can't say as Paul wrote: *Therefore I am content with weaknesses, insults, hardships, persecutions, and calamities for the sake of Christ; for whenever I am weak, then I am strong.* It is still tempting to complain, moan, and groan, especially when new "thorns" crop up, but I pray for the day that I can be fully content with all of those things for the sake of Christ.

Dear brother or sister in Christ, do you have "thorns" in your life? Maybe it's something similar to mine. Maybe it's some other physical condition. Possibly you are struggling financially like so many pastors. Or maybe your thorn is the difficult congregation you are serving right now. May I encourage you, as a fellow sufferer in Christ, that when we are weak, then the strength and power of God can truly manifest itself in and through us. If you haven't experienced this yet, then it might be hard to understand how marvelous this is. There have been times when I didn't think I could get up to preach or make it through the service, but I did. Some of those Sundays, people who had no idea what physical or mental agony I was going through, would comment on how that had been one of my best and most powerful sermons. There's only one explanation for that, as far as I'm concerned, and that is the *power* of God being *made perfect in weakness*, and he will do the same for you. I guarantee it!

A Pastor's Prayer:
Dear Lord,

Thank you for those weaknesses that just won't go away. Thank you that your *grace is sufficient* for me as your *power is made perfect in* [my] *weakness*. Help me to grow to that point where I can honestly be fully content with whatever hardship I am experiencing for your sake. Amen.

Proper 10

Mark 6:14-29

This text paints a vivid picture of the superstition and evil that existed in Jesus' day. His growing popularity was not only attracting more people, but was also getting the attention of leaders. Herod noticed the stir Jesus was creating and became interested in learning more about him, for he feared (and actually believed) that Jesus was John the Baptist raised from the dead.

His speculation in regards to Jesus was indicative of the superstition shared by many. Some thought Jesus was Elijah, others thought he was another prophet, but many believed he was, indeed, John the Baptist. This superstition, especially in Herod's case, was fueled by a guilty conscience; for he was responsible for John's death by beheading.

This brings us to the extent of evil in that day. If one studies the family history of the Herods, you'll find that they weren't all that different from the typical cast of a modern soap opera. Imagine having a president's wife with as much pull and wickedness as that of Herodias! We may get discouraged with our leaders from time to time, and there may well be a lot more wickedness that goes on behind closed doors than we are aware of, but I'm not aware of any pastor in America whose head is in danger of rolling because he preached a sermon that angered the president's wife! We still have the freedom in this country to preach God's Word in all its truth and authority. That is something to be very thankful for.

However, there are some similarities between what Jesus faced and what the church faces today. For example, many people are still confused in regards to who Jesus is. It seems that at least once a year, one or more major new magazines, or television networks, tackle the question: "Who is Jesus?" Some of these investigative reports have been enlightening, as they usually shed some light on what various people, both in and outside church, are thinking about Jesus. However, seldom, if ever, do they arrive at the truth of who he is. Our role is to faithfully proclaim the truth of Jesus for the sake of our people and all who will listen. When people in the church are unsure of who Jesus is, that is often an indicator that there is no consistent, clear teaching about Jesus in their church. Granted, some people sleep while we preach, but as a whole, if we are faithfully proclaiming God's Word, and if people are consistently coming to church, they should have a pretty good idea of who Jesus is. So never grow weary of proclaiming Christ, week after week, year after year. It is our most important responsibility and ought to be seen as our greatest privilege.

The other similar tension that the church faces is the increasing wickedness in our society. We have become somewhat immune and numb to much of it, for it has come gradually and tends to grow on us. What was once horrific to some Christians is now accepted by many. Standards have lowered and the degree of evil has risen. It seems, at times, like evil is prevailing and righteousness is losing.

What are we to do? We are to faithfully proclaim God's Word in regard to sin and righteousness. More and more pastors are afraid to preach on sin, for it is "offensive" to their congregations. Of course it is offensive, for no one likes to be told they are wrong. Sermons on what the Bible characterizes as sin, have been written off as "narrow-minded, out of date, and intolerant." Sin itself has been given new names, such as "mistakes, obsessive/compulsive disorders," and even "normal behavior." People justify their sinful behavior by saying, "Everybody's doing it!"

If we don't clearly and boldly proclaim God's definition of sin and what his standards for his children are, then how are people (both in and out of the church) going to have an idea of what sin is? It is a sad state of affairs when churches (pastors and parishioners alike) no longer take a stand for, nor defend, God's righteous and universal moral law.

A Pastor's Prayer:
Dear Lord,

Thank you for who you are and for clearly revealing yourself to us through your word. Help me to proclaim your truths in ways that people will come to know you and believe in you. Please forgive my sins, and forgive me for when I have excused sin in my life and in the life of others. Lord, help me to boldly preach on sin so that others might repent and follow you. Thank you. Amen.

Ephesians 1:3-14

I like to think of this text as being able to do for us spiritually and emotionally what a hot bath does for us physically and mentally. When our body aches and our mind is tired from stress, a long, hot, soaking bath seems to soothe both the body and the mind. So, too, when we feel weary from ministry and the battle against Satan; when our emotions are drained from dealing with people and their sins; a slow, soothing "bath" in this text can lift our spirits and calm the troubled heart. Let's look at some of the uplifting and calming elements in these verses.

The first thing we see is how *blessed* we are. I don't know that we are able to fully comprehend the extent of what Paul was trying to communicate here. We know heaven is going to be awesome and we know how we have been blessed in this life, but when it comes to fully grasping *every spiritual blessing in the heavenly places*, we hit a wall. Perhaps Paul's statement to the Corinthians says it best: *No eye has seen, nor ear heard, nor the human heart conceived, what God has prepared for those who love him* (1 Corinthians 2:9). How true that is!

Secondly, we see that God *chose us*. I'm fully aware that there are various views on what it means to be chosen, so I'll avoid wading into that debate. However, I'm sure we all agree it is an incredible truth that God wants us — sinful, selfish, conniving little people that we are — to be his children! That has always been his desire. God isn't like some selfish, self-centered individuals who feel obligated to take in an orphaned child. No, he wants us to be with him, now and forever. What a fantastic truth this is!

Thirdly, we have *redemption* in Christ. This goes hand in hand with the previous point, for the only way to be a child of God is through redemption. Redemption is not dependent on our performance or ability to buy our way into heaven, but on the basis of *his glorious grace that he freely bestowed on us in the Beloved*. So freely has he given us his grace that Paul described it as having been *lavished on us.* The generosity of God toward us is absolutely humbling, for we know we've done nothing to deserve it. We might illustrate it this way: Suppose a child has been especially naughty on his birthday. His parents feel there is just cause to withhold their gifts from him as punishment. However, instead of giving the child what he deserves (punishment) the parents give him what he doesn't deserve (a lavish amount of gifts). That is what God has done for us in Christ.

Fourthly, God has *made known to us the mystery of his will* in regards to the eternal reign of Christ. He didn't have to do this, but he did. He wants to share his kingdom with us — now and forever. This mystery was long withheld from his people, but in the fullness of time, God revealed his mystery through Jesus.

Last of all, we have been given the *promised Holy Spirit* as a guarantee of our future inheritance in heaven. Like all the previous points, God is the one doing the action. He blessed us. He chose us. He redeemed us. He made known to us the mystery of his will. And he has given us his Holy Spirit. Notice the significance of this, according to Paul: *In him you also ... were marked with the seal of the promised Holy Spirit; this is the pledge of our inheritance toward redemption as God's own people, to the praise of his glory.*

Are you currently spiritually and emotionally drained? Do you feel like "throwing in the towel"? If so, I urge you to read and re-read this text and allow the Lord to renew you spiritually and give you renewed strength emotionally.

A Pastor's Prayer:
Dear Lord,

Thank you for the countless blessings that are mine, simply by faith in Jesus. Thank you for choosing me to be your child and for all the rights and privileges that come with that. Thank you for redeeming my soul from hell. Thank you for revealing to me the mystery of your will, for me and the whole world. And thank you for giving your Holy Spirit as a guarantee of all you've promised to me. Amen.

Proper 11

Mark 6:30-34, 53-56

This week's lesson consists of both the introduction and conclusion to the familiar accounts of Jesus feeding the 5,000 and calming the storm. Pastors can identify well with this text, for it describes what we need at times.

In verses 7-13, we see that Jesus had sent the disciples out in groups of two. Their mission was to proclaim repentance, cast out demons, and heal the sick. As our text opens, we read that they had returned and were excitedly reporting to Jesus all that had taken place as a result of their ministry. It reminds me of a church convention, where pastors are excitedly reporting to others the great things God has been doing through them and their churches.

Ministry is exhausting, even when things are going well. Jesus recognized fatigue in his disciples and said to them: *Come away to a deserted place all by yourselves and rest a while.* How desperately we need that, too, for the very same reason that Mark identified: *For many were coming and going, and they had no leisure even to eat.* There are those days when it seems that the hectic pace of appointments, phone calls, meetings, and visitation prevent us from catching our breath, much less getting a chance to eat. Thank God for summers and the opportunities that vacations afford us to *come away to a deserted place all by yourselves and rest a while.*

As great as vacations are, I found that they don't come often enough to keep me rested. I had to plan time away in my weekly schedule. So I set Saturdays aside as my day for my wife and children. All my calls were screened. I still dealt with emergencies and did those occasional weekend weddings and funerals, but for the most part, that day was for my family, where they knew they would have my undivided attention.

However, that still wasn't enough to keep me going. I needed time away during the week to reflect on my ministry, to pray for God's wisdom and guidance, and to just listen. I informed my church board that I would be taking approximately four hours per week to do this. I would then retreat to solitary places, such as a state park, a friend's home, or somewhere that I could be all alone without interruption (with the cell phone off!). With an open Bible and notebook, I would listen to what God might be trying to tell me, whether about myself, other people, or the ministry of our church. As I read, prayed, and let my mind wander, I often sensed God leading me toward ideas and decisions that I may never have arrived at in any other way. Pastors need to get away in order to stay fresh and avoid burnout.

Verses 32-34 remind me of a movie titled, *What About Bob?* The main character, Bob, was a psychologically needy person. His psychiatrist became so exhausted from his clients that he took some time off. This threw Bob into a panic. He managed to find out where his doctor had retreated to, and, much to the doctor's shock and anger, Bob showed up on his doorstep. The balance of the movie is about Bob overcoming many of his phobias at the expense of the doctor going slowly insane!

I've never fully understood why Jesus took the disciples to a *deserted place by themselves*, only to allow thousands of needy "Bobs" to crowd in on them. Then, as if that wasn't enough, he capped off their day by sending them out on a lake where they encountered a violent storm. The best explanation I know is that only in a state of complete human exhaustion, when the disciples had come to the end of themselves, could Jesus' power be fully manifest. So it is with us. It isn't until we have come to the end of our physical and mental resources that it seems Jesus is free to do some astounding, even miraculous, things in our ministries.

Thank God he doesn't push us that hard every day, but when he does, know that he will get you through, and you might even see a miracle or two along the way. Just make sure that your fatigue is due to Christ's schedule and not yours.

A Pastor's Prayer:
Dear Lord,

Thank you that you won't ask me to do more than what you will give me strength to do. Help me to recognize when my fatigue is caused by my schedule and not yours. Help me to make time to get away to a solitary place and to make good use of that time to be alone with you. Amen.

Ephesians 2:11-22

What a powerful passage this is for the church. It is good to be reminded that Christ not only died for our sins, but that he has also *broken down the dividing wall* between Jews and Gentiles.

Those of us who are Gentile Christians were separated from God on two fronts: our sin and our race. The Apostle Paul described us as being, *by birth ... without Christ, being aliens from the commonwealth of Israel, and strangers to the covenants of promise, having no hope and without God in the world.* That's a pretty dismal picture, isn't it? I suppose one could say we were doubly damned, for not only were we victims of the Fall, but also *aliens* and *strangers*, due to being Gentiles.

This ought to give the Gentile church all the more reason to be thankful for God's grace. Our salvation is completely the result of God's decision. He chose to die for our sins and he chose to include us in the new covenant. Our inclusion is not the result of bargaining, peace talks, or negotiations. It is only the result of God's unmerited grace.

If God could bring down the dividing wall between man and God, and between Jew and Gentile, imagine what he can do in our churches. Tragically, there are many dividing walls in churches. Some walls are between family members, others are between people within the church, and there are those between pastors and parishioners. Jesus can tear down our walls. Nothing is too hard for him!

What hostilities exist in your church? Some of them we can do very little about. I've dealt with some bitter hostilities between people in the church. When one (or both) are unwilling to budge, most often one of them leaves the church. Other hostilities involve us. Are we being humble? Are we listening well to the other person's opinions? Or, are we being stubborn and insisting on having our way? Are we letting pride stand in the way of admitting we are wrong?

There are things we can do when the hostilities involve us; such as sitting down with those who are opposed to us and trying to talk out our differences. It is often helpful to have a third, independent party present — someone that you and your opponent trust. If we have wronged the individual, we can (and should) apologize to them, asking them to forgive us. We can be humble and warm, rather than proud and cold.

However, we can't do it all. The person we are at odds with has responsibilities, too. If they refuse to meet with us, or to forgive us, or to admit they were wrong, then there's little else we can do but pray for them.

It is in our church conflicts that this text is helpful, for there exists no *dividing wall* in the church that God cannot tear down. The key is in getting God involved. As we go back to the basics of who we are and what we have in common, we can realize, as Paul pointed out, that *in Christ Jesus you who once were far off have been brought near by the blood of Christ.* If this does not soften the hearts of those in conflict, then perhaps at least one of the parties is not in a right relationship with God.

The only true answer for peace in our relationships, in and out of the church, is in Christ: *For he is our peace; in his flesh he has made both groups into one and has broken down the dividing wall, that is, the hostility between us.* It is not an accident that he is called the Prince of Peace. For us to try make peace without him is a waste of time and breath.

The next time there is dissension in your church or division between you and someone else, remember this text and how God dealt with division. Ask him to do this again in your life and your church. If all parties will yield to him, peace and unity will come to all involved and your relationships will become stronger than ever before.

A Pastor's Prayer:
Dear Lord,

Thank you for removing the "double damnation" that hung over me. Thank you for bringing peace between you and me. Lord, where there is strife in my church, help me to lead us in your approach to bringing peace and unity. Wherever I am at fault, please forgive me and give me courage and humility to admit my faults and ask forgiveness. Thank you. Amen.

Proper 12

John 6:1-21

Last week's lesson, from Mark 6, was the introduction and conclusion to the two accounts in today's text. There we noted the fatigue factor in serving our Lord. In these two accounts, I want us to pay careful attention to Jesus' words. First of all, notice the leading question he asked Philip: *Where are we to buy bread for these people to eat?* Jesus was not stumped or overwhelmed by the enormity of this task. Nor was he looking to Philip for advice, but rather looking for signs of maturity and faith.

In our ministries, Jesus leads us into difficult situations and then asks us leading questions (through our thought processes) as to how we are going to carry out his mission. For example: Suppose you have planned a summer vacation Bible school and want to reach as many of the unchurched neighborhood children as possible. Your advertising efforts paid off, for the attendance is overwhelming. However, you didn't staff enough people, purchase enough crafts, nor prepare enough snacks. And Jesus "asks," "How are you going to share the gospel with all these children?"

How often do we come up with answers that sound similar to Thomas'? *Six months' wages would not buy enough bread for each of them to get a little.* What a typical reply based on human reason. We do the math, we think logically, and then we come up with some ridiculous, faithless, pessimistic response. You see, Jesus doesn't want us to think merely along the lines of reason when it comes to his kingdom work. He wants us to balance reason with faith.

Now Andrew was a little closer to this balance, for he came with an idea that would require faith and a miracle, even though he had no clue as to how it would work. *There is a boy here who has five barley loaves and two fish. But what are they among so many people?* Ah! Now we're getting somewhere! Jesus simply said, *Make the people sit down.* In other words, "Prepare to be amazed. You are about to witness a miracle." Jesus did not do what he could have done. He could have created a wonderful meal out of nothing. He could have sent manna and quail from heaven. Instead, he took something tangible that reason could take hold of, and applied it to a scenario that would require faith. Presto! A miracle! When Jesus leads us into seemingly impossible situations, he doesn't expect us to pull things out of thin air, nor does he tell us to just sit by while he does a miracle. He asks us to take tangible things, combined with a balance of reason and faith, and through that he accomplishes things we could never accomplish without him.

Going back to our earlier example with all the VBS children; the task seems impossible, but the Lord gives you the idea to call someone, who calls someone else and together they get others involved in helping, donating food and items for crafts, and praying. By the end of the week, you look back at a successful VBS program and hear the Lord whisper, *Gather up the fragments left over, so that nothing may be lost* and you realize you just witnessed a miracle! For there was enough of everything you needed and then some. That's how our Lord works in our ministries today.

I want us to hear one more brief statement from our Lord. It came late in the night while the disciples were leaning into their oars, battling a fierce storm on Galilee. They saw what appeared to be a ghost coming near them and they cried out in terror! But a voice came to them over the wind and the waves: *It is I; do not be afraid.* Pastor, are you afraid right now? Is there a "storm" in your church and you don't know how to deal with it? Is the time right for a miracle? Jesus is there. He knows all about it. He knows what you and others are feeling and thinking. He knows what it's going to take to bring peace and calm to the situation. He knows what miracles you need to encourage your faith and to carry on his work. Listen to his still, small voice: *It is I; do not be afraid.*

A Pastor's Prayer:
Dear Lord,

I need a miracle right now. Things are overwhelming and I don't know what to do. Please remove my doubts and fears. Help me to know what I am to say and do, and when I am to let you do your powerful work through me and others. Thank you that you care. Thank you for being in the midst of our ministry, especially during the storms. Amen.

Ephesians 3:14-21

This prayer, which Paul prayed for the Ephesians, is a wonderful, pastoral prayer. I mean that in two senses of the expression, for it is a wonderful prayer for pastors to pray for their parishioners, but is also a wonderful prayer for parishioners to pray for their pastors. Our people need prayer, but we most certainly need their prayers as well. Blessed is the congregation whose pastor prays for them, but in turn, blessed is the pastor whose congregation prays for him/her.

Paul first prayed that the Ephesians might be *strengthened in* [their] *inner being with power through* [God's] *Spirit.* Oh, how we need the power of God in our inner being to carry on his work. We need his power to love others as he loves them. We need his power to be patient with those who are slow to respond to his word. We need his power to preach boldly when Satan and others would want us to fall silent. Yes, we daily need to be strengthened in our inner being with power through God's indwelling Spirit.

Our people need to be strengthened as well. They need God's power to resist temptations. They need his power to serve faithfully in the church in accordance with the gifts God has given them. They need his power to be bold witnesses for Christ in the workplace and in their schools — places where pastors can seldom go and witness for Christ. Pray that your people will be strengthened in their inner being with power through God's Spirit.

Secondly, Paul prayed *that Christ may dwell in* [the] *hearts* [of the Ephesians] *through faith, as* [they were] *being rooted and grounded in love.* Just because we are pastors doesn't mean that we don't need this prayer. Our faith is shaken from time to time. We have questions and doubts about Christ, and to what extent he actually dwells in us when we face our struggles with sin. There's always room for improvement when it comes to being more deeply *rooted and grounded in love* — for God and people.

So, too, the people we minister to desperately need this prayer. It doesn't matter if they've been a Christian all their lives or are brand-new believers. Far too many Christians have a head knowledge of Jesus, but he does not dwell in their hearts by faith to the degree that God desires. If the church, as a whole, were more *deeply rooted and grounded in love,* what a difference that would make in the personal lives of Christians and the life and ministry of the church! Faithfully pray this for your people, and urge them to pray this for you.

Last of all, Paul prayed something huge for the Ephesians: *I pray that you may have the power to comprehend, with all the saints, what is the breadth and length and height and depth, and to know the love of Christ that surpasses knowledge, so that you may be filled with all the fullness of God.* Paul longed that the church in Ephesus might begin to comprehend that which cannot be fully comprehended — the love of Christ. We need this prayer prayed for us, too, for at the heart of every successful pastorate, is a love for God and a love for people. Both are dependent, to some degree, on our comprehending the love that Christ has for us. The more we can comprehend the *breadth, length, height, and depth* of Christ's love for us, the more we will *be filled with all the fullness of God.*

This is so true for our people as well. Few people truly grasp the extent of Christ's love for them. They know he loves them, and that warms their hearts and gives them hope, but they don't know how much. If they did, it would be more evident in their words, attitudes, and actions. It would be more evident in their service and giving to the church. We would see in them the *fullness of God.* Pray this prayer for your people, for they desperately need it.

It is easy for pastors to become cynical about prayer when they see so little fruit from it. But I encourage you to hear and believe what Paul said in his benediction: *Now to him who by the power at work within us is able to accomplish abundantly far more than all we can ask or imagine.* Never forget, that whatever you are thinking and actually asking of God, he can do infinitely more than that. Think large, dear friend, and by faith, pray even larger!

A Pastor's Prayer:

(Pray the text as a prayer for yourself and your parishioners.)

Amen.

Proper 13

John 6:24-35

Do you minister to people like these who were chasing Jesus around the lake? I'm referring to those who believe, not for the forgiveness of sins, but for what they can get out of him — in this life and in eternity. It's easy to detect some of these people, for they are ones who are bitter with God for he didn't answer their selfish prayers. They wanted money, they wanted a relationship, they wanted better health, they wanted whatever they thought would make them happier, but he didn't give it to them when and how they wanted it. They are people who are chasing after *food that perishes*, when what they really need is *food that endures for eternal life*.

Are we this way at times? Do we make bargains with God that sound something like this: "God, I'm working hard for you, day in and day out. I sacrificed a lot to serve you. Now God, please bless me." What are we working for: *food that perishes* or *food that endures for eternal life*?

Our most important work on earth, according to Jesus, is: *that you believe in him whom he* [God] *has sent*. What we do as a pastor counts for nothing if we don't believe in Jesus. What our people do at their jobs and the things they do in the church, count for nothing it they don't believe in Jesus. Apart from him, anything we do is merely working for things that perish. I'm not saying that everything else we do, whether as pastors or parishioners, is worthless. No, it is all important if it is first preceded by the work of believing in Jesus Christ.

Every unbeliever works hard at many things, but all they do will perish with them for all eternity. Believers, who take seriously what Christ taught in this text, see that the most important thing they can do in this life is to first of all believe in Jesus. Then everything else they do, whether at work, at school, or at church, is done to serve that primary purpose. This is why many unbelievers see life as meaningless and without purpose, for it's all coming to nothing anyway. But believers in Christ see all that they do in this life as important for serving God's primary purpose for them — faith in Christ.

The key to determining whether we are working for food that perishes or food that endures for eternal life is to check how *thirsty* and *hungry* we are. Jesus said: *I am the bread of life. Whoever comes to me will never be hungry, and whoever believes in me will never be thirsty.* Are we hungry; not for physical food, but for spiritual food? This spiritual hunger is seen in a dissatisfaction, or discontent, with what we have. Do we always need to be buying something to be happy? Do we find ourselves constantly wanting to move to another parish? Is the grass always greener somewhere else? That may well be a spiritual problem that only Jesus can satisfy.

The Apostle Paul, who spent the first part of his life working for *food that perishes*, wrote to the Philippians: *I have learned to be content with whatever I have. I know what it is to have little, and I know what it is to have plenty. In any and all circumstances I have learned the secret of being well-fed and of going hungry, of having plenty and of being in need. I can do all things through him who strengthens me* (Philippians 4:11-13). The Christian church today is desperately lacking for people who have learned to be content. This is a huge spiritual problem. The solution to it begins with the pastors and their own lives. When we have allowed the Lord to deal with us in this area, then we, like Paul, can share with others what we have learned.

May we get better and better at going to the Bread of Life for food that endures for eternal life; not just merely faith in him for salvation and eternal life, but to truly grow up in him. Yes, God wants us in heaven with him, but he wants more than that. He wants a meaningful relationship with people who aren't chasing after him for *food that perishes*, but are abiding in him for *food that endures to eternal life*.

A Pastor's Prayer:
Dear Lord,

Please help me to see where my priorities have been wrong and where I have been selfishly demanding of you *food that perishes*. Lord, help me to be a role model for others that they, along with me, might work for food that endures for eternal life. Thank you. Amen.

Ephesians 4:1-16

When teaching and preaching on the book of Ephesians, I like to compare this little epistle to a tractor and trailer. The first three chapters are the tractor. They contain the power to pull the trailer — the last three chapters. In other words, without the power of the gospel, we would be unable to live out the Christian life.

Verse 1 of our text is the hitch pin between the two sections: *I therefore, the prisoner in the Lord, beg you to lead a life worthy of the calling to which you have been called.* What we are called to be (a child of God), has been spelled out in the first three chapters. It is a life in Christ and he in us. Paul was urging the Ephesians to understand that if they profess to be children of God, then they are to live like children of God. They are to lead a life that is worthy of (or reflects) who they are as children of God.

Oh, how important this message is for the church today! We profess to be a "Christian nation," but is our nation as a whole leading *a life worthy of the calling to which* [it has] *been called*? I think not. Our churches are filled with people who profess to be Christians, but are they leading lives that are *worthy of the calling to which* [they] *have been called*? Far too many are not. What are we to do? We are to faithfully preach law and grace, but if all they are hearing is grace, we need to apply more law.

It is human nature to rebel against the law, which tells us what we should and should not do. But it is also human nature to take advantage of grace. That is why Paul raised this issue with the Roman church when he asked: *Should we continue in sin in order that grace may abound? By no means! How can we who died to sin go on living in it?* (Romans 6:1-2). You see, we want to drive the "tractor," but we don't want to pull the "trailer." Or put another way; we want God's grace, because we don't want to go to hell when we die, but we don't want to live the Christian life, because we want to do what we good and well please. Paul was telling the church in Ephesus that it doesn't work that way. If we want to be children of God, we are to live like children of God. We don't live godly lives to be saved, but rather we live godly lives because we are saved, by faith in Christ alone.

In addition, this text points out the purpose of our calling and the use of our gifts which God has given us. The gifts God gave each of us serve the purpose of equipping *the saints for the work of ministry,* [and] *for building up the body of Christ.* Our ministry is to be first and foremost a ministry of the word. We are to teach and preach God's Word so that the saints (believers in Christ) are equipped to serve God in his church. However, far too many congregations have this wrong. They think they hire the pastor to do all the work. And when he or she can't get it all done, they hire multiple staff. Is this really God's intention for the church? Is this really the most effective way to reach the lost? I think not, for the most effective churches are those where every believer is a minister, and the pastor is the one who trains and equips them to do the *work of ministry* and to *build up the body of Christ.*

The temptation for all too many pastors (including yours truly) is to do the work ourselves. We get frustrated with people who are too busy, so we just do it all ourselves. However, we are not doing them, nor the Body of Christ, any favors. Every time we let people off the "hook" of their God-given responsibilities, we are enabling them to remain immature Christians.

Preach on this text, fellow pastor, and pray that the Holy Spirit will convict people if they're failing to get involved in God's kingdom work. Also, pray for wisdom and time to train them; then set them free to use their gifts to serve the Lord.

A Pastor's Prayer:

Dear Lord,

Thank you for your power that has not only called me to be your child, but enables me to live like the child of God I am. Lord, thank you, too, for the gifts you have given me to equip the saints. Help me to know how to do that; and then to set them free to serve you, even if they don't do it exactly the way I would. Give me patience with those who refuse to get involved in the ministry at this time in their lives. Help me to know how to preach your word in a way that your Spirit might convict them and prompt them to serve. Thank you. Amen.

Proper 14

John 6:35, 41-51

Do you know people who complain about Jesus? They say things like: "How could he be God and man both? That's impossible! And if he is so good, and all he supposedly made is good, then why is there so much evil in the world?"

Jesus faced complainers all the time, for the things he said did not fit with how they thought. They knew who his family was, so how could he say that he had *come down from heaven*? That didn't make sense. And how could he be *the Bread of Life*? That didn't make sense either, so they complained about him.

We face complainers as well. Due to their ignorance about God and their worldly intelligence, they complain about Jesus, for he doesn't make sense to them. He doesn't fit with how they think. Do you struggle with this? Do you complain (at least to yourself, if not to others) about things that Jesus taught that don't make sense to you? Dear friend, we will never get to know Jesus by trying to figure him out. If we would do less complaining over difficult truths and Christian doctrines, and more time listening to Christ's words, we would find it easier to believe.

Imagine the impact it would have had on the Jewish community if the religious leaders had accepted Christ's words by faith and believed in him. They had a lot of control over the people, so what they said is what the majority believed. There were those who broke away from the Jewish teachings and traditions to follow Jesus, but they were a minority. As much as we hate to admit it, perhaps the majority of the people in our churches believe what we say, as well. They are followers, who think very little for themselves when it comes to spiritual and religious matters. On one hand, it is good, I suppose; for if everyone wanted to be a leader we would have a mess. However, we ought to encourage people to think for themselves, so that the beliefs and convictions they hold are theirs and not the pastor's.

Let's take the central teaching of this text as an example. How many of the people you minister to believe that Jesus is the Bread of Life? Do they even know what that means? If they were to say (as perhaps many would), "Yes, I believe Jesus is the Bread of Life," would they know why they said that? Would it be because that's what you and their church believes? Or, would they say they believe, because they have read and studied God's Word for themselves and find it to be true?

The point I'm getting at, which Jesus emphasized often, is that salvation comes through faith alone. But it is not faith alone that saves us. It is the object of our faith that saves us. The religious leaders of the Jews had faith and deep convictions in what they believed, but they were perishing with their beliefs, for their beliefs did not (nor do they yet today) give eternal life. To make matters worse, they were leading the majority of their people to hell with them, for most people were not thinking for themselves. They were merely following their leaders.

I believe it is possible for people to believe in something (and in this case, Jesus), not because they have studied him on their own and come to their own beliefs and convictions, but because they are followers. They think they are Christians, but they have little or no clue as to what it is they believe. This is extremely dangerous for them spiritually, for no one can get into heaven by hanging on to the coattails of another.

We must stress the importance of people reading and studying the Word of God on their own. They must believe for themselves that Jesus is the Bread of Life, and be able to explain what that means for them personally. There are no "group plans" when it comes to salvation and eternal life. Everyone will stand before the Father and give an accounting of what they personally believe. Pray for courage to preach this, for the good of your people and for the sake of him who died for them.

A Pastor's Prayer:
Dear Lord,

Please forgive me for when I have complained against you. Lord, help me to know how to do more than merely lead people in a belief system with rituals and traditions, but to lead them into your word where they can come to a personal knowledge and faith in you for salvation. Thank you that you are the Bread of Life, and that you give each of us who believe, all the life we need. Amen.

Ephesians 4:25—5:2

The NRSV Bible titles this text, "Rules for the New Life." We could, for the sake of this devotional, retitle it, "Rules for the Successful Pastorate." Do you want to be an effective and successful pastor in the eyes of God and people? Then this text holds many of the keys for that success. Let's reflect on it with an open and honest heart before God; asking his Spirit to convict us of where change is needed, and to help us make those changes.

First, a successful pastor puts *away falsehood*. If we are not honest with our spouse and children, if we are not honest with the synodical leaders, if we are not honest with our church council, and if we are not honest with the people we minister to, no one will trust us and we will be ineffective.

Secondly, a successful pastor knows how to *be angry* without sinning. Many pastors have destroyed their ministries due to uncontrolled anger. I have a bad temper which frightens me when I am pushed to the limit. I have had to ask God to help me to control my temper and to know when it is appropriate to express a righteous anger toward sin.

Thirdly, a successful pastor does not steal. Maybe you're not tempted to steal the offering, but do you steal time by wasting it on things that have nothing to do with the ministry? Pastors are notorious for this, especially pastors of small churches where there is no one around to hold them accountable for how they use their time. I have found that a planner and a "To Do" list help me to be disciplined with my time. I also provide a monthly report to my church leaders as a way of holding me accountable and showing that I wasn't trying to hide something.

Fourthly, successful pastors let *no evil talk come out of your mouths, but only what is useful for building up, as there is need, so that your words may give grace to those who hear.* This is so important! The effectiveness of our ministry rises and falls on this truth. If people are hurt by the remarks you make and the humor you enjoy, then change how you talk or talk less. Your hurtful remarks and humor may be "the way you are" and in keeping with your personality, but God does not excuse sin in any way. We can change, by the help of God's Spirit. As we think and speak more like him, we will more and more take on the very nature and personality of Christ, which is powerful when ministering to people.

In addition to withholding hurtful words, practice saying things to people that build them up, for their good and the good of those who hear you speaking to them. Compliment people who are serving well. Thank them for their help. Compliment a young person for some accomplishment you read about in the newspaper. This is a great way to build their trust and earn their respect. The words we say to people today are an investment into our relationship with them tomorrow. The better our relationships are, the more successful and effective our ministry will be.

Fifthly, a successful pastor works hard at being *kind, tenderhearted*, and *forgiving* just *as God in Christ has forgiven* them. It doesn't take a rocket scientist to see why this is important, and how damaging it is when we don't put these behaviors into practice. Notice that the motivating factor for this, and the previous behaviors, is the fact that Christ has forgiven us. With that truth always in the forefront of our minds, we will find it much easier to be kind, tenderhearted, and forgiving.

Last of all, a successful pastor loves others just as God loves them. This imitating, which Paul urged, is not simply looking at Christ and trying to do things the same way. It is an imitating that comes from a heart that has been changed by the blood of Jesus. Any changes that you need to make in how you minister to others, must *always* start in the heart. If not, you'll just be pretending and it won't take people long to identify a fake.

Therefore be imitators of God, as beloved pastors, and you'll be loved by your parish.

A Pastor's Prayer:
Dear Lord,
   Please forgive me for where I fall short of your perfect will for me. Lord, please help me to imitate you from the heart. Thank you for your love for me and the forgiveness of my sins. I want that to be what motivates me to be a successful pastor. Amen.

Proper 15

John 6:51-58

This week's lesson picks up where last week's left off, and is the conclusion to Jesus' discourse on the Bread of Life. His audience that day couldn't figure out what he was talking about, for it didn't make sense to them. How could he be the Bread of Life and how could he come down from heaven? These are, no doubt, difficult truths to comprehend, but our ability or inability to comprehend them doesn't make them any less true. It's similar to me and my computer; I'm amazed at the technology, but I don't understand how it works. Does my inability to comprehend it make it any less true or real? No. And so it is with the teachings of Christ. This is very important for us to grasp and to pass on to our parishioners.

Jesus wasn't done confusing them though. He also told them that they were to *eat* him. What? That didn't make sense at all! If they were to take him literally, it would be cannibalism!

When attempting to understand this text, I tend to agree with those who believe this is *not* in reference to the sacrament or Eucharist, for that would not be instituted until sometime later. So what did he mean? It seems most consistent with what Jesus said before this: to understand this *eating* and *drinking* as referring to believing.

Jesus contrasted himself to the bread that their ancestors ate while wandering in the wilderness in the days of Moses. All who ate that bread died. Not that the bread killed them, but it was unable to give them enduring and eternal life. It sustained life while in the wilderness, but it didn't extend their life beyond normal years.

However, *whoever eats of this bread* (or believes in Jesus Christ) *will live forever.* Jesus was offering them something far superior to anything their ancestors had ever eaten. Let us not forget we have something far superior to offer people than anything they can buy or do to extend life here on earth. People today are chasing after anything and everything they can get their hands on to try to stay young and add years to their lives. Why? Because this life is all they've got. If professing Christians are doing this, it means they have not thought enough about heaven nor the life that Christ has given them through faith in him.

I'm not suggesting that we neglect our bodies, or that it is wrong to keep ourselves physically fit and looking good. What I am saying is to be obsessed with this is wrong. Obsessions often grow out of a fear. When professing Christians are afraid to die and dread the future that God is preparing for them, there is something wrong. They don't seem to understand how real life from Jesus is. For when we understand his words and receive them by faith we begin to clearly understand that this life on earth is nothing compared to heaven!

We cannot overemphasize from our pulpits and when ministering one on one with people, the importance of sincere belief in Jesus Christ. Jesus was not requesting a superficial relationship with people whereby they identify themselves with a Christian church and confess the Apostles' Creed each time they worship. He was requesting and inviting people to an intimate relationship whereby *those who eat my flesh and drink my blood abide in me, and I in them.*

This term, *abide*, has come to mean a lot to me; as it suggests quality time, quantity of time, listening, loving, nurturing, security, friendship, empathy, comfort, and perhaps so much more. That is the relationship Jesus desires with us and the people we minister to. However, we cannot describe that kind of a relationship to others and teach them how to have it, if we don't have it ourselves.

I urge you today to "eat the flesh" and "drink the blood" of Jesus. In other words, get in him and let him get in you. Once you are there, stay there and abide with him and he will abide with you. It's a wonderful relationship that will greatly impact your ministry.

A Pastor's Prayer:
Dear Lord,

Thank you for initiating this intimate relationship with me. Help me to abide in you and allow you to abide in me. Please help me to not only model this relationship for others to see, but to know how to preach and teach it so others can enjoy it, too. Amen.

Ephesians 5:15-20

The Apostle Paul's advice to the church in Ephesus, as found in this text, could come right out of a pastor's handbook on ministry. It is sound, timeless advice; and not surprisingly so, as it is God's Word to the church.

The opening statement is strong and unmistakable: *Be careful then how you live, not as unwise people but as wise.* Oh, how much easier our ministries would be if we and our parishioners would follow this rule for Christian living! The problem is, we are not always careful how we live. We are too easily swept up by the momentum and values of the world around us. The fact that the divorce rate in the church is about the same as that of the unchurched is very telling. The fact that you can't tell much difference in the lifestyles of many Christians from that of the unbelieving world around them is reason to pause as well. Far too many Christians don't want to be told what to do, and use God's grace as an excuse to sin. Certainly God's grace does cover our sin, but what is the advantage of bringing all this pain upon ourselves and others in the name of "freedom"? This is unwise living, and makes a mockery out of grace and the one who has extended this grace to us.

If you and your parishioners want to live like wise people, then I urge you to read Proverbs, the words of Jesus, and the Apostle's letters. These are rich resources containing the best wisdom the world has ever known.

Our text then urges us to make *the most of the time, because the days are evil.* It wasn't then, nor is it now, the time to be lazy. There is much work for the church to do, starting with itself and reaching out into the community. I had a volunteer jail chaplaincy ministry for a couple years and was shocked at the number of men who had never read the Bible. Some didn't know anything about the name of Jesus, other than that it was a swear word. We have a huge mission field right around us.

Now, the first two statements we've looked at, if not taken seriously, lead to only one thing — foolishness. So we are warned: *do not be foolish, but understand what the will of the Lord is.* Do you know what the will of the Lord is for you and your ministry? Do the people in your church know what the will of the Lord is for them and their church? Many times we think we know, but if the truth be known, what we call *the will of the Lord* is really the pastor's agenda or the selfish and proud plans of a congregation.

It takes time, prayer, Bible reading, earnest discussion amongst sincere Christians, and more prayer to determine the will of God. One of the mistakes that many Christians and churches make (including pastors) is that we are impatient. We don't want to go through the hard work of determining the will of the Lord. I pity the pastor who wants to take time to determine the will of the Lord, but the congregation won't. If they want to press ahead without sufficient time for the aforementioned steps, move on and find a church that does want to understand the will of the Lord and leave the *foolish* church behind.

Last of all, we are encouraged to worship intentionally and diligently. I like how Paul introduced this, as he used the illustration of getting drunk. When a person is filled with alcohol, it takes over their mind, mouth, and motion. So, too, when we are filled with the Spirit of God, he will take over our mind, mouth, and motion in worship. He guides us into singing *psalms and hymns and spiritual songs among ourselves, singing and making melody to the Lord in our hearts, giving thanks to God the Father at all times and for everything in the name of our Lord Jesus Christ.* May we allow this pattern for private and public worship to guide us in the future. And may our worship come out of thankful hearts, for God has given us so much in the person of his Son, Jesus Christ.

A Pastor's Prayer:

Dear Lord,

Thank you for this set of rules on how to live my life, both in and out of the church. Help me to preach and teach these rules in a law/grace balance, that people might see the advantage of following these rules in their personal lives and in the ministry of their church. May they, and I, always remember that the motivation to live out these rules is the fact that you died for our inability to do it perfectly. Thank you. Amen.

Proper 16

John 6:56-69

Our text tells us of a deciding moment in the lives of Jesus' *disciples*. John seems to be referring to all of Jesus' followers, at this point, including the twelve. His teachings had become not only difficult to understand, but extremely difficult to accept.

I wonder what we would have done in this situation? The number of people following Jesus had been growing. More and more people were sitting up and taking notice of this extraordinary man. Church growth experts might advise that this would not be a good time to "rock the boat." But Jesus did, for he did not want anyone in his "boat" who did not believe in him, no matter how difficult his teachings were.

Far too many pastors are living under pressure to not say or do anything that will "rock the boat." As a result, they are avoiding preaching on difficult passages in God's word that speak directly to the sins in people's lives. By "difficult," I'm not necessarily referring to passages such as John 6, which are difficult to exegete and explain to our people. I'm referring to passages that are very clear and people know exactly what we are saying when we preach on them, for when we do, they are offended.

Now speculate with me as to what would have come of Jesus' ministry if he had avoided hard teachings so as to not offend anyone, for fear of losing any disciples. Look at our text again and notice what John wrote: *Among you there are some who do not believe ... one of you is a devil.* If Jesus had tried to humor everyone along and "tiptoed" around topics and issues that might have offended the nonbeliever, what would have become of his ministry? For one thing, its credibility would have been undermined by compromise. Jesus is absolute truth and so was his ministry. If he were not up front with the truth, the integrity of that ministry would have been lost. In addition, those followers who did believe wholeheartedly would have lost respect for him. Why follow someone who won't defend the very truths he claims to represent?

If you agree that it would have not have been good for Jesus to avoid the difficult issues in order to avoid losing followers, yet you are avoiding preaching on these very same issues, then you better look long and hard in the mirror and ask yourself: Is it right for me to steer clear of difficult issues in order to avoid losing parishioners? The answer you should be arriving at is, "No!" When you "tiptoe" around truths in God's word that you fear are going to offend people, and possibly result in people leaving, you are undermining the integrity of Christ's ministry through your church. If there are people in your church who want you to take a firm stand for the absolute truths of Christ, and not compromise or waver on those truths, you run the risk of losing the respect of the most valuable people in your congregation.

All too often, pastors give in to the reasoning that the most valuable people in their church are the biggest givers, and those who are the most gifted and visible in the community. However, if these people are unbelievers and therefore of the devil, then any pastor who continues to cater to these individuals so they won't leave the church, has his/her priorities mixed up. The church of Jesus Christ was not built on unbelievers, but on those who accepted the hard teachings of Jesus and stuck with him, no matter what. Jesus lost a bunch of followers that day, but he preferred that, so he might know exactly who the real believers were.

Dear Pastor, if you are avoiding preaching the hard truths of God's Word for fear of your people, you are not being true to your call or to the one who called you. Make sure, first of all, that you are a true believer of Christ like the eleven who stuck with him. Then preach his word boldly and don't flinch if people start leaving the church. If they are not true believers, you don't want them, nor do you need them, for they will destroy the integrity, and hinder the effectiveness, of your ministry.

A Pastor's Prayer:
Dear Lord,

These are hard truths! When faced honestly, I know what I have to do, but in so doing, I run the risk of offending people and watching them leave the church. Lord, I'm aware that your truths are offensive to the unbeliever, but help me to preach them boldly anyway, so that the true believers will be strengthened and hopefully the unbelievers will turn to you. Thank you. Amen.

Ephesians 6:10-20

This text is a serious reminder of how dangerous the ministry is. If you have some romantic idea that everyone should love and appreciate their pastor, think again. Being a pastor is, due to the one we serve, hard work and dangerous. When we accepted God's call to be a pastor, we stepped into the midst of a battle between God and the devil for the souls of humanity. If you are not feeling the tension and heat of that battle, then very likely you are not preaching all the truths of God's Word, as I wrote about in the devotional on today's Gospel Lesson.

A mistake that pastors make when tensions arise in the church is to think that people are the problem. Paul clarified that in this text: *Our struggle is not against enemies of blood and flesh, but against the rulers, against the authorities, against the cosmic powers of this present darkness, against the spiritual forces of evil in the heavenly places.* All believers in Christ, during Paul's day, experienced tremendous opposition. The unbelieving Jews and the pagan Gentiles, such as the Romans, were aggressively persecuting the church. When the believers looked into the faces of their accusers and torturers, they understood that their struggle was not against them, but against Satan and his kingdom.

How important it is for us to understand this, for we often meet opposition in our ministries as well. If you follow the example of Jesus and do what I suggested in the devotional on the Gospel Lesson, you will experience opposition. People will get angry with you. Some will leave the church and others will try to drive you out. When you look into their angered faces and hear their cutting words, remember that your struggle is not against them. Your struggle is against Satan and his kingdom. It is he who does not want the truths of God's Word boldly proclaimed from the pulpit. When he opposes you, how do you think he will do it? Do you really expect a guy in a red suit, with a long tail, horns, and a forked spear to show up? It would be great if he would, for then maybe there would be a spiritual awakening in our churches! No, Satan is not going to personally appear and oppose you. He's going to oppose you through people. That's the way he usually opposed Christ, so don't be surprised when he does the same thing to you.

Paul then urged his readers to put on the necessary armor to fight this battle. Notice, there is no mention of retreating. All too often that's what we want to do — run and hide. I'm not saying there aren't times when we need to leave a church, for Jesus himself taught that if people will not receive the word, then leave them and shake the dust out of your clothes on the way out the door. However, if God seems to want you to stay where you are, then do so. Faithfully preach his word in truth, with boldness, and with his authority, but be sure to put your armor on first.

Notice what the armor consists of: *truth, righteousness, the gospel of peace, faith, salvation, and the Spirit, which is the word of God.* If you step into the pulpit on any given Sunday morning without these, you are in for serious injury, for the devil is going to do all he can to silence you. Most often he will use the very people who are sitting in your pews on Sunday morning.

I urge you, fellow proclaimers of truth, to resist the temptation to try make everyone like you. Few of us enjoy having enemies, and one area of our ministry that we want people to like us is in our preaching. Criticism there deeply hurts us. We must be sure that we are trying to please God in our preaching, and not the people who are listening.

Preaching is hard work and very dangerous. That is why Paul urged the Ephesians to pray for him that he might declare the gospel boldly. You, too, need people to be praying for you when you preach. Seek out true believers who want you to preach the truths of God's Word without compromise or wavering. Their prayers will be a great source of comfort and strength to you each Sunday.

A Pastor's Prayer:
Dear Lord,

I know that preaching your word is hard and dangerous. Please help me not to be afraid of people, but to faithfully proclaim everything you want me to preach, whether it is received well or not. When I am opposed by people, help me to remember that it is really the devil who is opposing me and not them. Thank you. Amen.

Proper 17

Mark 7:1-8, 14-15, 21-23

Perhaps we could summarize the overall theme of our text this way: Human traditions count for nothing in the kingdom of God. In these verses, Jesus was harshly critical of the Pharisees' traditions and the hypocrisy that accompanied them.

Take a moment to reflect on the traditions of your church. If all those traditions were stripped away, what would be left? Suppose that next Sunday all the paraments, robes, banners, candles, and symbols of any kind were removed; all the rituals, ceremonies, and liturgies would be unavailable; everything of tradition totally gone from your church and your worship. What would you do? Would you be at a loss to lead the worship service? I think every Christian church and pastor, no matter what faith and tradition they are, whether High Church or Low Church, traditional or contemporary, would do well to review their traditions in light of this text.

The Jewish *tradition* that was at the center of this discussion had to do with *washing*. The Jews saw the rituals of *washing* as not only important for physical cleanliness, but also spiritual cleanliness. The Pharisees in our text were disturbed by the fact that Jesus' disciples had been eating without washing their hands. They were in violation of not just any tradition, but the *traditions of the elders*.

What I find the most convicting in this text, is Jesus' quote from Isaiah and his immediate comment afterward. *This people honors me with their lips, but their hearts are far from me; in vain do they worship me, teaching human precepts as doctrines. You abandon the commandment of God and hold to human tradition.*

I wonder how much of today's Christian worship is people honoring God *with their lips*, while *their hearts are far from* him? I fear there is much more of this than we would like to admit.

Jesus said such behavior is an exercise in vain worship. I have talked to countless people over the years who became disillusioned by their church's traditions in worship. They felt the worship experience was meaningless and failed to meet their spiritual needs. They may well be right for feeling this way, for churches have developed, whether centuries ago or in recent years, traditions that they teach as *doctrines* with little or no biblical basis. These *doctrines* are nothing more than *human precepts*.

To make the problem worse, many Christian churches have become as powerful as, if not more so than, the Jewish religion of Jesus' day. Such large, powerful institutions are intimidating. If a pastor or congregation wants to express a valid concern over a long-held tradition, they might be ostracized. Therefore these human precepts survive, for no one is able to stand up to them.

What did Jesus call those who emphasize tradition over truth? He called them *hypocrites*. From time to time we may have someone tell us they don't go to church because the church is full of hypocrites. They may be right, for there often are a few hypocrites in the pews; but are there hypocrites in the pulpits? Are there hypocrites in the headquarters of church denominations? Are there hypocrites teaching in seminaries around the globe? I fear the answer is "Yes."

I'm not anti-tradition, but I am anti-hypocrisy. If your traditions and how you observe them are causing hypocrisy, then I urge you to end the tradition. If your church won't allow you to do that, then maybe it's time to find a different church, where solid biblical truth is preferred over human tradition.

A Pastor's Prayer:
Dear Lord,

Please help me to re-evaluate our church's traditions and to recognize any that are contributing to hypocrisy, whether through me or the church. Help me to know how to deal with dead traditions. If my church will not cooperate with me, lead me to a church that will. Thank you. Amen.

James 1:17-27

This text is another one of those Epistle Lessons that contains solid principles for pastors who want to have a successful ministry in the eyes of God. A common thread running through this text, is the importance of God's Word. James reminds us in verse 18 that

God *gave us birth by the word of truth.* The Word of God is the essential element in spiritual birth. We cannot become righteous, nor grow in righteousness, through any other means. Therefore it is more than a means of salvation. It is also a word for sanctification. James makes several important points in that regard.

First he urges us to *welcome with meekness the implanted word that has the power to save your souls.* God's Word should always be received in an attitude of meekness and humility. After all, it is God who is speaking! Often, when God spoke in the days of Moses, there were great displays of power that accompanied that word. These displays of power gripped the hearts of the Israelites with fear. The church has lost that sense of awe and respect today, for God has chosen to speak in a still, small voice through his word, yet with no less power or authority.

One of the tendencies of our proud, selfish, human nature is to be quick to talk and slow to listen. Listen to the prayers that some people pray (even our own at times) and we will hear them telling God what to do. So James advised his readers: *let everyone be quick to listen, slow to speak, slow to anger; for your anger does not produce God's righteousness.* This is most certainly true in regards to our relationship with God. We will grow and mature as children of God much more quickly if we spend more time sitting quietly with an open Bible, reading and reflecting on his word, than if we spend an hour in prayer with little or no Bible reading.

This truth is also sound advice for everyone in regards to our relationships with others. I have found this to be so true in my relationship with my wife, my children, and in ministry. People want to be heard, and the person who is a good listener quickly gains the trust and confidence of others.

One of the challenges that every believer faces is that of following through with what God's Word has told us. Countless times, people have come up to me after a Sunday service and said something to this effect: "That was a good sermon, Pastor. Now if I can just do what you said." It is a universal problem, thus James wrote: *be doers of the word, and not merely hearers who deceive themselves.*

The Word of God is powerful, not only to save us, but to change us. However, God made himself vulnerable on both accounts, whereby he doesn't save any soul that doesn't want to be saved, nor does he change any person who won't cooperate with change. We're all guilty of looking at ourselves in the *mirror* and then walking away and forgetting what we were like. May we more and more be found amongst *those who look into the perfect law, the law of liberty, and persevere,* for in so doing, we *will be blessed.*

Last of all, James points us in the direction of a ministry that is *pure and undefiled before God, the Father.* It is not a ministry of talking and acting like we are more religious than others (like the Pharisees in the Gospel Lesson), but one of caring *for orphans and widows in their distress, and* [keeping] *oneself unstained by the world.* This type of ministry is often looked down on by the world (and even some in the church), but it is noticed by God and that's what counts. We can't go wrong in helping the disadvantaged in our society. To bring them hope, help, and happiness can be one of the more fulfilling and rewarding things we do as pastors.

A Pastor's Prayer:
Dear Lord,

Thank you for your word and the righteousness that it reveals to me. Help me to look intently into it and do what it says, so others might be blessed by my godly life and drawn to you for salvation and spiritual growth. Thank you. Amen.

Proper 18

Mark 7:24-37

When studying the miracles of Christ, I'm always struck by the unpredictability of God. The two miracles that are recorded in our text are prime examples of this. Jesus could have done all of his miracles the same way, using the same methods and the same words of authority, but he didn't. We may never fully know why until we get to heaven, but it is intriguing to take note of it now.

In the first incident, Jesus was approached by a Gentile woman about healing for her daughter who was possessed by a demon. Jesus' response appears derogatory, yet he was testing her faith. She more than passed his test by her reply, for Jesus commended her for what she said, and healed her daughter, who wasn't even present with them.

In the second incident, a man was brought to Jesus who was deaf and mute. In this case, Jesus healed the man in a rather unusual way. He took the man to a private place, *put his fingers into his ears, and he spat and touched his tongue.* Then, with a sigh, he commanded: *Be opened*, and the man's ears were opened and his tongue released.

Why did Jesus seem to test the faith of the mother and reward that faith, when there was no mention of faith when healing the man? It shows the unpredictability of God. I'm not suggesting that God is a God of change who goes back and forth on his word. No, for God's Word is clear — he does not change. However, he can be unpredictable. Just when we think we have him figured out, he does things a little differently. It's what helps preserve the environment of mystery that is so necessary for genuine faith. If God were predictable and we could figure everything out about him, what would happen to faith? There would be less and less need for it.

The church needs to be reminded again and again that God is unpredictable yet today. Rigged formulas and methods for saving souls and growing churches are risky, for they are not taking into account that God will work whenever and however he wishes.

When we put God in a "box" in our teaching and describe his activity in terms of a set pattern that can be counted on every time, we deceive ourselves and those we teach. We can't manipulate God with certain prayers, rituals, and activities. It frustrates me to no end when I get forwarded e-mails that say something to this effect: "Pray this prayer seven times and send it on to ten other people and a miracle will happen to you tonight." God does not operate that way.

When responding to the needs of individuals, God seems to take several factors into account. He takes faith into account. Sometimes it is the faith of the person in need. Sometimes it is the faith of the person asking. Other times there seems to be no faith at all, but once God acts on the individual's behalf, faith blossoms! God also takes his glory into account. He does what will bring him the most glory and honor, not because he has a big ego, but because he is God. Everything serves him, so everything he does will bring him glory and honor and praise in the eyes of his creation. God also takes our best interest into account. He sees the big picture, which we can't see. Why some people are healed and others are not is directly related to what God sees as best. Why some are healed one way and others healed another way is directly related to what God sees as best. Thus there is an unpredictability about God that we have no choice but to surrender to. To fight it is to fight God. To surrender to it, is to discover the joy and marvel of how God works in our lives in ways we could never have predicted.

May we respond to God's working in our lives and the lives of others in the same way that the people gathered around him that day responded: *He has done everything well.*

A Pastor's Prayer:
Dear Lord,

Thank you for your unpredictability that keeps the Christian life exciting! May I yield to you by faith at all times, but especially when I can't figure out what you are up to. Thank you for always doing *everything well*. Amen.

James 2:1-10 (11-13) 14-17

James could have written this letter to almost any church in America that has wealthy, upper-class members. The problem of partiality has plagued the church for a long time. How damaging it is to the witness of the church if the wealthy look down on the poor. It amazes me how quickly wealth and status can change some people from being caring and sensitive, to selfish and rude.

Perhaps one of the more difficult aspects of being a pastor is dealing with people who call or stop by the church office to ask for financial assistance. The easiest thing to do is turn them away — end of story. However, if one takes this Epistle Lesson seriously, then we have to admit that one of the *works* of a believer in Christ is to share with those in need. But are we to share with everyone, even those who are using and abusing the "system"?

One criterion I used was, if we were also ministering spiritually to the person(s) who were asking for help, we were more likely to help them. If they were randomly calling churches for help, then I refused to help them. Then there were those whom I felt had a legitimate need. We would help them financially, only to have them take advantage of us, or leave the area, without us having any opportunity to minister to them. This can sour a person and cause one to be cynical about helping the needy in the future. But the fact still remains; we are not to show partiality, for it is a sin.

James went on to make an interesting point about the poor. He wrote: *Has not God chosen the poor in the world to be rich in faith and to be heirs of the kingdom that he has promised to those who love him?* The financially poor are not automatically Christians because they are poor, but they often have more faith, when it comes to trusting God to provide, than the wealthy do. This may be because they can't trust in themselves, or others, to provide for their great need.

One of the downsides to being wealthy is that it is so easy to trust in self to provide. As a result, the wealthy forget what it's like to pray for provision, because they always have more than they need. Jesus taught that it is difficult for the wealthy to enter the kingdom of God, for there is a close correlation between financial wealth and not recognizing one's spiritual poverty. And, for some reason, the financially poor seem much quicker to recognize their spiritual poverty and need for Christ than the wealthy. So, God didn't choose the poor to be saved, but rather designed it that only those who recognize their spiritual poverty and need for Christ can be rich in faith (whether they are wealthy or poor).

Verses 14-17 are very sobering and, if we will take them seriously, force us to re-evaluate our attitude and behavior toward the poor. In our churches there are people who claim to have faith, attend church faithfully, maybe teach Sunday school or sit on the church board, but they won't lift a finger to help the poor. They will speak respectfully to them and wish them well, but they won't do a thing to help them financially. James called this kind of Christianity *dead* faith. This is a touchy issue, for we believe strongly that we are saved by grace and not by works. Martin Luther struggled with this, too; and allegedly at one point in his ministry labeled James' epistle "The Epistle of Straw," feeling it lacked solid, justification-by-faith theology.

However, if we believe in Christ for salvation, we cannot deny the fact that we, spiritually impoverished people that we are, have been recipients of the abundant riches of God's grace and mercy. For us to not help the poor amongst us is to demonstrate a self-centered faith that is really no faith at all.

May we honestly wrestle with this issue personally and, with God's help and courage, preach it to our parishioners for their good, and the good of the poor around us.

A Pastor's Prayer:
Dear Lord,

Please forgive me for when I have shown partiality between the rich and the poor. Thank you for how you have lifted me out of spiritual poverty and blessed me with the riches of your kingdom. Help me show this same generosity to others as an act of faith that reinforces the saving faith I have in you. Lord, also help me to know how to preach on this delicate subject to people who struggle with this as much or more than I do. Thank you. Amen.

Proper 19

Mark 8:27-38

How easy it is for any of us to fall into the same trap that Peter fell in; where we set our minds on *human things* rather than on *divine things*. That is, of course, the most natural thing for us to do, because of our inherited, sinful, human nature.

Jesus had to *rebuke* Peter for thinking incorrectly. How about you? Who is able to rebuke you when you think incorrectly?

One of the inherent risks of being a pastor is building up a wall of authority and control, whereby no one is able to hold us accountable and rebuke us. This is dangerous, for if our leaders are not allowed (or better yet — *encouraged*) to hold us accountable and rebuke us when we are thinking incorrectly, then we become untouchable. No longer are we team players, for we have isolated ourselves behind a veil of either absolute authority (where no one dares challenge us) or invisible existence (where no one has a clue what we are doing). Both scenarios can inflict serious damage on our church and will likely destroy our reputation.

Many pastors who fit one of the above scenarios, often carry this same mentality and behavior into the home. Their spouse is treated the same way, whereby they are not allowed to hold their husband or wife accountable, or rebuke them. Any attempts to do so are met with intimidation, severe rebuke, or the silent treatment. A marriage where at least one spouse does not have the freedom to rebuke the other spouse, and hold them accountable, is really no marriage at all. It is a contract where one spouse agrees to be controlled and manipulated by the other until "death do us part." If the "death" does not take place physically, it most certainly will emotionally, which is a miserable way for a husband and wife to live out their days in marriage. Not to mention it is a poor example to the church of what a godly marriage should look like.

Equally as damaging is the pastor who refuses to be held accountable and rebuked by his/her children. Children who have the freedom to hold their parents accountable, whether to promises they've made or to values in the home, grow up to be much healthier emotionally and have much better relationships with their parents and other authority figures. Those who don't have this freedom become angry with their parents, for they feel powerless to express their feelings. They become especially angry with the controlling parent, but also with the other parent, for they feel if anyone should be able to rebuke the controlling parent, it is the other adult in the home. When this doesn't happen, the child feels even more powerless, for what chance do they, a child, have of rebuking a parent who is in the wrong if another adult can't? As a result, the anger, rebellion, and possibly withdrawal, become more intense.

If we want to be pastors, spouses, and parents who are loved, respected, and effective, then we will make sure that at least someone knows they can hold us accountable and rebuke us when we are thinking incorrectly. Ideally, I believe at least one trusted individual in the church, plus our spouse and all of our children, should have the freedom to rebuke us, and they need to know that we want them to do this. But they also must know that we draw the line at disrespect and destructive criticism. If we encourage them to use the biblical principles in Ephesians 4:15 and 29, we will be helped by their words of rebuke and our relationship with them will deepen and strengthen.

Peter grew in knowledge of his Lord and in character that day when the Lord rebuked him. Rebuke and accountability from people we trust and love can do the same for us.

May this also encourage us to do the same for others. Our spouse and children need to be held accountable and rebuked, from time to time, as much as we do; as do our church leaders and parishioners. When we do this from a heart of love and humility, as Jesus did, much good can come from times that are otherwise tense and often painful.

A Pastor's Prayer:
Dear Lord,
   Please help me to swallow my pride and allow others to hold me accountable and rebuke me when necessary. Please help me to do this tactfully with others, whether in the church or at home. Thank you. Amen.

James 3:1-12

The first verse in our text is sobering, indeed. *Not many of you should become teachers, my brothers and sisters, for you know that we who teach will be judged with greater strictness.* Because of this verse, I wouldn't get up to preach and teach again if it weren't for Christ's promise that he will give us the words to say when we need them.

Having said that, however, a wise pastor never forgets how easy it is for things to slip out of his/her mouth that he/she shouldn't say. James said that *all of us make many mistakes*. That's not a fun thought, but it is the truth. Some of the worst mistakes pastors make are with their tongues. James couldn't have used a better illustration when referring to the damage that the tongue can do. I see several ways that a pastor's tongue can set *forest fires* in his/her ministry.

The most serious is preaching and teaching false doctrines or giving people false hope. Jesus said: *If any of you put a stumbling block before one of these little ones who believe in me, it would be better for you if a great millstone were fastened around your neck and you were drowned in the depth of the sea* (Matthew 18:6). That's how seriously Jesus takes it when we say or do something that would cause someone to stumble spiritually. How important it is to prayerfully prepare our sermons and Bible studies and *always* base them on God's Word. I've been amazed at how hungry people are for sound, biblical teaching. People today want to know what God's Word says, what it means, and how it applies to their lives. They don't want the opinions of others or nice, sentimental stories. They want something they can sink their intellectual and spiritual "teeth" into. Let's not disappoint them.

There's another way we can start *fires* and that is by using our loved ones (or people from the church) in illustrations without first getting their permission. This is a good way to ensure a cold and silent ride home after church and to lose the trust and confidence of people in our church.

Another way that we can start *fires* with our tongues is to talk about people behind their backs. I live in fear of this all the time, as these opportunities can catch us off guard. We might be having an innocent conversation with someone when they ask: "Oh, Pastor, I've been meaning to ask you; how's so and so?" Or sometimes it is the "innocent" prayer request: "How can I be praying for so and so?" And before we know it, we have shared more than we should. God help us to think before we speak, and to know how to respectfully withhold information from people who don't have a right to it.

Yet another way that we can start *fires* in our congregation is through our humor. I have a sanguine personality, which means I'm prone to talk too much, and much of the talking I do is for fun. I love to make people laugh! I love to kid around with people. And as a result, I have put my foot in my mouth countless times. Oh, how I constantly need to pray that God would put a filter over my lips so that I can still be a fun guy, but without saying things that I will regret, or that others might find offensive.

I can't possibly touch on all the ways that we as pastors can start *fires* in our churches and homes with our tongues, but one last one, in closing, is how we talk to our family in public. I have been appalled at how some pastors talk to their spouses and children in the presence of others. They shouldn't talk that way to them in the home, much less in public or in the church. What we say to our spouses and children, and how we say it, makes lasting impressions on all who hear. Are these lasting impressions building people's respect for us and giving them good examples to follow, or just the opposite?

May we begin each day by asking God to help us speak only what he wants us to speak, for his sake and the good of others.

A Pastor's Prayer:

Dear Lord,

How quickly I can start fires with my tongue! I ask you to please forgive me for when I have. Help me today, to say only that which will help others and bring honor and glory to you. Thank you. Amen.

Proper 20

Mark 9:30-37

Competition and power struggles can greatly hinder the effectiveness of a church's ministry. In our text, we read that Jesus saw this coming and, though the problem was in its early stages, he stopped it before it got out of hand. Even though the argument was between a few men, it had the potential to damage the spirit of the whole group. Perhaps we smile when we read the account, for it seemed like a silly argument, but it does emphasize the fact that those men were no different than any of us. For that reason, this text certainly speaks to the church today about competition and power struggles.

Pastors face this issue on several fronts, the first being our own internal struggles with competition and power. I'm sure I am not the first pastor who has felt a twinge of envy when other churches in town, or other churches in the synod, are doing better than mine. Perhaps I'm not the only pastor who has wondered why others get asked to speak at church gatherings and conventions, but I seldom am. However, does a growing church and an itinerary of speaking engagements make one pastor better than another? The devil would want me to think so. The fact is, a small minority of pastors have large churches and get asked to speak at church gatherings and conventions. That means that the majority of pastors are like me; working with small, struggling congregations, who are seldom noticed and recognized for what they accomplish or what they have to say. And Jesus said: *Whoever wants to be first must be last of all and servant of all.*

Pastors also face competition and power struggles with their parishioners. Many churches seem to have "patriarchs" and "matriarchs" who have been around since the church was founded. They seem to know what is "best" for the church and make sure everyone knows that. If they do not currently hold an office in the church, they will try to "throw their weight around" at congregational meetings, often causing division in the church. Often these people engage in power struggles with the pastor, which can polarize church members against one another. What are we to do?

Pastors can address these power struggles by preaching on this text (and others like it) and remind people what Jesus said: *Whoever wants to be first must be last of all and servant of all.* We also would do well to honestly evaluate our own attitudes and make sure we are not getting swept into their competition and power struggles. If preaching on and modeling servanthood doesn't bring about changes and if the constitutional process of dealing with leadership issues doesn't bring improvement, then maybe it's time for the church to be without a pastor for a while.

Last of all, pastors face these issues on the synodical level. This is the actual living out of a pastor's internal struggles that I mentioned earlier. It is one thing to think competitively; it is quite another to become competitive in the politics of the church in an effort to be the greatest. Many pastors struggle with big egos. It feels good to be promoted and assume more responsibility, but if we are doing it for no other reason than to be the greatest, watch out, for we may be headed for a downfall.

I am, by nature and personality, susceptible to pride and a big ego. I know how easy it is for me to talk "big" and brag about my accomplishments. I know how quickly power and prominence can go to my head. Therefore, serving small churches and seldom being asked to speak at large church gatherings may well be God's answers to my prayers, for I am so fearful of falling into a similar situation as those disciples. If being first really means being last and a servant of all, then that's what I want. I pray God will keep me there, whether anyone notices or not.

A Pastor's Prayer:
Dear Lord,

My pride scares me. Please don't let me hinder your work through me by getting involved in competition and power struggles. Help me to know how to preach and teach this text to the people in my church so they, too, will understand the value of being last and servant of all. Thank you. Amen.

James 3:13—4:3, 7-8a

I saw a cute saying on a church sign recently that read: "If God is your co-pilot, switch seats." I've since thought of another one: "If the devil is your co-pilot, switch planes!"

Something which no pastor should take lightly is the ongoing need for God's wisdom. Any time we start depending on our own wisdom to carry us along in ministry, we are no longer "flying" with God. We are bound to "crash," for like a terrorist hi-jacker, that's exactly what the devil wants to see happen to us.

In this text, James effectively compared a person without God's wisdom to one with it. This applies to the church as well.

Beginning with the dark side of this issue, let's look at what characterizes a person, or congregation, who is operating under the devil's wisdom. They will *have bitter envy and selfish ambition in their hearts.* They will *be boastful and false to the truth. There will also be disorder and wickedness of every kind.* Sadly, this not only describes unbelievers, but some pastors and churches as well. If this describes you or your church, it's time for some serious spiritual house cleaning, involving the confession of sins, true repentance, and yielding once again to God's gracious will for you and your church.

"But," we might ask, "where did these things mentioned above come from? I was doing so well before." Well, James may have the answer to that: *Those conflicts and disputes among you ... come from your cravings that are at war within you. You want something and do not have it ... you covet something and cannot obtain it; so you engage in disputes and conflicts.* Can we not see, in these statements from James, the root causes of a lot of church conflicts? When pastors or congregations (or both) start thinking selfishly, apart from God's wisdom, things get messy real fast.

James went on to point out that there is also a problem with the prayer life of the pastor and/or congregation: *You do not have, because you do not ask.* [If you do ask], *You ... do not receive, because you ask wrongly, in order to spend what you get on your pleasures.* I inserted a few words for emphasis, for that is basically what James was saying. When we rely on our wisdom, or the wisdom of others, we quit praying before, during, and after our meetings. If we do still pray, the prayers start to sound more like this: "Dear God, please bless our church and help us raise lots of money so we can become the biggest and best church in town. Amen." I think you get the point.

On the brighter side of this issue, are the characteristics of a person, or congregation, who operates under God's wisdom. God's wisdom looks like this: *Show by your good life that your works are done with gentleness born of wisdom ... wisdom from above is first pure, then peaceable, gentle, willing to yield, full of mercy and good fruits, without a trace of partiality or hypocrisy. And a harvest of righteousness is sown in peace for those who make peace.* What a sharp contrast to the person or congregation operating under human wisdom (which, I remind you, is really the devil's wisdom). Which set of characteristics would you like yourself and your church to be known for?

If our life and ministry, and that of our church, have resembled the first set of characteristics more than the latter, but we really want to change, then listen to James' directive on what to do next: *Submit yourselves therefore to God. Resist the devil, and he will flee from you. Draw near to God, and he will draw near to you.*

You've already been impacted by God's Word through this text, so the very next thing to do is talk to God about what you've discovered. If this is something your congregation needs to do, then preach this text and at the end of the sermon lead them in prayer, maybe even inviting others to pray as well.

A Pastor's Prayer:

Dear Lord,

I know I have sinned repeatedly by following the devil's wisdom and not yours. Please forgive me and my congregation. I want, from this day on, to seek your wisdom and be guided by you. I want my life and my church to show the characteristics of people who are living according to your wisdom. I ask this for Jesus' sake and your honor and glory. Thank you. Amen.

Proper 21

Mark 9:38-50

In last week's devotional on the Gospel Lesson, I wrote about the danger of being competitive and caught up in power struggles. As I indicated, those can take many different forms. In this text, we have Jesus' disciples coming to him with an almost childish concern: *Teacher, we saw someone casting out demons in your name, and we tried to stop him, because he was not following us.* As silly as their concern might seem, it is a concern being replayed in one Christian church after another. One thing I have never been able to understand is why some pastors, churches, and denominations imply that they are the only true church. Both major and minor church bodies have done this down through the years, and some still continue to.

The Bible makes it clear that there is only one true church — the church of Jesus Christ (and I'm not referring to the Mormons!). This is the church universal; consisting of believers in Christ from various Christian denominations around the globe. Why are we at odds with each other when we are about the same mission; proclaiming the good news of Jesus Christ to a spiritually lost world? Granted, I'm fully aware that there are both major and minor differences in doctrines and practice, but if the gospel is at the heart of what we profess and the main purpose of our ministry, then I believe Jesus would say to all of us: *Do not stop* [them]; *for no one who does a deed of power in my name will be able soon afterward to speak evil of me. Whoever is not against us is for us.*

What many pastors and churches are doing is putting each other down to try make themselves look better. So maybe you think your doctrine is better than someone else's; good for you! You should, or how else can you keep teaching and preaching it with confidence? But the truth is, any church with a set of doctrines that is Christ centered, believes in the Trinity, holds to Christ's words that he is the only way to the Father, and sees the primary purpose of the church as carrying out Christ's Great Commission, is on the right track. They are for Christ and not against him. So how can any of us presume to be so much smarter than Christ, and be against them when he isn't?

What this separatist mentality and isolation is doing, is confusing young and immature believers and creating a stumbling block for unbelievers. Time and again I have tried to share the gospel with skeptics who raise this one question over and over again: "Why can't Christians get along?" Good point! Why can't we? Either it's Jesus' fault for instituting a shabby organization such as the Christian church, or else it the church's fault for doing such a shabby job of running this pure and holy body which he instituted. I hope you will humbly agree with me that it is, without a doubt, the latter of the two. In part, due to differing interpretations of scripture and deep convictions, and in large part due to arrogance and pride, we have continued this same attitude of the disciples where *we tried to stop* [them], *because* [they were] *not following us.*

Brothers and sisters in Christ, I'm not proposing one big Christian church, for that would be ridiculous. I'm urging us to follow Christ's advice. Let's quit bad-mouthing one another and back-stabbing each other. Let's pray for, and with, one another now and then. Let's do a better job of educating our children on our differences and similarities and let them decide where they want to go to church. Intimidating them with unbiblical fear and consequences if they leave the fellowship of our church is only keeping the conscientious ones; it drives the others away, not only from the church but from God.

Much of the Christian church has become a *stumbling block*, for it has *lost its saltiness*, and you know what Christ recommends for those who are a stumbling block. Let us not take this lightly, but do something about it. Change can, and must, begin with us.

A Pastor's Prayer:
Dear Lord,

Please forgive my petty grievances with other Christians, pastors, and churches. Help me to see the church through your eyes as one body, under one head; and not in competition, but serving one commission. Thank you for my fellow Christians in other churches. I ask your blessings on them today. Amen.

James 5:13-20

The final text from James sheds light on a key element in successful and effective church ministries. This applies not only to pastors, but church members as well. All the various components in this text add up to one main, overarching point: "Care for one another. Let's see what a caring church looks like."

First, it cares for those who are *suffering*. How? By encouraging them to *pray*, and praying with them. Bring in those who are *cheerful*, and have them *sing songs of praise* for, and with, those who are suffering. The elderly love this! For those who are suffering with a serious illness, bring in the *elders of the church and have them pray over them, anointing them with oil in the name of the Lord.*

To effectively care for others in this way takes several things. It takes an awareness of needs. Do you know who is suffering? How long, on the average, does someone in your parish suffer until you know about it? Is it minutes, hours, days, weeks? How long until the rest of the church family knows?

A caring church is not only aware, but also quick to respond with compassion. This caring compassion involves prayer, encouragement, and, if it seems appropriate, anointing with oil.

This care requires some things that are seriously lacking in today's culture; selflessness, time, and good health. If we want to do this well, we will think less of ourselves and more of others. If, while caring for others, we are constantly thinking about all the things we should be doing or want to do, it will show in our attitude, and lack of concern and attention. To be an effective caregiver, we will want to make time for those who are suffering. We can't be holding their hand and looking at the clock at the same time (unless we're checking their pulse!).

Caring people also take good care of themselves. This not only applies to the obvious, of taking good care of ourselves physically (for the sick cannot care for the sick), but also taking care of ourselves mentally, emotionally, and spiritually. Are we in a good state of mind? Are we thinking rightly about those who need our care? If we are too tired, for example, we will probably be less patient with those we are caring for than if we are well rested.

How are we doing emotionally? I find that people who are drained emotionally from stress in their lives, such as marriage problems, are hindered in their ability to care for others; no matter how much time they have available. As much as possible, we will want to be emotionally strong and healthy to care for those who are suffering, or we will crash emotionally. Depression has become a major problem for pastors, especially those whose emotional "tank" is running on empty much of the time. The way to fill that "tank" is in solving issues that are causing undue stress and spending time with healthy people.

And how are you doing spiritually? A major aspect to caring for those who are suffering is spiritual care. When it comes to this, we cannot give what we do not possess. James urged that the confession of sin be associated with prayer and anointing with oil. However, if we are living in sin and operating in a spiritual vacuum, we lose our nerve to confront sin and our prayers are hindered. On the other hand: *The prayer of the righteous is powerful and effective.* That is exciting, for if we are in a right relationship with God, he is going to use us in powerful ways to accomplish his eternal purposes!

The main purpose in caregiving is not to make people laugh or feel good, but to bring them to *the truth.* Notice what James wrote about this: *You should know that whoever brings back a sinner from wandering will save the sinner's soul from death and will cover a multitude of sins.* That, my friends, is what spiritual caregiving is all about, and should be the primary goal of every pastor and congregation.

A Pastor's Prayer:

Dear Lord,

It is a tremendous privilege to serve you by caring for the needs of those who are suffering. Grant me good health, in every possible way, so you can accomplish your purposes through me. Help me to know how to encourage my congregation to be a caring church, so we might effectively accomplish the mission you have given us. Thank you. Amen.

Proper 22

Mark 10:2-16

This text addresses two critical issues in the church, the first being the difficult issue of divorce and the other being the exciting issue of blessing our children!

With the divorce rate reaching epidemic proportions, both in and out of the church, how does one preach on this text? I have become convinced that we won't slow the divorce rate by preaching on the sin of divorce. Nor will people avoid remarriage by being told that Jesus calls it *adultery*. I believe the only possibility of turning this thing around (as painfully slow as this approach is) lies in us doing a better job of educating the church on what a strong, godly marriage consists of.

To begin with, I think the fault for the decline in respect for the God-ordained institution of marriage lies largely with men. Fathers and husbands, since earliest times, have failed to follow God's plans and have neglected their God-given responsibilities. Many men have done this willfully. Countless others didn't even know there existed divine plans and responsibilities that they were to follow. They just took a shot in the dark and if they got it right, they were lucky; if they got it wrong, there was pain.

Jesus touched on the problem in general when he said: *Because of your hardness of heart he wrote this commandment for you.* He was referring to the certificate of divorce that Moses permitted men to give their wives. Notice again what the root of the problem was; *hardness of heart*. This problem rose primarily in the men. If we study the history of Israel during the days of Moses, we will find that the men failed miserably.

The same holds true today. Behind every divorce is a hardened heart. I say that from experience, as I have given spiritual care to many couples who were on the verge of divorce. Those who didn't end their marriage were those where the man took up the humble, servant-like role of spiritual leader in his home. Those that ended in divorce were those who continued to harden their hearts. In some cases the husband's heart was hardened toward the will of God for him and his marriage. In other cases the wife's heart was hardened because of her husband's sin or her father's sin. She then added to that her own sin, which made her heart harder. This may be an over-simplified solution, but I believe it is biblical: If there were no hard hearts, there would be no divorce.

So how do we soften hard hearts? We give people law and grace. If they respond positively to that, their hearts will soften and so will their attitudes toward each other and their marriage. The key to this is the cross, and no one lays this out better than the Apostle Paul in Ephesians 5:21-33. I urge all pastors to get a good grasp on this text. Get your men to read it, study it, and allow the Lord to apply it to their hearts and marriages. God can, through his word of law and grace, greatly reduce the divorce rate, especially in the church.

In closing, I want to touch on the exciting issue of blessing our children. What a breath of fresh air they are after talking about divorce! Jesus loved the children and saw in them the greatest faith that exists. In fact, he said: *whoever does not receive the kingdom of God as a little child will never enter it.* What a powerful, revolutionary statement that was! The "wisdom" and "maturity" of adults is nothing compared to the faith of a child. But those adults who receive the kingdom of God with the same uncomplicated faith of a child, will receive much more than salvation. They will enjoy all of God's blessings, including stronger relationships and better marriages.

Thank God for our children. May we love them sincerely and make sure they feel welcome and highly valued in our church. The future of the church rests, not in hard-hearted adults, but in the faith and innocence of children.

A Pastor's Prayer:

Dear Lord,

Thank you for our children. May we learn from their faith and innocence how to relate to you. Please soften any hardness that exists in my heart. Give me wisdom and boldness to teach your principles for lasting and loving marriage relationships. Thank you. Amen.

Hebrews 1:1-4; 2:5-12

Of the many good truths contained in this text, I want us to focus primarily on that of God's providential care for his creation.

The author immediately introduces us to Christ, for the primary purpose of the letter seems to be that of helping the Hebrew Christians get a better grasp of how Christ fulfilled the sacrificial system. In doing so, he first introduced Christ as *a Son*. He is God's Son whom God *appointed heir of all things*. Christ is so much more than a mere man. He is the Son of God who is over all things. Therefore he is in the highest place of authority over all God's creation.

Speaking of creation, the author also identified Christ as the one who *created the worlds*. He is not the first Bible author to point out this truth about Christ. John, at the beginning of his gospel wrote this: *In the beginning was the Word, and the Word was with God, and the Word was God. He was in the beginning with God. All things came into being through him, and without him not one thing came into being* (John 1:1-3a).

The Apostle Paul also wrote about this in his letter to the Colossians: *He is the image of the invisible God, the firstborn of all creation; for in him all things in heaven and on earth were created, things visible and invisible, whether thrones or dominions or rulers or powers — all things have been created through him and for him. He himself is before all things, and in him all things hold together* (Colossians 1:15-17).

Christ is, indeed, so much more than a mere man. He is the Son of God who not only created everything, but he continues to sustain it. How does he do this? Our text tells us that *he sustains all things by his powerful word*.

One of the unfortunate outcomes of Darwin's theory of evolution is that many people (at least those who whole-heartedly embrace this theory as the explanation for the origin of all that exists) have lost sight of God's purpose and meaning for their existence. When we remove God and his Son from the equation of our origin we immediately lose all sense of purpose, for our lives seem pointless. Gradually, the origin of sin and the need for the cross become blurred, for they don't fit with the theory of chance. When we allow science to determine our purpose and meaning, these important truths get lost in theories, equations, and billions of years. But when we allow God's word to reveal to us our purpose and meaning, it all begins to make sense and gives us something to live for!

It was for this reason that God had this author, and the others I quoted earlier, clearly explain to us who was overseeing things from the beginning. It was God, working together with his Son. They had a plan and design for the whole universe long before it ever came into existence. They had a plan and design for each and every one of us, as well, long before we were born.

Our text tells us that God, in planning out our salvation, brought all things into existence *for* himself. Since we were made by him, and for him, then it is safe to say that he will provide for us as well. When we attempt to harmonize Darwin's atheistic theory of origin with God's word, we face the difficult task of trying to figure out when and where God became involved with humanity and why or how he cares for it. But if we will believe what the Bible says, that God and his Son were in the beginning with an eternal plan already in place, then that gives us, not only purpose and meaning for this life and all eternity, but also great assurance that he is indeed caring for us and providing for our every need.

A Pastor's Prayer:
Dear Lord,

Thank you for making me and having a plan for my life long before I was even conceived. Thank you that you provide for me, because you are personally interested in me. Thank you for making me for your enjoyment. Help me to obediently live out your purposes for me and to have faith to believe what your word teaches us in regards to the origin of all things. Amen.

Proper 23

Mark 10:17-31

In ministry, we often encounter people who are fully convinced that they are "good enough" to get into heaven. This text clarifies for us what God's definition of "good" is, and how far superior it is to the world's definition.

In the church, we use this word a lot. We talk about how certain people are "good people." We teach our children to "be good kids." We tell them that people who obey the Ten Commandments are "good," yet they hear us call people "good," who fall way short of that perfect standard of goodness. Clearly, even the church's definition is inferior to Christ's definition.

Our text is the familiar account of a rich man who approached Jesus to find out what he must *do to inherit eternal life*. The man addressed Jesus as a *Good Teacher*. Apparently he had some foreknowledge about Jesus. But Jesus quickly corrected him, saying: *Why do you call me good? No one is good but God alone.* That statement is the clearest definition of what it means to be "good." It means to be God! And that rules out all of us, doesn't it?

Jesus tested the man's own ideas in regards to his own goodness by asking how well he was keeping the Ten Commandments. When we hear the man's description of his lifestyle, any of us would be quick to characterize him as a "good man." In fact we would probably welcome people like him on our church council and ask him to teach Sunday school. After all, we are always looking for some "good" people to fill these positions, right?

Well, the rich man failed the test, for although he had been a "good boy," one thing he lacked; complete obedience to the First Commandment. When faced with making a choice between his wealth or following Jesus, his wealth proved to be his god. And he went away grieving. He wasn't good enough, was he?

How important it is that we correct our own thinking in terms of what true, biblical goodness is, and help our parishioners to see goodness from this perspective as well. We should be doing all we can, with the help of the Holy Spirit, to be good people by keeping the Ten Commandments; but the truth of the matter is, we'll never keep them perfectly. We just can't be good enough to please God. What Jesus was asking of the man, he asks of each of us, too — complete abandonment to him. In the attitude of our hearts, we are to *sell everything and follow him*. This complete "selling out" is what is required for salvation. It isn't a work we do, as much as an attitude we have, so God can be first and foremost in our lives.

Peter began to question our Lord as to what would come of this complete abandonment to follow him, and Jesus replied: *Truly I tell you, there is no one who has left house or brothers or sisters or mother or father or children or fields, for my sake and for the sake of the good news, who will not receive a hundredfold now in this age — houses, brothers and sisters, mothers and children, and fields, with persecutions — and in the age to come eternal life.*

Perhaps there is no one group of people who find more comfort in this than pastors and missionaries. There is, in one sense, an abandonment of all these things in the attitude of our heart to follow Jesus and allow him to have first place over all our other affections. But then there is the actual, physical abandonment of many of these things and people, due to his call in our lives. He may call us to serve a church on the other side of the nation from our loved ones. He may call us to serve in a mission field halfway around the world. He may ask us to leave our jobs and financial security to serve him in a church that can barely meet our needs.

Does such sacrifice make us "good" people? No, it is merely the obedient response of people who believe, by faith, that Jesus has more to offer them than anything, or anyone, else.

A Pastor's Prayer:
Dear Lord,

Thank you that you are the ultimate standard of goodness. Forgive me for my puffed-up attitudes when I have thought myself to be a good person. Thank you, that on the basis of Christ's blood, you see his goodness in me rather than the sinner that I am. Amen.

Hebrews 4:12-16

This text beautifully presents to us a balance of law and grace. Verses 12 and 13 contain law and certainly don't beat around the bush when describing the activity of God's Word. Verses 14 through 16 apply the salve of God's grace to the wounds inflicted by the necessary surgery of the law. Let's look closer at both passages.

As people whose primary calling is to proclaim God's Word in a variety of settings, through a variety of means, let us never underestimate its power. Our text describes God's Word as *living and active*. When we read the Bible, we are not reading something that is dead, out-of-date, and ineffective. No! We hold in our hands something that is alive! Like holding a lion cub who wants to get away and pounce on its enemies, so the Word of God is alive and "squirming" — wanting to get away from our lips to reveal sin and unbelief and bring grace to the broken hearted.

The author uses the metaphor of a sword when describing the activity of God's Word: *The word of God is ... sharper than any two-edged sword, piercing until it divides soul from spirit, joints from marrow; it is able to judge the thoughts and intentions of the heart. And before him no creature is hidden, but all are naked and laid bare to the eyes of the one to whom we must render an account.*

May we not take lightly what God is doing when we share his word. When it is proclaimed in all its truth and authority, God is cutting deep into the hearts of the listeners. He is speaking to consciences and trying to cut away the hardness of hearts that have grown cold from sin and unbelief. David is a good example of this when the Prophet Nathan came and boldly spoke God's Word to him. The word of God cut deep into David that day, revealing his sin. It did that, because one man obediently spoke what he was told to speak, "Thus saith the Lord...!" He did it with the authority that God's Living Word possesses. He did it for the good of David and the nation, and for God's honor and glory. Was it fun? I'm sure Nathan would have rather done just about anything else that day, but the fact is, he did it; and through him God accomplished much with the law that day. David responded favorably to the law so that God was then able, through his word, to apply the "salve" of grace to David's "wounds."

The author of Hebrews then turns our attention from the horrific picture of God's Law at work to that of his grace bringing forgiveness and healing. He does this through the imagery of Christ as the *great high priest*. He wants us to know that Jesus is far superior to any earthly high priest. Jesus *has passed through the heavens*; making him a divine, all-powerful high priest. Yet, in spite of that power and glory, he is not so high and mighty that he *is unable to sympathize with our weaknesses*. This is where grace begins to get really beautiful!

We don't deserve to have him sympathize with us. We deserve swift judgment and punishment for our sins, but not our great high priest. He is one who *in every respect has been tested as we are, yet without sin*. That means he identifies with us. He is one who can say to us, "I understand what you are going through. I know it is hard. I felt like giving up, too, but I didn't."

What a beautiful, gracious invitation closes out this text: *Let us therefore approach the throne of grace with boldness, so that we may receive mercy and find grace to help in time of need.* He invites us to approach his throne of grace after we have sinned against him. This is God's grace at its purest and best! We don't deserve that, nor do the people to whom we proclaim his grace. That is why it is called grace and mercy. That is what we get to share with people after they have been injured, sometimes severely, by God's Law.

Preaching the law is never fun, but when you do it with God's grace in view, your listeners are more likely to respond positively and feel loved by both you and the Lord.

A Pastor's Prayer:

Dear Lord,

Thank you for your word — that it is alive and active. Thank you, that as I proclaim your law, you are revealing to people their problem with sin; and as I proclaim your grace, you are forgiving their sins and bringing healing to their souls. Lord, help me to faithfully proclaim a balance of both for your sake. Amen.

Proper 24

Mark 10:35-45

James and John remind me of some of the people we encounter from time to time. Like those who call our office and ask something to this effect:

"Say Pastor, can you do me a favor?"

"Well, I'll see. What is it you would like me to do?"

"You see, Pastor, my boyfriend and I would like to get married this weekend. Would that work for you?"

"Ah. No. I'm sorry. I have to brush my cat this weekend." (I probably wouldn't say that, but I would indicate as politely as I could that their request was not reasonable.)

James and John were asking for something much bigger and more impossible than an instant wedding. They wanted "the best seats in the house" when Jesus entered his kingdom. It's pretty clear that they really had no clue as to what they were asking, and perhaps that is the lesson for all of us in this text. Since we are finite human beings, we ask God for some pretty crazy things at times, because we just don't have a clue what we are really asking for.

What are some things that you ask God for? Might it be a different group of people to minister to? More pay? A larger church? A higher position in your denomination? Maybe you ask him to change your spouse, or your children, or the people in your church. Maybe you're asking for a miracle of healing for yourself or someone else. We ask God for some really big things at times and that is okay, for he has invited us to do so. Jesus told the disciples to ask for big things, so these guys probably thought: "Hey, what do we have to lose? Never hurts to try."

I find it interesting what happened to these two disciples as a result of their big request. Their prayer was answered, all right. The answer was, "No." Along with that, they got something they hadn't asked for but needed more than they realized. They received knowledge about Jesus, learned something about themselves, and had their eyes opened in regard to their relationships with others.

Perhaps this is the best thing that could happen to us as a result of our wild and crazy prayers. They don't seem wild and crazy at the time we pray them, in fact they seem quite legitimate. But as time goes by, and we realize more and more that the answer seems to be, "No," we start to learn some things that we didn't know before.

We learn more about God. We learn about his patience and that he really has our best interest at heart. We learn that he must have a sense of humor (he has to in order to put up with us!) and is very loving toward his children.

We learn more about ourselves. We learn that we aren't as smart as we thought we were. We learn how selfish and proud we can be. We learn how impatient we are with God and other people. We learn that we're always learning how to pray.

We learn more about others. We learn what it means to serve, rather than be served. We learn that everyone, no matter how much they irritate us, is created in the image of God and we are to look for that potential in them. We learn that people are not rungs on the ladder to success, but are the ones who will help us be successful if we love them, care for them, and put their interests and needs before our own.

Those were some of the hard lessons that James and John learned, but never saw coming when they asked this huge favor of Jesus. May we also learn from our prayers, both the wise prayers and the crazy ones. May we not get bitter with God when we don't get what we ask for. Instead, let's be quick to ask ourselves (and God, perhaps): "What can I learn from this?" And let's be quick to help others learn these valuable lessons from their prayers, too.

A Pastor's Prayers:
Dear Lord,

Please forgive me for all the times that I have asked selfish, ridiculous things of you. Help me to learn more about you, others and myself through my prayers — both the good ones and the crazy ones. Thank you for your patience with me and your willingness to help me grow and mature. Thank you that you always answer my prayers as you see best. Amen.

Hebrews 5:1-10

The author of Hebrews seems to have wanted his original readers to understand how Jesus had fulfilled the priestly system in the temple. The old order of things was passing away, as Jesus had ushered in the new. The Old Covenant was giving way to the glorious New Covenant.

The description of the temple priests and their ministry, in verses 1-4, gives us some idea of the huge responsibility they had, and how inadequate they must have felt while serving God before the people. The feelings of inadequacy would have resulted from being weak, sinful mortals like the people they served. They needed the sacrifices for sin as much as the people did.

When contrasted with these temple priests, Jesus stands head and shoulders above them in terms of qualification, perfection, and strength. He fulfilled, in a glorious way, all that they did. Their ministry, preceding Christ for centuries, was a "shadow" of the glorious atoning work of Christ. What they did, day after day, could never fully satisfy God's righteous demands, but what Christ did, once for all, completely satisfied God's demands.

We are the "priests" of the church today. Just as the temple priests were a mere "shadow" of the much greater reality to come, so, too, we are mere "shadows" of the greater reality who has come. The temple priests served God in view of the future cross. We serve God in view of the historical cross. Their ministry was a dim reflection of Christ's ministry to come. Our ministry is a dim reflection of Christ's ministry that was.

Reread with me, verses 1-4, as I would like us to try identify personally with this text and see how it can apply to us today. *Every* [pastor] *chosen from among mortals is put in charge of things pertaining to God on their behalf, to offer* [prayers] *for sins. He is able to deal gently with the ignorant and wayward, since he himself is subject to weakness; and because of this he must offer* [prayers] *for his own sins as well as for those of the people. And one does not presume to take this honor, but takes it only when called by God, just as* [the apostles were]. Fits our situation amazingly well, doesn't it?

The thing that strikes me most, as I connect personally with this text, is the issue of inadequacy. How humbling that God has called us, from amongst our fellow *mortals*, to serve him on Christ's behalf. How humbling to be in charge of *things pertaining to God on behalf* of our parishioners. How humbling to be in the position to pray and offer absolution for the forgiveness of our parishioner's sins. Granted, the process and ceremony is much different from that of the temple priests, but the end result is the same, or better — sins are forgiven once and for all.

May the following statement characterize each of us in our ministries: *He* (or she) *is able to deal gently with the ignorant and wayward, since he himself is subject to weakness.* Never forget that we are as ignorant and wayward as the worst sinners we deal with, for we possess the genetic tendencies, through our sinful nature, to sin as they have sinned. No matter how gross some people's sins might be, may God help us to deal gently with them, if for no other reason than the fact that Christ has dealt gently with us and our sins.

May we find great comfort, knowing that we have been preceded by the greatest high priest that ever lived. He was perfect and therefore accomplished what we can never accomplish. What we do in ministry is always on the basis of what he has done, and never on the basis of who we are or our qualifications. What we offer people — the forgiveness of sins — is always on the basis of Christ's shed blood for them and the power of his resurrection. Our "priestly" position and authority can add nothing to that.

Thank God for Jesus, who is the power behind all we do, and makes it effective and life changing for us and those we serve.

A Pastor's Prayer:
Dear Lord,
Thank you for being the great high priest. May I serve you faithfully as a "priest" to those whom you have placed in my spiritual care. Help me to always remember that I am no better than the worst sinner alive. Only by your grace, am I your child. Amen.

Proper 25

Mark 10:46-52

Imagine this scene with me: Jesus and his disciples exiting Jericho followed by a large crowd. Apparently Jesus has been quite popular in that community. Alongside the road sits a beggar who has apparently been overlooked by those who had been bringing people to Jesus. Perhaps he didn't have any friends or family to lead him to Jesus. Since no one will help him, he uses the only means he has — his lungs! Shouting to Jesus for mercy, the man begins to get the attention of some people. Unfortunately there isn't much compassion in the crowd, for they tell him to be quiet. The man becomes desperate. Maybe he fears this will be his only chance to get help from Jesus, so he yells louder. This time he gets Jesus' attention.

Notice how Jesus handles the situation. He sends for the man and, upon his quick arrival, Jesus asks him, *What do you want me to do for you?* It is obvious that the man is blind, so there must be some reason why Jesus asked the man this question. The man blurts out: *My teacher, let me see again.* Much to our amazement, there is no spit, no mud, no prayers, no commands to be healed, nothing except one simple statement from Jesus: *Go; your faith has made you well.* And to further our amazement, the man immediately regains his sight!

As I reflect on this scene, I find myself asking: "What faith? Where is the evidence of faith in what this man said? Is there something that we, as ministers of the gospel, can learn from this scene?"

Perhaps there is evidence of faith in the names he used when calling to Jesus: *Jesus, Son of David; teacher.* There would have to be some things that he believed in advance of this scene in order to address Jesus in those ways.

Maybe there are signs of faith in what he cried out to Jesus; *have mercy on me!* In order to plead for that, he would have to have some idea about Jesus' ability to show mercy to him.

Maybe the strongest sign of faith is seen in his request: *let me see again.* "Let me"? Do you suppose this blind man believed that Jesus had control over other people's sight? It seems like he did believe that, and perhaps that takes more faith than I have given him credit.

In our ministries, we encounter people (provided we get out of our offices and engage with the world) who are looked down on by others. They seem simple in mind and lacking in social skills. Society shuns them, other than to give them a handout and tell them to be quiet until they are eligible again next month. Many in the church push them aside, because their smell, mannerisms, or overall appearance (or all of the above) make them uncomfortable.

But these people are crying out for a chance to meet Jesus. Maybe they have more faith than we give them credit for. Maybe they have more faith than some of our most prominent church leaders. Maybe, just maybe, they have more faith than us. Is that intimidating? Does that make us uncomfortable? Does that make us squirm in our chair and wish we could change the subject?

Our world is full of people like blind Bartimaeus, who Jesus values just as highly as us. Why do we ignore them, when Jesus doesn't? May God help us to swallow our pride (or fears) or whatever it is that is keeping us from reaching out to these people in Jesus' name. Let us make every effort to educate our parishioners on what Jesus' will and mandate for the church is, in regards to these people.

Just as Bartimaeus very likely became a productive member of society after he was healed, so too, many people who seemed odd and worthless can, once they've been touched by Jesus, contribute a lot to society and the church. Let's give them a chance, by giving Jesus a chance to heal them.

A Pastor's Prayer:
Dear Lord,

Please forgive me for all the times I have shunned people like Bartimaeus. Give me love for them and faith to believe that you can make a difference in their life. Help me to know how to educate others in the church so we can, as one group, reach out to the broken and needy around us. Thank you. Amen.

Hebrews 7:23-28

This text continues the discussion about how Jesus is an infinitely greater high priest than those who faithfully served in the temple. The author was making a case for the fact that Jesus had replaced the necessity for all that had been tradition and religious practice for hundreds of years. Can you imagine being a priest at that time and being told that your services were no longer needed? A similar situation for us might be if we were told that our pastoral services were no longer needed, for someone much greater than us had replaced all that we had been doing, with something much more powerful and effective. That's basically what the author of Hebrews was saying.

As scripture and history have shown, the priestly system did not cease its duties overnight. In fact, it took a foreign army to bring it to an end, not the preaching of Christ's followers. How thankful we can be that it did come to an end. How thankful we should be that Christ completely fulfilled it, so there is no need to go back to something so inadequate and ineffective. Can you imagine trying to carry out the sacrificial laws today?

Our text, then, points out some major differences between Christ and the old system. First of all, there is the difference in the life span of the priests. The old priestly system was served by priests who died. They were not able to serve forever. However, our great high priest, Jesus Christ, *always lives to make intercession for* us. How much better is that? Thank God that Jesus never dies, but is a living priest who will serve his Father faithfully forever. And because of this, *he is able for all time to save those who approach God through him.* When leading people to faith in Christ, we never have to worry that we'll get a "busy signal," or that he is "out to lunch," or worse yet, dead! Christ is always available to save those who come to him by faith.

Another difference is that, *unlike the other high priests,* [Jesus] *has no need to offer sacrifices day after day, first for his own sins, and then for those of the people; this he did once for all when he offered himself.* No temple priest could have offered himself for others and had his death effectively cover their sins. Only Jesus could have done that. We can be assured, and assure others, that what he did on the cross was completely sufficient for them. There is nothing we can add to this to make our sins more forgiven or to further guarantee that they are. What Christ has done is done and never needs to be repeated nor have anything added to it. What wonderful good news that is for us and for those to whom we minister!

A temptation for many people is to want to try to add something to what Christ has already done, to help insure that their sins are really paid. It might be to do something to pay for their sin, such as withhold some pleasure from themselves, or go to church more, or pray more, or pray certain prayers, or give more money to church or some charity. These may well be commendable things, but they are totally ineffective in adding anything to God's grace. If we are going to do any of those things, or things like them (and we should), they should always be done in response to grace and never in addition to grace.

How privileged we are to be ministers of grace today. What the priests did, day after day, was nothing compared to what Christ did. Yet if they did not faithfully continue in that service, or if they made the least little error in carrying out the sacrificial laws, they could have been struck dead by God. The gospel message we get to proclaim is infinitely more powerful and effective than the old sacrifices, and we can proclaim it without fear, for Jesus, our great high priest, *always lives to make intercession for* us.

May we never take our role lightly; but may we never take it so seriously, either, that rituals, ceremonies, and traditions once again replace the good news of the gospel.

A Pastor's Prayer:

Dear Lord,

Thank you for abolishing the old sacrifice system. Thank you for the tremendously powerful gospel message I can proclaim, that is always completely effective in forgiving my sins and the sins of those I minister to. Help me to see, and remove, anything that I have been trying to add to your grace; and instead, do those things that are worth doing, in response to your grace. Thank you. Amen.

Proper 26 (All Saints)

Mark 12:28-34

This text summarizes the sum total of all that a Christian should believe and be. A person's attitude toward these two commands directly impacts their behavior in every day life. If this is true of the people to whom we preach, then it is most certainly true of us as well. The main purpose of this devotional is to stir the hearts and minds of pastors so they wrestle with each text personally before entering the pulpit to preach it. This text is a prime example of the importance of doing so.

Jesus summarized all of God's commands into these two: *love the Lord your God with all your heart, and with all your soul, and with all your mind, and with all your strength. The second is this, you shall love your neighbor as yourself.*

Do you love God with all your heart, soul, mind, and strength? That is a good question for us to ask ourselves on a regular basis, for the devil is constantly trying to break down our relationship with God. It is so easy for other things to sneak in and hinder our love for him. If we begin to lose this love, it will soon become evident in our ministry. It will affect our attitude toward what we do and the people we minister to. It will affect our attitude toward material things and how we live our life. It will have a "snowball" effect on our devotional life, for as our love begins to slip, so does the quality and quantity of time with God, which in turn results in more slippage and so on.

Early on in my ministry, I had someone tell me something that has stuck with me ever since: "Minister out of the overflow." In other words, if we begin our day with God, in Bible reading and prayer, much of what he reveals to us in those times becomes exactly what we need for ministering to others — whether in that day or some day down the road. I have found this to be so true. However, when we let our love relationship with God slip, we also neglect time with him. The result is less and less overflow from which to minister to others. Pretty soon we are standing in a hospital room "grasping at straws," trying to think of something to read and share with the person in need of comfort. How frightening to realize you are drying up spiritually because you have not been loving God with all your heart, soul, mind, and strength.

Do you love others as yourself? This, too, is a critical question to ask ourselves often, for if we lose our love for people, we won't last long in ministry. We can fake our love for God and fool some people for a while, but we can't fool people when it comes to loving them. If you are having trouble loving others, ask yourself "Why?" Maybe it is because you are having trouble loving yourself.

Some people don't love themselves because they weren't loved as a child. Other people struggle with self-love due to physical or verbal abuse. There are those who don't love themselves because of sin in their life — past and present. They can't believe they did what they did, nor can they believe God would forgive them, so they hate themselves for this. If we don't love self, we won't be able to love others.

An even bigger issue in all of this is that we can't love others if we don't love God. Yes, there are many people who don't love God, yet seem to have no trouble loving others. However, the real test of this love, which Jesus spoke of, is whether or not we can love our enemies and pray for those who persecute us. The greatest example of what the actual living out of this command should look like is Jesus on the cross, praying for his enemies: *Father, forgive them; for they do not know what they are doing* (Luke 23:34).

Do you find yourself wavering in your love for God and your parishioners? I urge you to take some time right now and talk to the Lord about that, before you try to preach this text to others.

A Pastor's Prayer:
Dear Lord,

Please forgive me for allowing things to come between you and me, hindering my love for you. I want to love you more than anyone or anything. Help me, too, dear Lord, to love those whom you have placed in my life. May my love be Christlike so that all who meet me will meet Christ through me. Thank you. Amen.

Hebrews 9:11-14

Again, our epistle for this week continues the discussion on how Christ sufficiently and completely fulfilled the old sacrifice system. In this particular text, the author explains how the *blood of Christ* was infinitely better at cleansing us from sin than the *blood of goats and bulls*. He acknowledges that the blood of the sacrificial animals did accomplish something, as it sanctified *those who [had] been defiled so that their flesh [was] purified*. These sacrifices satisfied God's demands at that time; however, they were little more than an imperfect shadow of the great and powerful reality to come — the blood of Christ. His sacrifice was *without blemish*, and served to *purify our conscience from dead works*. This enables us to now worship the living God without fear, whereas the worshipers under the old sacrifice system worshiped in fear all the time.

I can't emphasize enough how precious this relationship is, which God has made possible for us through Christ. It is our only hope for salvation. It is *the way, the truth, and the life* (John 14:6). It is the most important message we have to share. If we do not share it, everything else we share, through teaching, preaching, and private conversation, is pointless. Everything we do in ministry comes out of this and finds its ultimate purpose in this.

Notice how the author emphasizes, in this text and in previous texts, how Christ fulfilled everything about the old sacrifice system. None of it had a purpose any more. Something that had been loaded with symbolism and significance had been reduced to nothing by the perfect sacrifice and atoning work of Christ in connection with his victorious resurrection. I stress this, for since this time, the Christian church has once again complicated the simple and basic, yet incredibly powerful, gospel message.

The church of today has become filled with symbols, icons, statues, art, stained glass windows, banners, vestments, candles, incense, liturgies, rituals, ceremonies, prayers, traditions upon traditions, to the point that it is easy to lose sight of the basic gospel message. Although they might deny it, some churches would rather compromise the truth of God's Word than give up a human tradition. Sounds real familiar, doesn't it? That was the very problem that the author of Hebrews was addressing. The new had come and the old was to pass away, but it didn't want to.

The temptation for the church today, is to consider the basic gospel message as the old thing which can pass away and introduce new thoughts, doctrines, and practices to replace the old. However, these new ideas are as ineffective as (perhaps even less than) the blood of goats and bulls. How does this happen? How do we develop religious systems that crowd out the proclamation of the pure gospel message?

The development of new religious ideas and formation of complicated religious systems, comes not from God, but from people. Sometimes people innocently start with something that is good, in and of itself, but then it develops into something that is false teaching and possibly outright heresy. Pretty soon people are putting more faith into some one, some thing, or some activity than they are into Christ himself. There is no doubt in my mind who is behind this. It is the "father of lies" himself — Satan — who wants the church to get sidetracked once again and get our eyes and our hearts off of Jesus, who is the only one who can save us.

Ministers of the gospel, please watch carefully over your churches. Make sure that all you do serves the gospel rather than distracts from it. Never force the gospel to be subservient to anything else, for it and it alone is *the power of God for salvation* (Romans 1:16).

A Pastor's Prayer:
Dear Lord,

Please help me to recognize, both in my own life and in the life of the church, anything that is distracting me or others from the basic, powerful gospel of Jesus Christ. Thank you that faith in you is all we need for salvation. Help my church and me to make sure everything we do serves the gospel, and not the other way around. Amen.

Proper 27

Mark 12:38-44

Our Gospel Lesson touches on two extremes; the proud and the humble. Just as both extremes were in the temple that day, so too, we often see both extremes in our churches.

The proud group, which in this case was the *scribes*, was known as the religious elite. When I read Christ's description of them, I get a knot in my stomach, for I've seen far too many of these types in the church as well. These men loved fine clothes that drew attention. They liked being greeted in the marketplaces and recognized for their "importance." They selected the best seats at the synagogues. By *devouring widows' houses*, Jesus probably meant they exploited the generosity of people of humble means, like the widow in the second half of our text, and their prayers were something else! Apparently these went on and on, no doubt in an attempt to impress people with their religiosity.

Do you see any of yourself in this description? We are all prone to pride at times. Depending on our personality, and possibly our position in the church, it doesn't take much for some of us to start swaggering either. There's nothing wrong with dressing well. In fact, a pastor should always use good taste in what he/she wears; but if we are dressing up so people will notice us, we are more likely to offend them than impress them.

Do we like to be noticed when we are out in public? There's nothing wrong with being noticed and conversing with others, but if we're on a popularity "trip," and wanting to impress people because we are a pastor, we will turn people off. Do we enjoy being in front of the congregation? There's nothing wrong with being in front of people, unless we are there largely because we like attention. Pastors who try to be "cute," so people will be impressed with their humor, intelligence, or good looks, will lose people's trust rather than gain it.

Do you make it a point to talk often about money and giving to the church? There's nothing wrong with preaching and teaching on stewardship, but if we are trying to get money out of people in order to fund our pet programs or make ourselves look good (which a strong financial report often does), then we are going to lose people's trust even further.

What about your prayers? Are they long, drawn-out efforts to impress people? There's most certainly nothing wrong with pastors praying, for it is a vital part of our ministry. However, a pastor who doesn't know how to pray a prayer that is appropriate for the setting which he/she is in, will soon be written off as a fake.

Second only to the importance of faith in Christ and love for God and people, a good, effective pastor possesses much humility. The pastor who dresses nicely, yet modestly; who is friendly in the church and in public, but not overly so; who is basically inconspicuous in front of others; who does not take advantage of people financially; and who prays prayers that fit the occasion, is more likely to be trusted and loved by their parish and much more effective in the community, than one who is careless.

In addition to humility, is the important quality of generosity, as brought out by Jesus in reference to the poor widow. She didn't have much, but she gave what she had by faith. That is all Jesus expects of us, too. Some people he blesses with abundance and others with very little, but he does expect cheerful generosity in proportion to what he has given us. This goes not only for our money, but our time as well. Generous pastors, compared to those who are selfish and stingy, quickly gain the trust and respect of the parishioners. May God help us to be pastors who reflect the person of Christ, both in the church and in the community.

A Pastor's Prayer:
Dear Lord,

I desire to be humble before you and all to whom you would have me minister. Help me to see anything about me that is offensive and immediately correct that, so I do not turn people away from hearing the gospel. Give me faith to be generous, as a faith response to your blessing upon me. Thank you. Amen.

Hebrews 9:24-28

This is now the fourth lesson, in a series of five Epistle Lessons from Hebrews. The emphasis in each text has been on the superiority of the atoning, sacrificial work of Christ in comparison to the old sacrificial system. With each lesson we have been reminded of how blessed we are to live on this side of the cross, historically speaking. I've also cautioned us to be careful not to let church traditions, rituals, and ceremonies, overshadow the glory and power of the cross. For if we are not careful, we could find ourselves going, not "back to the future," but forward to the past; to a religious system as weak, or weaker, than that of the old sacrificial system. It is crucial to the ministry of the church, that everything in the church of human origin must serve the gospel, and not the other way around.

The emphasis in the first half of this text is once again on the superiority of Christ. How good to know *that he has appeared once for all at the end of the age to remove sin by the sacrifice of himself.* Christ did not have to die over and over again for each new generation. Unlike the activity in the temple, which had to be repeated again and again, Christ was sacrificed *once to bear the sins of many.*

We shift our attention, for the balance of this devotional, to a couple of key points that the author made and that have great significance for the church. The first is found in verse 27 and reads: *it is appointed for mortals to die once, and after that the judgment.* One of many spiritual ideas floating around in the world, is that of reincarnation. It is a philosophy on death that has absolutely no biblical basis. People who do not believe in Christ's death and resurrection, have fashioned this idea out of their own theories of death and the afterlife. The belief was intended to give them hope, but instead it has robbed them of any hope they might have had.

This passage couldn't be clearer; we *die once.* Not twice, not three times, not seven times, or more. We have but one life to live and *after that the judgment.* Yes, there will be a judgment for everyone. Those who are found with faith in Christ will be given eternal life. Those without faith will be given eternal death in hell. There is no cycling through, again and again, to try to get it right.

This life is the only shot we have. We must not believe otherwise, if we are to properly prepare our parishioners for death and the afterlife. We must educate them on this, for they are being influenced by a lot of different ideas in the world on death.

The other key point the author made was that Christ *will appear a second time, not to deal with sin, but to save those who are eagerly waiting for him.* The justification part of sanctification is done, but we are not completely sanctified until Christ comes the second time. We could compare this to a concert we want badly to attend, but we have no idea how or where to get tickets. In fact, we heard that the tickets were so expensive, no one could afford them anyway. How would anyone get into the concert? Only if the artist were to throw the doors open wide and let everyone in — free of charge. But we still need a ticket, albeit a free one, to get into the concert. We have no idea how to find or obtain one. One day, some one comes up to us and offers us a free ticket! Would we believe it was for real? Would we trust them, that they had the authority to extend this great act of grace and mercy to us?

Dear friends, the eternal, heavenly "concert" has been bought out by the artist who holds all the "tickets." They are free for the asking. There is nothing we can do to improve our chances of getting one, nor is there anything we can pay or do to ensure that the tickets are good, once we get them by faith. Everything has been taken care of. The preparations have been made. The big event is all that remains, and we wait for it to be announced. Are you ready? Are your parishioners ready? May it not take any of us by surprise.

A Pastor's Prayer:

Dear Lord,

Thank you that you are all sufficient for my sins and the sins of the whole world, past, present, and future. Lord, help me to believe in you alone for salvation, and to rest in the fact that there is nothing I can add to what you have done to increase my chances of entering heaven, or to make it surer. I look forward to your glorious return! Amen.

Proper 28

Mark 13:1-8

This text reveals a significant difference in how Christ looks at things compared to how we see them. The one disciple, who was struck by the beauty of the temple buildings, represents all of us. We are so easily caught up in beautiful things that won't last. Perhaps the disciples wondered if Jesus had gotten up on the wrong side of his mat when he said: *Do you see these great buildings? Not one stone will be left here upon another; all will be thrown down.* His response reminds me of someone who always has a negative comment about everything. It can be the most beautiful day, but for them it is either too hot or too cold. I struggle with this from time to time as a pastor. Being a sanguine personality, I'm generally a pretty up-beat guy, but I know I can get pessimistic about things at times, especially about people. However, it isn't realistic to always pretend everything is a "bed of roses," either.

Is Jesus a pessimist or a realist? Being God, he sees things as they are (and as they are going to be, which, thank God, we can't). I'm sure Jesus saw the beauty of the temple, but he wanted to direct their attention to a greater reality; something more important than buildings.

One of the important roles we have is helping people see a bigger reality beyond the buildings and grounds of their church. Many congregations struggle with wanting larger, more beautiful buildings that will attract people. They want full-service facilities that will meet everyone's needs. Pastors like it when people say: "Wow! What a beautiful building, Pastor!" We might feel it reflects our leadership skills if we lead the congregation through a building program, or maybe it says something about who we are. If the people of such a beautiful facility would call us to be their pastor, we must be doing something right!

The truth of the matter is: *not one stone will be left upon another; all will be thrown down.* Are we putting as much (or more) effort in building a "church" that lasts for all eternity, as we are in building one that will crumble? That seems to be Christ's concern in this text. For he went on to warn the disciples: *Beware that no one leads you astray. Many will come in my name and say, "I am he!" and they will lead many astray.* You see, while we are focused on building and maintaining things that won't last, the "church" that lasts for all eternity (the people) may well be going *astray.* You may be thinking: "That's a pessimistic thing to say." Yes, maybe it is, but I also try hard to be a realist in ministry, even in writing this devotional, which is based on both the reality of God's Word and real experiences.

If we are not careful about how focused we are on things that won't last, the things which God intends should last forever could be lost. I know it is an area of ministry that can be difficult to balance. We are often called upon to give leadership and direction during a building program; all the while continuing to give spiritual care. It's like asking the contractor of a large building project to start holding Bible studies and worship services on the job site and offer spiritual care to all their employees; all the while overseeing a construction project. Since they are not trained to give spiritual care, they will have to work hard at doing it well, at the risk of neglecting what they were trained to do — construction.

When we, who were trained to teach and preach the word of God and care for the spiritual needs of our parishioners, allow ourselves to be put into the position of supervising a construction project, something has to give. Enormous pressure is put on us to do something well, that we don't know how to do. Our work load increases with additional meetings, more decisions to make, and having to encourage tired, crabby people; all at the expense of neglecting what we were trained to do — ministry.

Forgive me if our text has little to do with the point I just made. However, I do believe it says this to us; if we want to reflect the character and care of our Lord, we will want to be less impressed with things that crumble and more focused on people, to make sure they are not being misled by false "christs."

A Pastor's Prayer:
Dear Lord,
    Help me to keep my priorities in line with yours. When called upon to do things that will distract me from caring for your people, help me to know when, and how, to say, "No." Thank you. Amen.

Hebrews 10:11-14 (15-18) 19-25

This is the last text in a series from Hebrews, that has served to help the reader understand how Christ is a better sacrifice for sins than the old sacrifices. These texts have also shown how he fulfilled every aspect of the old sacrificial system, making it obsolete and no longer necessary. For the purpose of this devotional, I would like to look at verses 22-25, where the author encourages his readers to do three things, with each of his pleas beginning with the words, *let us.*

First, he wrote: *Let us approach with a true heart in full assurance of faith, with our hearts sprinkled clean from an evil conscience and our bodies washed with pure water.* That which we are to approach is *the sanctuary*, or the presence, of God. In verse 19 he wrote that *we have confidence* to enter this sanctuary because of the blood of Christ. This is in sharp contrast to the fear that went hand in hand with the temple activities under the old sacrificial system. Up to this time, to approach the sanctuary of God, and in particular the holy of holies, was a fearful thing. The God of the old covenant and sacrificial system was a holy and righteous God who struck fear in the hearts of everyone. How thankful we can be for this wonderful, approachable relationship that Christ made possible for us to have with God. He still demands obedience and righteousness of us, but the confidence we have to approach him, in worship and in prayer for his grace and mercy, is always on the basis of Christ's obedience and righteousness, not ours.

The second *let us*, is found in verse 23 and reads: *Let us hold fast to the confession of our hope without wavering, for he who has promised is faithful.* Anytime we waver in our confession of faith, it is *not* a result of something going wrong in heaven. It is either the result of sin in our own lives or the evil around us, which might be causing us doubts and fears. God made unconditional promises to us that he will never go back on and that can never fail, because, by the very nature of his being, he is faithful. Therefore, we can, and ought to, *hold fast* to what we believe. What a comfort to know that God is unshakable and his promises unbreakable. Since he is always faithful to us, let us always be faithful to him. In addition, when our parishioners see us holding fast *to the confession of our hope without wavering,* that encourages them to do the same.

Last of all, the author of this text wrote: *Let us consider how to provoke one another to love and good deeds, not neglecting to meet together, as is the habit of some, but encouraging one another, and all the more as you see the day approaching.* This is an important task of the pastor in any church. As we reflect upon, and pray over, our ministry and the people that make up our ministry, let us be always considering these matters. How can we encourage them to love each other more, and also love those who are outside the church family? Perhaps we could preach more on the subject. Maybe we could encourage some fellowship opportunities where they can practice putting their love into action.

How can we encourage our people to do good deeds? Again, we could preach on it. We could tell them about needs that exist in the church where they could get involved. Above all, it is so important that we stress the purpose of good deeds. They are not something we do for salvation, or to increase our chances of eternal life. Good deeds, done for the right reason, are always done in response to God's gracious gifts of salvation and eternal life. We love (and serve) because he first loved (and served) us.

We can also stress the value of meeting together in worship and fellowship for the same reason. We don't go to church to get to heaven, but rather to worship our great high priest who has gone to heaven before us and made it possible for us to join him there later.

A Pastor's Prayer:
Dear Lord,

Thank you for your blood that was shed for me, so I can come near your throne in confidence and without fear. Please strengthen my faith, that I may hold to what I confess without wavering. Help me to know how to provoke my parishioners to love and to do good deeds and to keep meeting together in fellowship with you until you return. Thank you. Amen.

Christ The King/Proper 29

John 18:33-37

Pilate is in a real predicament in this scene that our text describes. He is trying to ascertain just exactly who Jesus is. The Jews say one thing, Jesus says another, and Pilate's wife is telling him not to get involved! It was quite a predicament for this Roman governor who was trying to keep everyone happy, yet treat Jesus "fairly" as well. When he asked Jesus: *Are you the King of the Jews?* Jesus replied: *Do you ask this on your own, or did others tell you about me?*

I would like us to consider that reply for a moment in light of our own professions of faith and those of our congregations. When we profess, in the words of the Apostle's Creed, "I believe ..." and go on to state "our" beliefs; are we saying these things on our own, or because others told us about him? Another way of asking that is; do you truly believe in your heart what you profess to believe, or are you just saying it because that's what people expect you to say?

Creeds, liturgies, prayers, rituals, and ceremonies have their place and can add much to our worship experience, provided we are repeating the truths they contain, from the heart, and not the lips only. It's one thing to have these things memorized in our head, and quite another to have them uttered from the deep convictions in our heart. Pilate was not questioning what he believed, but rather what Jesus and others were saying.

We would do well to consider this for our parishioners, too. We may have deep convictions about what we confess and the things we preach on, but do they? If not, is it because these truths are not their own but merely what others (and more specifically we) are telling them?

When the Apostle Paul was preaching in Beroea, the *Jews were more receptive than those in Thessalonica, for they welcomed the message very eagerly and examined the scriptures every day to see whether these things were so. Many of them therefore believed* (Acts 17:11, 12a). Did they believe the word on the basis of what Paul said, or on the basis of their own study which supported what Paul had told them? It was the latter of the two. But how many of our parishioners go home after a Bible study, or Sunday sermon, and *examine the scriptures every day to see whether these things were so*, as we told them? Not very many, I'm afraid. As a result, if some one, or some thing, comes into their life and challenges their beliefs, immediately they are faced with the issue; do they believe Jesus and his words on their own or on the basis of what others have told them about him? If it is the former, they are less likely to be led astray. If it is the latter, unless they are very loyal to the person who told them about Jesus, they are much more likely to be led astray.

What are we to do about this? We must, for the good of our people, strongly urge them to read their Bibles. I'm amazed at how few professing Christians read the Bible on a daily basis — even weekly, for that matter. What this failure to read the Bible has left us with, is a church that is largely biblically illiterate. How sad, for they are missing out on rich blessings of fellowship that come from reading God's Word and professing faith in truths that are truly their own because of their diligent study of his word.

I also want to briefly point out another question that Pilate asked Jesus, which comes immediately after our text in verse 38: *What is truth?* So many people are asking that today, and many of them grew up in the church. This question was preceded by a statement from Jesus, reading: *Everyone who belongs to the truth listens to my voice.* My question is this, how can they belong to the truth if they are not listening to his voice? And how will they "hear" his voice if they don't read his word in addition to what they hear from us? It's an issue that is of utmost importance to the future of the church, if the church is going to truly believe what it professes to believe.

A Pastor's Prayer:
Dear Lord,

Help me to make it a top priority every day to read your word, and to listen to your voice. In so doing, I will know better what I believe and why. Please help me to know how to encourage my people to do the same. Thank you. Amen.

Revelation 1:4b-8

What a glorious text this is, and what a glorious scene it portrays for us! Oh, how we need to be reminded of the glory that surrounds our king, now and for all eternity. The everyday cares of life and ministry cloud the glory of Jesus in us. We become weighed down by people's problems, our own problems, sin (whether ours or that of others), schedules, demands, and the like. As a result, it is difficult to see the glory of our great and coming king. Texts like this one can help restore our awe for the majesty of Jesus. Let's take a closer look.

Grace to you and peace from him who is and who was and who is to come. Here we are reminded that our king is alive and eternal. The gods of many world religions are dead. They never were alive. The concept of them is alive and has possibly been around for thousands of years, but there is no eternal and living existence on the part of their god. But our God and king is eternal — he always was and will always be! That is a good reminder for us when we consider who it is that we are serving and worshiping. It gives renewed meaning to what we do and why we do it, week after week.

Jesus Christ, the faithful witness, the firstborn of the dead, and the ruler of the kings of the earth. Our king is a faithful witness of truth, a faithful witness of the Father, and a faithful witness of all that makes up his kingdom. We can know and stake our ministries and our futures upon his faithful witness. That's a lot more than can be said for the kings of the earth! Speaking of which, our king rules over them, too. It may seem like they are in control, but ultimately, they can't do anything (good or evil) other than what our king allows them to do. Our king is also the firstborn of the dead. He was the first to rise from the dead and is our guarantee that all who believe in him will do the same. What a great and glorious promise that is for us and for all to whom we minister!

To him who loves us and freed us from our sins by his blood, and made us to be a kingdom, priests serving his God and Father, to him be glory and dominion forever and ever. Amen. This sounds like a benediction, but is actually a part of John's greeting to the churches. Notice the glorious truths he identified about our king:

he loves us, he freed us from our sins, and he made us to be a kingdom of priests who serve our God and Father. May we never lose sight of the glory that is ours through his love for us. Who deserves that? None of us do, but that is the desire of his heart to love each and every one of us fully.

Oh, the glory of being set free from our sins! They are some of the heaviest baggage that weighs us down; if not our sins, then the sins of others. Thanks to our king, he has set us free; and what a privilege we have to pass that good news on to others; whether through our teaching, preaching, or pastoral care.

What a glorious position he has given us! It is not a position that we have worked hard for or earned, like our earthly positions; it is a gift. This position is to be a *priest* who serves our God and Father, in his kingdom. We do it now in this life, but will do it in a much fuller way in heaven. Once there, our duties will have changed from caring for the spiritual needs of people, to joining them in worship of our king.

Because of these glorious truths, John calls us to join him in acknowledging our king, and the fact that all *glory and dominion* are his *forever and ever. Amen.* May both our private and public worship be a taste of what it will be like in heaven. Not that I think we will be sitting around singing hymns and praise choruses all the time, for I don't think we will. But all that we will do (whatever that is), will be done as an act of worship. That is no different from how our life is to be lived now. Worship extends far beyond the worship hour on Sunday morning. It is to be a lifestyle lived for God's honor and glory, for he richly deserves it all the time, not just once a week.

A Pastor's Prayer:
Dear Lord,

Thank you for your glory and majesty. Daily renew that image in my mind so I never lose sight of who it is that I am worshiping and serving. I love you and adore you! Amen.

Textual Index

Passage	Page
Matthew 2:1-12	43
Mark 1:1-8	19
Mark 1:4-11	47
Mark 1:9-15	80
Mark 1:14-20	55
Mark 1:21-28	59
Mark 1:29-39	63
Mark 1:40-45	67
Mark 2:1-12	71
Mark 4:26-34	143
Mark 4:35-41	147
Mark 5:21-43	151
Mark 6:1-13	155
Mark 6:14-29	159
Mark 6:30-34, 53-56	163
Mark 7:1-8, 14-15, 21-23	188
Mark 7:24-37	192
Mark 8:27-38	196
Mark 8:31-38	84
Mark 9:2-9	75
Mark 9:30-37	200
Mark 9:38-50	204
Mark 10:2-16	208
Mark 10:17-31	212
Mark 10:35-45	216
Mark 10:46-52	220
Mark 11:1-11	101
Mark 12:28-34	224
Mark 12:38-44	228
Mark 13:1-8	232
Mark 13:24-37	13
Luke 1:26-38	25
Luke 2:1-14 (15-20)	30
Luke 2:22-40	34
Luke 24:36b-48	113
John 1:6-8, 19-28	21
John 1:(1-9) 10-18	39
John 1:43-51	51
John 2:13-22	88
John 3:1-17	139
John 3:14-21	92
John 6:1-21	167
John 6:24-35	171
John 6:35, 41-51	175
John 6:51-58	180
John 6:56-69	184
John 10:11-18	117
John 12:20-33	96
John 15:1-8	121
John 15:9-17	125
John 15:26-27; 16:4b-15	134
John 17:6-19	129
John 18:33-37	236
John 20:1-18	105
John 20:19-31	109
Acts 2:1-21	136
Acts 19:1-7	49
Romans 4:13-25	86
Romans 8:12-17	141
Romans 16:25-27	27
1 Corinthians 1:3-9	15
1 Corinthians 1:18-25	90
1 Corinthians 6:12-20	53
1 Corinthians 7:29-31	57
1 Corinthians 8:1-13	61
1 Corinthians 9:16-23	65
1 Corinthians 9:24-27	69
1 Corinthians 15:1-11	107

2 Corinthians 1:18-22	73	James 3:1-12	198
2 Corinthians 4:3-6	77	James 3:13—4:3, 7-8a	202
2 Corinthians 5:6-10		James 5:13-20	206
(11-13) 14-17	145		
2 Corinthians 6:1-13	149	1 Peter 3:18-22	82
2 Corinthians 8:7-15	153		
2 Corinthians 12:2-10	157	2 Peter 3:8-15a	19
Galatians 4:4-7	36	1 John 1:1—2:2	111
		1 John 3:1-7	115
Ephesians 1:3-14	41, 161	1 John 3:16-24	119
Ephesians 2:1-10	94	1 John 4:7-21	123
Ephesians 2:11-22	165	1 John 5:1-6	127
Ephesians 3:1-12	45	1 John 5:9-13	131
Ephesians 3:14-21	169		
Ephesians 4:1-16	173	Revelation 1:4b-8	238
Ephesians 4:25—5:2	177		
Ephesians 5:15-20	182		
Ephesians 6:10-20	186		

Philippians 2:5-11	103
1 Thessalonians 5:16-24	23
Titus 2:11-14	32
Hebrews 1:1-4; 2:5-12	210
Hebrews 4:12-16	214
Hebrews 5:1-10	218
Hebrews 5:5-10	98
Hebrews 7:23-28	222
Hebrews 9:11-14	226
Hebrews 9:24-28	230
Hebrews 10:11-14	
(15-18) 19-25	234
James 1:17-27	189
James 2:1-10 (11-13)	
14-17	194

Topical Index

(G) - Gospel; (E) - Epistle

Abiding in Christ
Easter 5 (G) — 121
Easter 5 (E) — 123
Easter 6 (G) — 125
Proper 7 (G) — 147
Proper 12 (E) — 169
Proper 15 (G) — 180

Accountability
Proper 19 (G) — 196

Alert and Watchful
Advent 1 (G) — 13

Alone with God
Epiphany 5 (G) — 63
The Transfiguration
Of Our Lord (G) — 75
Easter Day (G) — 105
Easter 5 (G) — 121
Proper 11 (G) — 163

Anger
Proper 14 (E) — 177
Proper 17 (E) — 189

Apathy
The Epiphany
Of Our Lord (G) — 43
Proper 13 (E) — 173

Arrogance
Proper 21 (G) — 204

Assurance
Easter 7 (G) — 129

Authority
Proper 19 (G) — 196

Belief
Christmas 1 (G) — 34
Easter 2 (G) — 109
Proper 13 (G) — 171
Proper 15 (G) — 180

Blessings
Proper 10 (E) — 161

Burnout
Easter 4 (G) — 117
Proper 12 (E) — 169

Busyness
Epiphany 6 (E) — 69

Caregiving
Proper 21 (E) — 206

Changed Lives
Epiphany 7 (G) — 71
Proper 6 (E) — 145
Proper 15 (E) — 182

Child of God
Christmas 1 (E) — 36
Easter 3 (E) — 115
Proper 13 (E) — 173

Comfort
Advent 4 (G) — 25
Easter 4 (G) — 117

Compassion
Epiphany 6 (G) 67
Proper 14 (E) 177
Proper 21 (E) 206

Competition
Proper 20 (G) 200
Proper 21 (G) 204

Complaining
Proper 14 (G) 175

Confidence
Christmas 1 (G) 34
The Holy Trinity (G) 139

Conformity
Epiphany 4 (G) 59
The Transfiguration
Of Our Lord (E) 77
Lent 3 (E) 90
Lent 4 (G) 92
Easter Day (E) 107
Proper 15 (E) 182
Proper 16 (G) 184
Proper 16 (E) 186
Proper 26 (E) 226

Contentment
Advent 3 (E) 23
Proper 9 (E) 157
Proper 13 (G) 171

Conviction
Epiphany 2 (G) 51
Epiphany 4 (G) 59
Epiphany 4 (E) 61
Proper 29 (G) 236

Courage
Lent 4 (G) 84
Easter Day (E) 107
Easter 3 (G) 113
The Holy Trinity (G) 139
Proper 16 (G) 184

Death
Lent 5 (G) 96
Proper 27 (E) 230

Defeat
Easter 6 (E) 127

Devotion
Christmas 1 (G) 34
Proper 23 (G) 212

Discernment
Proper 15 (E) 182
Proper 19 (E) 198

Discipline
Epiphany 6 (E) 69
Easter 5 (G) 121
Proper 14 (E) 177

Division
Proper 11 (E) 165
Proper 20 (G) 200
Proper 20 (E) 202

Divorce
Proper 22 (G) 208

Doubt
Epiphany 2 (G) 51
Easter 2 (G) 109
The Holy Trinity (G) 139

Evil
Easter 6 (E) 127
Proper 16 (E) 186

Exaltation
Sunday Of The
Passion (E) 103

Exhaustion
Easter 4 (G) 117

Faith
Lent 2 (E) 86
Lent 3 (E) 90
Easter Day (G) 105
Easter Day (E) 107
Easter 2 (G) 109
Easter 6 (E) 127
Easter 7 (G) 129
Proper 6 (E) 145
Proper 8 (G) 151
Proper 18 (G) 192
Proper 18 (E) 194
Proper 22 (G) 208
Proper 25 (G) 220
Proper 26 (E) 226
Proper 28 (E) 234

Fear
Advent 4 (G) 25
Epiphany 4 (G) 59
The Transfiguration
Of Our Lord (E) 77
Easter 5 (E) 123
The Holy Trinity (G) 139
Proper 7 (G) 147
Proper 12 (G) 167
Proper 15 (G) 180
Proper 16 (E) 186

Forgiveness
Epiphany 7 (G) 71
Easter 3 (E) 115
Proper 7 (E) 149
Proper 14 (E) 177
Proper 23 (E) 214
Proper 24 (E) 218
Proper 25 (E) 222
Proper 29 (E) 238

Friendship with God
Easter 6 (G) 125

Giving
Proper 8 (E) 153
Proper 27 (G) 228

Glory to God
Advent 4 (E) 27
Proper 29 (E) 238

Godliness
The Nativity
Of Our Lord (E) 32
Proper 20 (E) 202
Proper 23 (G) 212

God's Promises
Epiphany 7 (E) 73
Lent 2 (E) 86

God's Provision
Lent 2 (E) 86
Proper 22 (E) 210

God's Word
Christmas 2 (G) 39
Epiphany 7 (G) 71
Lent 2 (G) 84
Lent 2 (E) 86

Easter Day (G)	105	Proper 24 (E)	218
Easter 2 (G)	109	Proper 25 (E)	222
Easter 5 (G)	121		
Easter 7 (G)	129	**Guilt**	
Proper 14 (G)	175	Lent 1 (E)	82
Proper 17 (E)	199		
Proper 22 (E)	210	**Healing**	
Proper 23 (E)	214	Epiphany 7 (G)	71
Proper 29 (G)	236	Proper 8 (G)	151

Goodness
Proper 23 (G)   212

Health
Proper 21 (E)   206

Good News
The Epiphany
  Of Our Lord (G)   43
Proper 25 (E)   222

Holy Spirit
Christmas 1 (G)	34
Advent 3 (E)	23
Epiphany 1 (E)	48
Easter 4 (E)	119
Easter 5 (E)	123
The Day Of Pentecost (G)	134
The Day Of Pentecost (E)	136
The Holy Trinity (G)	139
The Holy Trinity (E)	141
Proper 6 (E)	145
Proper 10 (E)	161

Good Works
Lent 4 (E)	94
Proper 6 (E)	145
Proper 18 (E)	194
Proper 28 (E)	234

Grace
Advent 1 (E)	15
The Nativity Of Our Lord (E)	32
Christmas 2 (G)	39
Christmas 2 (E)	41
Epiphany 6 (G)	67
Lent 1 (E)	82
Lent 4 (E)	94
Easter Day (E)	107
Easter 3 (E)	115
Proper 7 (E)	149
Proper 11 (E)	165
Proper 13 (E)	173
Proper 23 (E)	214

Honesty
Proper 14 (E)   177

Humility
Advent 2 (G)	17
Advent 4 (G)	25
Sunday Of The Passion (E)	103
Proper 11 (E)	165
Proper 19 (G)	196
Proper 20 (G)	200
Proper 27 (G)	228

Hypocrisy
    Proper 17 (G)   188

Joy
    Advent 3 (E)   23
    The Nativity
        Of Our Lord (G)   30
    The Epiphany
        Of Our Lord (G)   43
    Easter 3 (E)   115
    Easter 6 (G)   125

Law
    Easter 3 (E)   115
    Proper 7 (E)   149
    Proper 13 (E)   173
    Proper 23 (E)   214

Legalism
    Epiphany 4 (E)   61

Love
    Easter 4 (E)   119
    Easter 5 (E)   123
    Proper 8 (E)   153
    Proper 12 (E)   169
    Proper 26 (G)   226
    Proper 28 (E)   234

Loyalty to Christ
    Epiphany 3 (E)   57
    The Holy Trinity (G)   139
    Proper 6 (E)   145

Maturity
    Lent 5 (E)   98
    Easter 5 (G)   121
    Proper 13 (G)   171

Mercy
    Epiphany 6 (G)   67
    Proper 14 (E)   177

Miracles
    Epiphany 7 (G)   71
    Proper 12 (G)   167

Mystery
    Advent 4 (G)   25
    Advent 4 (E)   27
    The Epiphany
        Of Our Lord (E)   45
    Proper 6 (G)   143
    Proper 14 (G)   175
    Proper 15 (G)   180
    Proper 18 (G)   192

Obedience
    Lent 5 (E)   98
    Sunday Of The
        Passion (E)   103
    Easter 6 (G)   125
    The Holy Trinity (G)   139
    Proper 6 (E)   145
    Proper 17 (E)   189

Opposition
    Proper 16 (E)   186

Our Calling
    Advent 2 (G)   17
    Advent 3 (G)   21
    Advent 4 (G)   25
    The Epiphany
        Of Our Lord (E)   45
    Epiphany 3 (G)   55
    Lent 5 (E)   98
    Proper 7 (G)   147
    Proper 13 (E)   173
    Proper 24 (E)   218

Our Identity
    Advent 1 (E)   15
    Proper 10 (E)   161
    Proper 29 (E)   238

Our Inheritance
    Christmas 1 (E)   36
    Proper 6 (E)   145

Our Mission
    Easter 3 (G)   113
    Easter 5 (E)   123
    Proper 6 (G)   143
    Proper 21 (G)   204
    Proper 24 (E)   218
    Proper 25 (E)   222
    Proper 28 (G)   232

Partiality
    Proper 18 (E)   194
    Proper 21 (G)   204
    Proper 25 (G)   220

Passion
    Epiphany 5 (E)   65
    Lent 5 (E)   98
    Sunday Of The
        Passion (G)   101

Patience
    Advent 2 (E)   19

Peace
    Proper 11 (E)   163

Perspective
    The Nativity
        Of Our Lord (G)   30

Perseverance
    The Transfiguration
        Of Our Lord (G)   75

Pity
    Epiphany 6 (G)   67

Pleasing God
    Epiphany 1 (G)   47
    The Holy Trinity (G)   139
    Proper 14 (E)   177

Power Struggles
    Proper 20 (G)   200

Prayer
    Advent 3 (E)   23
    Lent 5 (E)   98
    Easter 5 (G)   121
    Easter 7 (G)   129
    Proper 12 (E)   169
    Proper 20 (E)   202
    Proper 21 (E)   206
    Proper 24 (G)   216

Preaching
    Advent 3 (G)   21
    The Epiphany
        Of Our Lord (E)   45
    Epiphany 4 (G)   59
    Epiphany 5 (E)   65
    Epiphany 7 (G)   71
    The Transfiguration
        Of Our Lord (E)   77
    Easter Day (E)   107
    Easter 2 (E)   111
    Easter 3 (G)   113
    Easter 5 (E)   123
    Easter 7 (G)   129

The Day Of		
Pentecost (G)	134	
Proper 7 (E)	149	
Proper 8 (G)	151	
Proper 8 (E)	153	
Proper 9 (G)	155	
Proper 10 (G)	159	
Proper 16 (G)	184	
Proper 16 (E)	186	

Preparation
  Advent 2 (G)   17
  Advent 2 (E)   19

Pride
  Lent 5 (G)   96
  Proper 9 (E)   157
  Proper 20 (G)   200
  Proper 21 (G)   204
  Proper 27 (G)   228

Priorities
  Advent 2 (E)   19
  The Holy Trinity (E)   141
  Proper 11 (G)   163
  Proper 28 (G)   232
  Christ The King (G)   236

Purpose
  Sunday Of The
    Passion (G)   101

Rebellion
  Lent 2 (G)   84
  Proper 22 (G)   208

Redemption
  Christmas 1 (E)   36
  Proper 10 (E)   161

Reputation
  Sunday Of The
    Passion (E)   103
  Proper 14 (E)   177
  Proper 19 (E)   198

Rest
  Epiphany 5 (G)   43
  Proper 11 (G)   163

Return of Christ
  Epiphany 3 (E)   57
  Proper 27 (E)   230

Salvation
  Advent 4 (E)   27
  Lent 3 (E)   90
  Lent 4 (E)   94
  Easter 2 (G)   109
  Easter 7 (E)   131
  Proper 7 (E)   149
  Proper 27 (E)   230

Sanctification
  Easter 7 (G)   129
  Proper 27 (E)   230

Self
  Lent 4 (E)   94
  Lent 5 (G)   96
  Sunday Of The
    Passion (E)   103
  Proper 24 (G)   216

Self-control
  Epiphany 6 (E)   69
  Proper 14 (E)   177
  Proper 17 (E)   189
  Proper 19 (E)   198

Sensitivity
  Epiphany 4 (E) — 61
  Proper 19 (E) — 198

Servanthood
  The Epiphany
    Of Our Lord (E) — 45
  Sunday Of The
    Passion (E) — 103

Sin
  The Nativity
    Of Our Lord (E) — 32
  Epiphany 2 (E) — 53
  Epiphany 6 (G) — 67
  Lent 4 (G) — 92
  Easter 3 (G) — 113
  Proper 10 (G) — 159
  Proper 14 (E) — 177
  Proper 23 (E) — 214
  Proper 27 (E) — 230

Skepticism
  Epiphany 2 (G) — 51

Speech
  Proper 19 (E) — 198

Spiritual Gifts
  Proper 13 (E) — 173

Strength
  Advent 4 (E) — 27
  Easter 4 (G) — 117
  Proper 7 (G) — 147
  Proper 11 (G) — 163
  Proper 12 (E) — 169

Suffering
  Lent 1 (E) — 82

  Lent 5 (G) — 96
  Lent 5 (E) — 98
  Proper 9 (E) — 157

Temptation
  Epiphany 2 (E) — 53
  Lent 1 (G) — 80
  Easter 6 (E) — 127

Thankfulness
  Advent 3 (E) — 23

Traditions
  Proper 17 (G) — 188
  Proper 26 (E) — 226

Truth
  Advent 4 (E) — 27
  Christmas 2 (G) — 39
  The Transfiguration
    Of Our Lord (E) — 77
  Lent 4 (G) — 92
  Easter Day (G) — 105
  Easter 7 (G) — 129
  Easter 7 (E) — 131
  The Day Of
    Pentecost (G) — 134
  Proper 10 (G) — 159
  Proper 16 (G) — 184
  Proper 17 (E) — 189
  Proper 26 (E) — 226
  Christ The King (G) — 236

Unbelief
  Lent 2 (E) — 86
  Easter Day (G) — 105
  Easter Day (E) — 107
  Easter 2 (G) — 109
  Proper 9 (G) — 155

Unity
    Proper 11 (E)   165
    Proper 21 (G)   204

Victory
    Epiphany 2 (E)   53
    Lent 1 (G)   80
    Easter 6 (E)   127

Wisdom
    Lent 3 (E)   90
    The Holy Trinity (E)   141
    Proper 15 (E)   182
    Proper 20 (E)   202

Worship
    The Epiphany
        Of Our Lord (G)   43
    The Transfiguration
        Of Our Lord (G)   75
    Lent 3 (G)   88
    Proper 17 (G)   188
    Proper 26 (E)   226
    Proper 28 (E)   234
    Proper 29 (E)   238

Zeal
    The Nativity
        Of Our Lord   32

Lectionary Preaching After Pentecost

The following index will aid the user of this book in matching the correct Sunday with the appropriate text during Pentecost. All texts in this book are from the Revised Common Lectionary. (Note that the ELCA division of Lutheranism is now following the Revised Common Lectionary.) The Lutheran designations indicate days comparable to Sundays on which Revised Common Lectionary Propers or Ordinary Time designations are used.

(Fixed dates do not pertain to Lutheran Lectionary)

Fixed Date Lectionaries *Revised Common (including ELCA)* *and Roman Catholic*	Lutheran Lectionary *Lutheran*
The Day Of Pentecost	The Day Of Pentecost
The Holy Trinity	The Holy Trinity
May 29-June 4 — Proper 4, Ordinary Time 9	Pentecost 2
June 5-11 — Proper 5, Ordinary Time 10	Pentecost 3
June 12-18 — Proper 6, Ordinary Time 11	Pentecost 4
June 19-25 — Proper 7, Ordinary Time 12	Pentecost 5
June 26-July 2 — Proper 8, Ordinary Time 13	Pentecost 6
July 3-9 — Proper 9, Ordinary Time 14	Pentecost 7
July 10-16 — Proper 10, Ordinary Time 15	Pentecost 8
July 17-23 — Proper 11, Ordinary Time 16	Pentecost 9
July 24-30 — Proper 12, Ordinary Time 17	Pentecost 10
July 31-Aug. 6 — Proper 13, Ordinary Time 18	Pentecost 11
Aug. 7-13 — Proper 14, Ordinary Time 19	Pentecost 12
Aug. 14-20 — Proper 15, Ordinary Time 20	Pentecost 13
Aug. 21-27 — Proper 16, Ordinary Time 21	Pentecost 14
Aug. 28-Sept. 3 — Proper 17, Ordinary Time 22	Pentecost 15
Sept. 4-10 — Proper 18, Ordinary Time 23	Pentecost 16
Sept. 11-17 — Proper 19, Ordinary Time 24	Pentecost 17
Sept. 18-24 — Proper 20, Ordinary Time 25	Pentecost 18

Sept. 25-Oct. 1 — Proper 21, Ordinary Time 26	Pentecost 19
Oct. 2-8 — Proper 22, Ordinary Time 27	Pentecost 20
Oct. 9-15 — Proper 23, Ordinary Time 28	Pentecost 21
Oct. 16-22 — Proper 24, Ordinary Time 29	Pentecost 22
Oct. 23-29 — Proper 25, Ordinary Time 30	Pentecost 23
Oct. 30-Nov. 5 — Proper 26, Ordinary Time 31	Pentecost 24
Nov. 6-12 — Proper 27, Ordinary Time 32	Pentecost 25
Nov. 13-19 — Proper 28, Ordinary Time 33	Pentecost 26
	Pentecost 27
Nov. 20-26 — Christ The King	Christ The King

Reformation Day (or last Sunday in October) is October 31 (Revised Common, Lutheran)

All Saints (or first Sunday in November) is November 1 (Revised Common, Lutheran, Roman Catholic)

U.S. / Canadian Lectionary Comparison

The following index shows the correlation between the Sundays and special days of the church year as they are titled or labeled in the Revised Common Lectionary published by the Consultation On Common Texts and used in the United States (the reference used for this book) and the Sundays and special days of the church year as they are titled or labeled in the Revised Common Lectionary used in Canada.

Revised Common Lectionary	Canadian Revised Common Lectionary
Advent 1	Advent 1
Advent 2	Advent 2
Advent 3	Advent 3
Advent 4	Advent 4
Christmas Eve	Christmas Eve
The Nativity Of Our Lord / Christmas Day	The Nativity Of Our Lord
Christmas 1	Christmas 1
January 1 / Holy Name Of Jesus	January 1 / The Name Of Jesus
Christmas 2	Christmas 2
The Epiphany Of Our Lord	The Epiphany Of Our Lord
The Baptism Of Our Lord / Epiphany 1	The Baptism Of Our Lord / Proper 1
Epiphany 2 / Ordinary Time 2	Epiphany 2 / Proper 2
Epiphany 3 / Ordinary Time 3	Epiphany 3 / Proper 3
Epiphany 4 / Ordinary Time 4	Epiphany 4 / Proper 4
Epiphany 5 / Ordinary Time 5	Epiphany 5 / Proper 5
Epiphany 6 / Ordinary Time 6	Epiphany 6 / Proper 6
Epiphany 7 / Ordinary Time 7	Epiphany 7 / Proper 7
Epiphany 8 / Ordinary Time 8	Epiphany 8 / Proper 8
The Transfiguration Of Our Lord / Last Sunday After The Epiphany	The Transfiguration Of Our Lord / Last Sunday After Epiphany
Ash Wednesday	Ash Wednesday
Lent 1	Lent 1
Lent 2	Lent 2
Lent 3	Lent 3
Lent 4	Lent 4
Lent 5	Lent 5
Sunday Of The Passion / Palm Sunday	Passion / Palm Sunday
Maundy Thursday	Holy / Maundy Thursday
Good Friday	Good Friday

The Resurrection Of Our Lord / Easter Day	The Resurrection Of Our Lord
Easter 2	Easter 2
Easter 3	Easter 3
Easter 4	Easter 4
Easter 5	Easter 5
Easter 6	Easter 6
The Ascension Of Our Lord	The Ascension Of Our Lord
Easter 7	Easter 7
The Day Of Pentecost	The Day Of Pentecost
The Holy Trinity	The Holy Trinity
Proper 4 / Pentecost 2 / O T 9*	Proper 9
Proper 5 / Pent 3 / O T 10	Proper 10
Proper 6 / Pent 4 / O T 11	Proper 11
Proper 7 / Pent 5 / O T 12	Proper 12
Proper 8 / Pent 6 / O T 13	Proper 13
Proper 9 / Pent 7 / O T 14	Proper 14
Proper 10 / Pent 8 / O T 15	Proper 15
Proper 11 / Pent 9 / O T 16	Proper 16
Proper 12 / Pent 10 / O T 17	Proper 17
Proper 13 / Pent 11 / O T 18	Proper 18
Proper 14 / Pent 12 / O T 19	Proper 19
Proper 15 / Pent 13 / O T 20	Proper 20
Proper 16 / Pent 14 / O T 21	Proper 21
Proper 17 / Pent 15 / O T 22	Proper 22
Proper 18 / Pent 16 / O T 23	Proper 23
Proper 19 / Pent 17 / O T 24	Proper 24
Proper 20 / Pent 18 / O T 25	Proper 25
Proper 21 / Pent 19 / O T 26	Proper 26
Proper 22 / Pent 20 / O T 27	Proper 27
Proper 23 / Pent 21 / O T 28	Proper 28
Proper 24 / Pent 22 / O T 29	Proper 29
Proper 25 / Pent 23 / O T 30	Proper 30
Proper 26 / Pent 24 / O T 31	Proper 31
Proper 27 / Pent 25 / O T 32	Proper 32
Proper 28 / Pent 26 / O T 33	Proper 33
Christ The King (Proper 29 / O T 34)	Proper 34 / Christ The King / Reign Of Christ
Reformation Day (October 31)	Reformation Day (October 31)
All Saints (November 1 or 1st Sunday in November)	All Saints' Day (November 1)
Thanksgiving Day (4th Thursday of November)	Thanksgiving Day (2nd Monday of October)

*O T = Ordinary Time

www.ingramcontent.com/pod-product-compliance
Lightning Source LLC
Chambersburg PA
CBHW071152160426
43196CB00011B/2058